The Grounds For Divorce
IN
Hindu and English Law

(A Study in Comparative Law)

P. K. VIRDI, LL.M., PH.D. (LOND.)
of the Middle Temple, Barrister

MOTILAL BANARSIDASS
DELHI : VARANASI : PATNA

© MOTILAL BANARSIDASS
Indological Publishers & Booksellers
Head Office : BUNGALOW ROAD, JAWAHARNAGAR, DELHI-7
Branches : 1. CHOWK, VARANASI-1 (U.P.)
2. ASHOK RAJPATH, PATNA-4 (BIHAR)

First Edition 1972

Printed in India
BY SHANTI LAL JAIN, AT SHRI JAINENDRA PRESS, BUNGALOW ROAD, JAWAHARNAGAR, DELHI-7, AND PUBLISHED BY SUNDARLAL JAIN FOR MOTILAL BANARSIDASS, BUNGALOW ROAD, JAWAHARNAGAR, DELHI-7

ACKNOWLEDGEMENTS

This work was accepted as a thesis for the award of Ph.D. in Law by the University of London in 1966.

I am grateful to Professor J. D. M. Derrett and Professor A. Gledhill for their guidance, help and patience during the preparation of this thesis. Professor T. E. James of King's College deserves my sincere thanks for his help and valuable criticisms on English Law. I am thankful to Dr. Olive M. Stone, Reader in Law, of the London School of Economics and Political Science, for reading and commenting on the section, 'reasonable cause'.

My thanks are also due to Messrs Motilal Banarsidass for bringing this work into publication.

P. K. V.

CONTENTS

Chapter I

INTRODUCTION

Under both the Hindu and the English systems of law marriage was formerly a sacrament and, therefore, indissoluble, but the nature of the marriage was different in that, while an English marriage was a voluntary union for life of one man and one woman to the exclusion of all others, a Hindu marriage was a gift of the bride by her father to her husband. According to Hindu religious belief the marriage subsisted not only during the life time of the spouses but also in subsequent existences; a Hindu widow was not allowed to remarry, as her previous marriage was not dissolved by the death of her husband. An essential element in English marriage is consent of the partners. It was not so in a *sastric* marriage. Under S. 5 of the Hindu Marriage Act, 1955 consent is not enumerated among the "conditions" essential to the validity of a Hindu marriage, though S. 12 (c) of the same Act renders a marriage voidable if consent has been obtained by force or fraud, which might be regarded as implying that such consent is required. Presumably no mention of consent is made in S. 5 of the Hindu Marriage Act, 1955 because marriages in India are still arranged by the parents of the partners and consent of the parents is regarded as consent of the couple.

Unlike English marriage a Hindu *sastric* marriage was a religious necessity for the procreation of a son, whose funeral oblations were essential to his salvation in his next existence. A Hindu was allowed to remarry and supersede his first or subsequent wife, if she failed to bear him a son. Even in present Hindu society much importance is attached to the birth of a son. The Hindu *sastric* marriage imposed many disabilities on the wife, for a man could abandon or supersede his wife without just cause. He could be polygamous, while a second marriage was not allowed even to a widow until the Hindu Widows' Remarriage Act, 1856, was passed and the harshness of this rule was mitigated. The standard of morality required of women was higher than that permitted to men. The lower status accorded to the wife was inconsistent with modern democratic ideas, which stress equality of the sexes.

The tendency to move away from *sastric* notions of marriage led to the passing of the Hindu Marriage Act, 1955, which brought about fundamental changes in the Hindu matrimonial law. The purely sacramental character of the Hindu marriage has been replaced by the English concept of marriage in so far as it allows divorce when it is not reasonable to expect the husband and wife to live together and perform their marital duties. The amendments introduced into English law by A.P. Herbert's Act of 1937 assume that marriage is a sacrament and an institution essential for the preservation of morality and social integrity; so that divorce should only be granted in circumstances which strike at the root of the institution. The provisions of the Hindu Marriage Act, 1955 seem to have adopted a similar approach.

Before 1937 divorce was impossible without proof of adultery; this was prejudicial to public morality, as a person who wished to bring an end to his marriage had either to commit adultery or perjury; the law was an incitement to immorality. The development of the English law of divorce will be dealt with in brief outline in chapter III, as the Hindu Marriage Act, 1955, The Hindu Marriage and Divorce Ordinance, 1960 (Kenya) and the Hindu Marriage and Divorce Ordinance, 1961 (Uganda) have borrowed the provisions for divorce largely from the English Matrimonial Causes Acts, 1937—1950 (as amended and consolidated by the (English) Matrimonial Causes Act, 1965). The above legislation brought revolutionary changes in the Hindu matrimonial law by introducing divorce and making marriage a civil contract, which can be terminated on prescribed grounds. As we shall see in chapter II), a Hindu *sastric* marriage was purely of a sacramental nature and did not admit divorce, so there is no Indian case-law to which courts can look for precedents in applying the modern Hindu law of divorce, which is still in process of development. The question is how far the Hindu courts can resort to English precedents? The following observations of Gajendragadkar, J. (as he then was) can be of some help in this respect. "When we are dealing with the problems of construing a constitutional provision which is not too clear or lucid, you feel inclined to inquire how other judicial minds have responded to the challenge presented by similar provisions in other sister constitutions."[1]

Since the Hindu Marriage Act, 1955 is based largely on the English Matrimonial Causes Act, 1950 there is a great tendency to rely upon English decisions. However, there are differences between the two Acts and great care has to be taken while acting upon the English law and practice of divorce; for instance, English decisions ordering medical examination of an alleged lunatic can have no application in a case arising under the Hindu Marriage Act, 1955, because, under the Matrimonial Causes Rules in England, specific provision has been made for examination by medical inspectors. There is no such provision in India.[2] There are other important considerations. There are differences in the social conditions between Hindu and English society and in the language of the English and Hindu Acts. Hindu law is quite different from English law in the following respects. Suffering from a virulent form of leprosy for a period of at least one year, and suffering from a venereal disease in a communicable form for a period of not less than three years are grounds for judicial separation, but there is no such provision in English law, though the communication of venereal disease may amount to cruelty. Ceasing to be a Hindu by conversion to another religion and renunciation of the world by entering a religious order are grounds for divorce peculiar to Hindu law, which will be defined and discussed in chapter X

All the statutory provisions relating to the grounds for divorce will be considered with special reference to their interpretation against the social background of Hindu society. It will be shown that, although some of the provisions of the Hindu Marriage Act, 1955 and the Kenya and Uganda Ordinances appear to be identical with provisions of the English Matrimonial Causes Act, 1950, the practical result is not always the same, when the law is applied to Hindu society, e.g., the definition

1. *Atiabai Tea Co. Ltd.* v. *State of Assam*, A.I.R. 1961 S. C. 232 at p. 257; see also *Umri Bai* v. *Chittar*, A.I.R. 1966 Madh. Pr. 205 (a warning to guard against the tendency to follow English precedents blindly).

2. *Bipinchandra* v. *Madhurben*, A.I.R. 1963 Guj. 250; S.S. Nigam, "*Hindu Law*" (1964) 6 J.I.L.I. 545 at p. 550.

of 'desertion' has been construed by reference to English case-law but what amounts to a just cause for an English wife living apart from her husband may not be sufficient in case of a Hindu wife. It is impossible to reproduce the whole English case-law here but reference will be made to English decisions, which have been accepted by the Indian courts as contributing to the interpretation of the Indian Statute. The concepts of adultery, desertion, cruelty and the effect of insanity both as a ground for divorce and in relation to other matrimonial faults will be studied in the light of social conditions in English and Hindu society.

In the words of M. C. Chagla[3] law in India must be considered in the context of a developing country, which is determined to forge ahead from an agricultural and poor society to an industrial and prosperous one. Sometimes society has evolved and propagated notions in advance of the law but in India the law has given a head to society by placing before it new ideals and values and providing sanctions for their support. One criterion of a civilised society is the position it accords to the women. When one remembers that Hindus look upon marriage as a sacrament one must concede that the Act of 1955 has achieved a great revolution.

Compulsory monogamy and the punishment of polygamy is a notable achievement of the Hindu Marriage Act, 1955[4] and the parallel provisions in the Kenya[5] and Uganda[6] Ordinances. They have put husband and wife on terms approaching equality. The revolutionary character of the grounds for divorce, as introduced into Hindu law by legislation based on the principles of English matrimonial law, will be considered as they operate in Hindu society, with a view to find out the similarities and differences between the two legal systems, and

3. M.C. Chagla, former High Commissioner for India in U.K., "*Indian Law : An Introduction*", Some Aspects of Indian Law today, published by the British Institute of International and Comparative Law, London, at p. 1.

4. Sections 13 (2) and 17 of the Hindu Marriage Act, 1955.

5. S. 10 (1) (g) (i) (ii) of the Hindu Marriage and Divorce Ordinance, 1960 (Kenya).

6. S. 9 (1) (b) (i) (ii) of the Hindu Marriage and Divorce Ordinance, 1961 (Uganda).

whether the legislation has made allowance for the discrepancies which are likely to occur when the English law is adapted to Hindu society. This study is confined to the grounds for divorce, but the following two chapters, which deal with the institution of marriage in English and Hindu law in general will facilitate comprehension of the problems which are created by the statue.

CHAPTER II

THE INSTITUTION OF MARRIAGE AND THE PRE-STATUTORY HINDU LAW OF DIVORCE

1. *THE NATURE OF HINDU MARRIAGE*

In Hindu law, that is to say in the *dharma-sastra* or 'orthodox' juridical theory of India, marriage (*vivaha*) was one of the ten *samskaras* necessary for men of the twice born classes and the only *Vedic* sacrament for women.[1] As in canon law and moral theology *matrimonium* is treated under *sacraments*, so in Hindu law *vivaha* is not treated under *vyavahara* (litigation) but under *samskara*. A *samskara* is a sacrament or a purificatory act. Marriage is considered sacred because it is said to be complete only on the performance of the sacred rites attended with sacred procedure. This *samskara* gives rise to the status of wifehood and its performance cannot be annulled by the fact that the husband or wife lapses from virtue, i.e., by committing adultery.[2]

It is almost impossible to define marriage in legal terms but the *sastric* concept of marriage would seem to be as a union between a man and a woman which arises at the time when the ceremony of marriage (i.e., *samskara*) has been completed, the bridegroom having the requisite qualifications for taking a girl in marriage and the bride the qualifications for being given in marriage, and this procedure having been completed before the nuptial fire.[3] Marriage is a sacramental rite, which is performed for the girl for the purpose of making her a wife and is marked by the holding of hands, along with its entire procedure

1. Manu II, 67-68, F. Max Müller, *Sacred Books of the East*, vol. 25; K.M. Kapadia, *Marriage and Family in India*, O.U.P., 1959, p. 168; S. V. Gupte, *Hindu Law of Marriage*, Bombay, 1961, p. 6; K. Srinivasa Iyengar, "*Powers of the Managing Member of a Mitakshara Joint Hindu Family*" (1905) 15 M.L.J., Journal, 211 at p. 224.

2. P.V. Kane, *History of Dharmasastra*, Poona, 1941, vol. II, part I, p. 620; Dwarka Nath Mitter, *The Position of Women in Hindu Law*, Calcutta, 1913, p. 195.

3. J.D.M. Derrett, *Hindu Law Past and Present*, Calcutta, 1957, p. 86.

and subsidiary details.[4] It gives the status of husband and wife to the married couple. The *mantras* used in the ceremony of wedding create a wife. The sacrament becomes complete by the use of those *mantras*. As regards the marriage of a *Sudra*, there are no *mantras* but other rites apply excluding the *mantras*.[5]

2. *THE PURPOSE OF THE SAMSKARAS*

The exact purpose of *samskaras* was left rather vague in our authorities. A critical look at the list of *samskaras* will reveal that their purposes were manifold. According to ancient Hindu religious belief man was surrounded by superhuman influences which were powerful for good or evil consequences. These influences could interfere in every important occasion in man's life. Therefore, the Hindus tried to remove hostile influences and attract beneficial ones, so that man might grow and prosper without external hindrances and receive timely directions and help from gods and spirits. Another purpose of the *samskaras* was the attainment of heaven. It had also a psychological value, impressing on the mind of the person concerned that he had assumed a new role and must strive to observe its rules.[6] The *Vivaha-samskara* consists essentially in an acceptance, which produces the mental impression that this girl is the man's wife, and wifehood arises from her having undergone the *samskara*, which *samskara* itself could not occur but for the marriage.[7]

4. Medhatithi on Manu XX, *Manu-Smriti* translated by G. Jha, vol. II, part I, Calcutta, 1921, p. 45.

5. Medhatithi on Manu, *The Principles of Hindu Law—The Commentaries* translated by J.C. Ghose, vol. II, Calcutta, 1917, p. 46; see also J.D.M. Derrett, "*The Discussion of Marriage by Gadadhara*", The Adyar Library Bulletin (1963), vol. XXVII, p. 171 at 187.

6. P. V. Kane, *History of Dharmasastra*, vol. II, part I, p. 193; R.B. Pandey, *Hindu Samskaras*, Banaras, 1949, ch. III, pp. 40-41; K.V. Rangaswami Aiyangar, *Aspects of the Social and Political System of Manusmriti*, Lucknow University, 1949, pp. 84-86; K.V. Rangaswami Aiyangar, *Some Aspects of the Hindu View of Life according to Dharmasastra*, Baroda, 1952, pp. 129-136; J.R. Gharpure, *Hindu Law*, Bombay, 1931, p. 69.

7. J.D.M. Derrett, "*The Discussion of Marriage by Gadadhara*", The Adyar Library Bulletin, 1963, vol. XXVII, at p. 180.

During the *samskara* of marriage a bridegroom is said to be an active receiver of the bride, who is taken by him and given by her father or other guardian. From the *sastric* point of view the religious aspect of marriage was so highly rated that a father was supposed to be under a sacred duty to give his daughter in marriage at the appropriate age, neglect of which duty was regarded as a sin.[8] A critical look at the concept of Hindu *sastric* marriage will show that it underwent changes from time to time.

3. *MARRIAGE IN THE VEDIC PERIOD*

It was a simple religious ceremony consisting of grasping the hand of the bride by the bridegroom. The Rigveda enjoins, "I take thy hand for good fortune, that thou mayest attain old age with me as thy husband; the gods have given thee to me that I may be the master of the household."[9]

4. *MARRIAGE IN THE SUTRA PERIOD*

The procedure of marriage became complex during the *sutra* period. The bridegroom was to lead the bride three times round the nuptial fire, and the ceremony was completed on taking the seven steps by the couple, The wife was shown the Pole Star, which was symbolic of the fact of her stability in her husband's home.[10]

8. Gautama XVIII, 21-23, S.B.E., vol. II; Manu IX, 4, S.B.E., vol. 25; Vasishtha XVII, 70, S.B.E., vol. 14 (the details of this orthodox juridical theory are beyond the scope of this thesis).

9. Rig-Veda X.85, 36 in S.B.E., vol. 30, p. 189; The Atharva-Veda XIV. I. 49-50, R.T.H. Griffith; *The Hymns of the Atharva-Veda*, vol. II Benaras, 1917, p. 169.

10. Paraskara-Grihya-Sutra in S.B.E., vol. 29, Oxford, 1886, pp. 283, 285; Grihya-Sutra of Hiranyakesin in S.B.E., vol. 30, p. 191; Khadira-Grihya-Sutra in S.B.E., vol. 29, p. 384; see also *N.C.* Sen-Gupta, *Evolution of Ancient Indian Law*, London, 1953, p. 119; A. S. Altekar, *The Position of Women in Hindu Civilisation*, Benaras, 1956, p. 80; P. H. Prabhu, *Hindu Social Organisation*, Bombay, 1958, p. 167.

5. *MARRIAGE IN THE SMRITI PERIOD*

During this period we meet with various forms of marriage,[11] eight of which will be briefly dealt with below.

(i) *The Brahma*

The gift of a daughter, after decking her with costly garments and honouring her by presents of jewels, to a man learned in the Vedas and of good conduct, whom the father himself invites, is called the *Brahma* rite. Medhatithi[12] on Manu XXVII comments that there is nothing to indicate the connection of special dressing with either the bride only or with the bridegroom only; hence they should be taken as relating to both. This seems to be the correct view, because in practice even today both the bride and the bridegroom are specially dressed and adorned for the wedding.

(ii) *The Daiva*

This was a gift of a daughter whom her father had beautifully clothed when the sacrifice had already begun, to the officiating priest, who performed that act of religion.

(iii) *The Arsha*

When the father gave away his daughter according to the rule, after receiving from the bridegroom, for the fulfilment of the sacred law, a cow and a bull or two pairs, that marriage was termed the *Arsha*. On the face of this text it appears that the taking of the consideration from the bridegroom rendered this form inferior to the above two and the *Prajapatya* below. But this is doubtful, for Medhatithi[13] on Manu III, 29 comments that such receiving of the cattle by the father was done in obedience to law, and not with the idea of receiving it in exchange for the price of the girl.

11. Apastamba II.5.11, 17-20, S.B.E., vol. 2; Gautama IV, 6-13, S.B.E., vol. 2; Manu III, 27-34, S.B.E., vol. 25; Narada XII, 38-43, S.B.E., vol. 33; Vishnu XXIV, 18-26, S.B.E., vol.7, Dwarka Nath Mitter, *The Position of Women in Hindu Law*, pp. 210-216; G. Banerjee, *The Hindu Law of Marriage and Stridhana*, Calcutta, 1923, p. 86; K.P. Jayaswal, *Manu and Yajnavalkya*, Calcutta, 1930, pp. 236-240; V.M. Apte, *Social and Religious Life in Grihya Sutras*, Bombay, 1954, pp. 20-21.

12. Medhatithi on Manu, III, 27 translated by G. Jha, *Manu-Smriti*, vol. II, part I, Calcutta, 1921, p. 51.

13. Medhatithi on Manu, III, 29, ibid., p. 55.

(iv) *The Prajapatya*

When the father gave away his daughter with honour saying distinctly, "May both of you perform together your civil and religious duties." Again Medhatithi[14] comments that the formula implies the condition that the daughter is to be given to the bridegroom only if he fulfills his duty, property and pleasure along with her. Therefore, this form was regarded as inferior by reason of this condition. Ludwick Sternbach,[15] whose study is based on the *Dharmasastra*, *Arthasastra*, *Kamasutra*, *Grihya-Sutras* and the *Mahabharata*, concludes that when the forms of marriage are closely examined there existed in ancient India not eight but eleven forms of marriage. The difference between the *Prajapatya* and the *Brahma* is that the bridegroom in the former is the suitor, i.e., he has solicited the girl, and is not invited by the father of the bride. He is an applicant for the bride's hand, and this makes it inferior to the *Brahma* form, where the bridegroom is voluntarily and respectfully invited by the father of the bride to accept his daughter. A Hindu marriage, being a gift of the bride, loses a part of its merit if it is not voluntary or wilful, but has to be applied for.

The *Prajapatya* was probably used only for a monogamic marriage and the husband could not renounce his wife and take to the order of *sanayasa* or *vanaprastha* without her consent or her company. In fact the *Brahma* was originally identical with the *Prajapatya*, because Apastamba and Vasishtha do not mention *Prajapatya* at all. The *Prajapatya* was added later, therefore, the *Smriti* writers fail to bring out the difference between the two.[16] *Prajapatya* is the second best and approved form.[17] As in the *Brahma* form so in the *Prajapatya* one the bridegroom is invited and honourably received by the father of the bride.[18]

14. Medhatithi on Manu III, 30 translated by G. Jha, *Manu-Smriti*, vol. II, part I, pp. 55-56.

15. Ludwick Sternbach, *Juridical Studies in Ancient Indian Law*, Delhi 1965, part I, pp. 347-348, 375-376.

16. A.S. Altekar, *The Position of Women in Hindu Civilisation*, pp. 46-47.

17. Baudhayana I. II. 20, 3, S.B.E., vol. 14; Gautama IV, 7, S.B.E., vol. 2.

18. Narada XII, 40, S.B.E., vol. 33.

(v) *The Asura*

The bridegroom having given as much wealth as he could afford to the father, paternal kinsman and to the girl herself took her as his bride. This being a sale of the bride was regarded as a base form of marriage and was prohibited by Manu.[19] This form was recognised by the Hindu law during the British period. In *Kailasanatha* v. *Parasakthi*[20] it was held that the distinctive feature of the *Asura* form of marriage is the giving of money or money's worth to the bride's father for his benefit or as consideration for his giving the girl in marriage. However, a courtesy or complimentary present given to the bride or her family has to be distinguished from bride-price.[21] Money paid by the bridegroom for the specific purpose of making jewellery for the bride is not bride-price and does not make the marriage an *Asura* one.[22] Now after Indian Independence the whole situation was reviewed by the Supreme Court,[23] which held that the *Asura* is an unapproved form of marriage and the test of it is that there shall be not only benefit to the bride's father, but that benefit shall form a consideration for the sale of the bride.

(vi) *The Gandharva*

This was a marriage arising out of mutual desire of a man and a woman, and can be compared with the modern love marriage. It was enjoined by the *sastra* that a *Brahmana* could contract a marriage legitimately in one of the first four forms.[24] However, in practice at least according to the Mithila School of law the *Gandharva* was recognised amongst the Brahmins.[25]

19. Manu III, 51, S.B.E., vol. 25. For a critical study of the *Asura* see J. Gonda, "*Reflections on the Arsa and Asura forms of Marriage*", *Sarupa-Bharati* edited by J.N. Agrawal and B.D. Shastri, Hoshiarpur, 1954, p. 223 ff.

20. *Kailusanatha* v. *Parasakthi*, A.I.R. 1935 Mad. 740; see also *Authikesavulu* v. *Ramanujam* (1909) 32 Mad. 512 (to the same effect); *Ratnathami* v. *Somasundra*, A.I.R. 1921 Mad. 608 (there must be an element of material benefit to the bride's parents); *Samu* v. *Anachi*, A.I.R. 1926 Mad. 37.

21. *Sivanagalingam* v. *Ambalavana*, A.I.R. 1938 Mad. 479.

22. *Velayutha* v. *Suryamurthi*, A.I.R. 1942 Mad. 219.

23. *Veerappa* v. *Michael*, A.I.R. 1963 *S.C.* 933; see also comments by S.S. Nigam, "*Annual Survey—Hindu Law*" (1964) 6 J.I.L.I. at p. 548 ff.

24. Vishnu XXIV, 27, S.B.E., vol. 7.

25. *Kamani Devi* v. *Kameshwar* (1946) 25 Pat. 58 (a case which contains some anomalous propositions beyond the scope of this thesis).

In *Bhaoni* v. *Maharaj*[26] the *Gandharva* was equated with concubinage. It was held that this form had become obsolete as a form of marriage giving the status of wife and making the issue legitimate. This case is unlikely to be followed in view of the Hindu Marriage Act, 1955 and changing public opinion, which tends to encourage grown up persons to make their own decision in the choice of their life partners.

(vii) *The Rakshasa*

This was a marriage by seizure of a girl by force from her house while she wept and called for assistance, after her kinsmen and friends had been slain in battle or wounded and their houses broken open.

(viii) *The Paisacha*

Where the suitor secretly seduced the girl while she was asleep or drunk or disordered in intellect that sinful marriage was called *Paisacha*. This is the eighth and the basest.

The first four marriages are regarded as "approved" marriages. It was a Hindu religious belief that sons born of these marriages were radiant with knowledge of the Vedas and were honoured by good men. Having these qualities of beauty and goodness, possessing wealth and fame, obtaining as many enjoyments as they desire and being most righteous, they would live a hundred years. The remaining four are regarded as blameworthy, from which spring sons who are cruel and liars, who hate the Vedas and the sacred law.[27] *Rakshasa* and *Paisacha*, which were condemned by Manu as base and sinful,[28] however did not legalise force or fraud as the marriage ceremony had in theory to be performed with sacred rites,[29] without which the marital relationship did not arise. Their recognition can be justified on the ground that they existed in order to validate the circumstances of which the unfortunate woman

26. *Bhaoni* v. *Maharaj* (1881) 3 All. 738; see also M.L. Jain, "*Validity of Hindu Marriage Solemnised without performing any Customary Ritual or Ceremony*" A.I.R. 1961, Journal, p. 84.

27. Manu III, 39-41.

28. Manu III, 33-34.

29. Vasishtha XVII, 73, S.B.E., vol. 14; see also J.D. Mayne, *A Treatise on Hindu Law and Usage*, Madras, 11th. ed., 1950, pp. 123, 127-128; P.N. Sen, *The General Principles of Hindu Jurisprudence*, Calcutta, 1918, pp. 269-270.

was the victim. The jurists were concerned with the results flowing from the circumstances preceding the marriage and classified those circumstances accordingly.

According to the *sastra* inferior forms of marriage, namely, *Asura*, *Gandharva*, *Rakshasa* and *Paisacha* do not involve a change of the *gotra* of the bride,[30] which is an essential part of the ceremony of the *Vedic* marriage, because in such forms there is no voluntary gift of the bride by her father to the bridegroom. Approved forms were meant for *Brahmans*[31] who were an important caste. According to Manu the first six forms of marriage were lawful for a *Brahmana*, the four last for a *Kshatriya*, and the same four, excepting the *Rakshasa*, for a *Vaisya* and a *Sudra*.[32] The significance of the approved and unapproved forms of marriage was that it determined the devolution of a woman's property on her death. In the former the husband and his family, while in the latter the father and his family succeed to her *Stridhana*.[33] Where a woman was married in the unapproved forms, her death ceremonies were to be performed by a member of the *gotra* of her father, whereas in case of the approved marriage, they might be performed either by her husband's *gotra* or her father's. The reason for this distinction seems to be that approved marriages were authorised by the families of the couple concerned, while the unapproved were contracted against the wish of family of the woman concerned, if we reserve the case of the *Asura* marriage, which originally did not imply a sacramental transfer but only a sale—spiritually (so the *sastra* seems to imply) she remained a member of her natal *gotra*. That is why she retained the *gotra* of her father.

If we look critically at the above mentioned eight forms of marriage, it will be evident that they were a mere elaboration of the concept of marriage (*vivaha*). They took account

30. *Vivada Tandava* translated by J.C. Ghose, *The Principles of Hindu Law : The Commentaries*, vol. II, Calcutta, 1917, p. 1142.

31. Vishnu XXIV, 27, S.B.E., vol. 7.

32. Manu III, 23, S.B.E., vol. 25.

33. Narada XIII, 9, S.B.E., vol. 33; *Moosa* v. *Haji* (1906) 30 Bom. 197; see also Surinder Singh, "*The Hindu Law of Marriage : Old and New*", The Law Review, Panjab University Law College (1965), vol. XVII, 24 at pp. 111-112; P.W. Rege, "*The Development of Woman's Proprety in India*" in Legal Essays—I by T.K. Tope, Bombay (1961-1962) 46 at pp. 49-50.

of local custom and usage, which were developing alongside the *sastra*. A survey of the *dharma-sastras*, *smritis*, *Nibandhas* and the Commentaries will prove that Hindu law was never static, but was modified by the practice of the time to suit the just demands of the people. With the advent of the British rule, the ancient sources of Hindu law began to be modified by judicial decisions and legislative enactments, while Hindu society assumed a new character because of its contact with the Western education, civilisation, economic and scientific progress.[34] In fact the Hindu Marriage Act, 1955 is the result of the influence which had started in the British period. Thus the *dharma-sastra's* contact with actual usage, though sometimes difficult to trace, has been, in practice, continuous.

According to Kautilya, whose *Arthasastra* (a predominantly secular book), reflects practical usages, there can be no divorce in case the marriage is contracted in one of the approved forms. But if the marriage is in an unapproved form, then it can be dissolved by mutual consent, if both have come to hate each other. There can be no release at the instance of only one party to the marriage who has begun to feel aversion to the other party in whatever form the marriage may have been performed.[35] Kautilya actually says *amokso dharma-vivahanam* "The law does not allow the dissolution of marriage between spouses who have undergone a *dharmic vivaha*."[36] The first four marriages are *dharmya*, i.e., connected with righteousness, because they are brought about under the authority of the father. Such marriages do not admit divorce.

6. *NUPTIAL CEREMONIES*

According to the plain *smriti* texts marriages in the un-

34. M.K. Lakshmipathi Chetty, "*A Survey of the Hindu Code Bill*" (1953) 105 M.L.J., Journal, p. 1 ff. ; U.C. Sarkar, "*Hindu Law : Its Character and Evolution*", The Law Review, Panjab University Law College (1965), vol. XVII, 1 at pp. 3, 16-17; J.D.M. Derrett, *Hindu Law Past and Present*, pp. 42-43.

35. Kautilya III, 3, 15-19, R.P. Kangle, *The Kautilya Arthasastra*, Part II, University of Bombay, 1963; P.V. Kane, *History of Dharmasastra*, vol. II, part I, pp. 621-622; S.R. Sastri, *Women in Sacred Laws*, 1950, p. 49.

36. Kautilya III, 3, 19, translated by J.D.M. Derrett. This translation differs slightly from that of R.P. Kangle, Bombay, 1963 ("there is no divorce in pious marriages").

approved forms do not require the performance of the religious ceremony, but the *sastric* law as applied by the courts during the British period in India held that such ceremony was essential for the validity of the marriage.[37] This is so even in modern Hindu Law. It was held in *Deivani* v. *Chidambaram*[38] that there are two essential elements to constitute a valid marriage, viz., a secular element, which is the gift of the bride in the four forms, the transference of dominion for consideration in the *Asura* form, and mutual consent of the spouses in the *Gandharva* form. These must be supplemented by the actual performance of marriage by going through the forms prescribed by the *Grihya-Sutras*, of which the essential elements are '*panigrahana*' (joining of hands of the bride and the bridegrooms) and '*saptapadi*' (taking of seven steps by the bridal couple). In the case of *Rakshasa* and *Paisacha* forms also (should these be capable of validity in modern times), there should be a marriage ceremony prescribed by the *sastras*. In *Bhaurao* v. *State of Maharashtra*[39] it was laid down that solenmisation of the marriage with proper rites and ceremonies was essential in the *Gandharva* 'form'. Similarly it was recently held by the Supreme Court[40] in a case of bigamy that in order to prove the validity of the second marriage it is necessary to prove that the essential nuptial ceremonies were performed.

The performance of rites and ceremonies according to religious beliefs (e.g., *saptapadi*) or according to custom and usage has been preserved by the Hindu Marriage Act. 1955.[41] The modern law has been developed in such a way as to show that the ceremony though vital to the religious purpose is no

37. *Brindavana* v. *Radhamani* (1899) 12 Mad. 72.

38. *Deivani* v. *Chidambaram*, A.I.R. 1954 Mad. 657; followed in *Kunta* v. *Siri Ram*, A.I.R. 1963 Punj. 235; see also *Ayodhya* v. *Shanti* I.L.R. 1963 Madh. Pr. 917 (where the validity of the marriage itself is in dispute, the performance of the necessary rites and ceremonies has to be proved).

39. *Bhaurao* v. *State of Maharashtra*, A.I.R. 1965 S.C. 1564.

40. *Kanwal* v. *H. P. Administration*, A.I.R. 1966 S.C. 614; relied on in *Venkata* v. *Tanguturu*, A.I.R. 1968 Andh. Pr. 107; see also *Phankari* v. *the State*, A.I.R. 1965 J. & K. 105 (to the same effect).

41. S. 7 (1) (2) of the Hindu Marriage Act, 1955; *Dutta* v. *State*, A.I.R. 1969 Cal. 55; K.S. Mathur, "*Validity of Hindu Marriage solemnised without performing any Customary Ritual or Ceremony*". A.I.R. 1962, Journal, p. 27.

longer vital to the working of the secular rights. Thus where a man and woman live as husband and wife and have children who are recognised as such by their community by the custom the rights of the spouses and their children will not be destroyed merely by someone's attempting to bring forth evidence that no ceremonies of marriage were performed on the couple.[42]

Whether or not such ceremonies are essential, their non performance or wrong performance can be excused under certain circumstances by the doctrine of *factum valet*, e.g., where the *saptapadi* (taking of seven steps) is not completed because of an accidental fire or some other mishaps, the validity of such a marriage cannot be upset subsequently. Where a marriage takes place under a custom according to which *saptapadi* is not an essential ceremony, the non-performance of *saptapadi* does not invalidate the marriage. In considering the validity of a marriage it is necessary to distinguish between the essentials and non-essentials of the custom.[43] The presumption that a valid marriage took place can be raised where it is established that the marriage was duly solemnised but some unessential ceremony was not performed or there was some defect in the completion of the rite.[44] Thus the sacramental and *sastric* characteristic of the Hindu marriage so far as the performance of the religious ceremonies is concerned is still in existence.

According to the *sastric* view the spiritual aspect of marriage was so important that the husband was said to have received his wife from the gods and not wedded her according to his own will, for he was doing what was agreeable to gods.[45] The consequence of marriage was that man and woman became one person, as the Veda expresses, "Her bones become

42. *Shivalingiah* v. *Chowdamma*, A.I.R. 1956 Mys. 17; D.F. Mulla, *Principles of Hindu Law*, Bombay, 1960, pp. 615-616, 807; see also *Rewaram* v. *Ramratan*, A.I.R. 1963 Madh. Pr. 160.

43. *Rakappa* v. *Chockalingam*, A.I.R. 1964 Mad. 126; Re *Raghave Reddy*, A.I.R. 1968 Andh. Pr. 117.

44. *Parbia* v. *Thopali*, A.I.R. 1966 Him. Pr. 20.

45. Grihya-Sutra of Hiranyakesin, S.B.E., vol. 30, pp. 189-190 ; Paraskara-Grihya-Sutra, S.B.E., vol. 29, p. 282; Manu IX, 95, S.B.E., vol. 25; N.C. Sen-Gupta, *Evolution of Ancient Indian Law*, London, 1953, p. 91.

identified with his bones, flesh with flesh, skin with skin."[46] From the time of the marriage, they are united in body and mind as well as in religious ceremonies.[47] As a river loses its identity by merging itself into the ocean, so a wife was supposed to merge her individuality with that of her husband. In the revealed texts of the *Veda*, in the traditional laws of the *Smritis*, and in the popular usage, the wife is declared to be half the body of her husband, equally sharing the outcome of good and evil acts.[48] So a Hindu marriage was a sacred union of two personalities into one for the purpose of the continuance of the society and for the uplift of the two by self-restraint, self-sacrifice and mutual co-operation for the performance of holy rites.[49] This is a central concept of Hindu ethics and law.

7. *THE OBJECT OF MARRIAGE*

It was threefold, namely *dharma* (the performance of religious and righteous duties), *praja* (progeny) and *rati* (pleasure). Where the Hindu lawgivers regarded *dharma* as the first and the highest aim of marriage, and procreation as the second, *dharma*, according to the *sastra*, dominated marriage. Marriage was a means not merely for satisfying sexual desire or to obtain progeny, but to secure a partner for the perfor-

46. Dayabhaga, ch. IV, sec. II, 14; *Tekait Mon Mohini* v. *Basanta Kumar* (1901) 28 Cal. 751 at 758 (the union is a sacred tie and subsists even after the death of the husband); P.H. Prabhu, *Hindu Social Orgnanisation*, pp. 172, 228.

47. Apastamba II 6. 14, 16, S.B.E., vol. 2; Prof Indra, *The Status of Women in Ancient India*, Banaras, 1955, p. 82; K.M. Kapadia, *Marriage and Family in India*, p. 169; Clarisse Bader, *Women in Ancient India*, London, 1925, p. 57.

48. Brihaspati XXV, 46, S.B.E., vol. 33; Manu IX, 45; Pratapa Rudra Deva, *Sarasvati-Vilasa*, translated from the original Sanskrit by Thomas Foulkes, London, 1881 (492-493) p. 99; G. Banerjee, *The Hindu Law of Marriage and Stridhana*, p. 150; Golapchandra Sarkar Sastri, *A Treatise on Hindu Law* Calcutta, 1927, p. 168; T.P. Gopalakrishnan, *Hindu Marriage Law*, Allahabad, 1957, p. 42; Gyan Prakash, *The Hindu Code*, Allahabad, 1958, pp. 258-259; H. Cowell, *The Hindu Law*, Calcutta, 1870, p. 165.

49. P.V. Kane, *History of Dharmasastra*, vol. II, part I, p. 193; Jaim. VI, 1. 3. 18 cited in K.T. Bhashyam Aiyangar, *Women in Hindu Law*, Madras, 1928, p. 11.

mance of religious duties. It enabled a man, by becoming a householder to perform religious sacrifices to the gods and to procreate sons.[50] It was the duty of the husband to require and the right of the wife to give co-operation in all religious acts. Manu[51] on the authority of the *Veda* declares that religious rites must be performed by the husband and wife together. Women were not allowed to perform any sacrifice, vow or fast apart from their husbands. They could obtain heaven merely by being obedient to their husbands.

It was a Hindu belief that a Hindu from his birth is born with three debts,[52] i.e., he owes *brahmacarya* (study of the *Vedas*) to the sages, sacrifice to the gods, and progeny to *pitris* (ancestors). The second purpose of the marriage was to procreate sons, who were supposed to save a man from hell. A son is called *putra* because he delivers his father from the hell called *Put*.[53] So much importance was attached to the birth of a son that a man was said to have conquered the spiritual worlds and obtained immortality and heaven by having a son.[54] Immediately upon the birth of his first-born son a man was freed from his debt to the ancestors.[55] Legitimate progeny being the objective, marriage was a religious necessity.[56]

The purpose of the marriage is further evidenced by the procedure of the marriage ceremony, when the bridegroom addresses the bride as, "I am heaven, you are earth, Come! Let us join together so that we may generate a male child, a

50. Rig-Veda X. 85, 36 in S.B.E., vol. 29, p. 282; Clarisse Bader, *Women in Ancient India*, p. 27; K.M. Kapadia, *Marriage and Family in India*, pp. 167-168; P.H. Prabhu, *Hindu Social Organisation*, pp. 165-166, 173.

51. Manu IX, 96; Manu V, 155; P.V. Kane, *History of Dharmasastra*, vol. II, part I, p. 556; R.M. Das, *Women in Manu and his Seven Commentators*, Arrah, 1962, pp. 164, 171-172; N.K. Dutt, *Origin and Growth of Caste in India*, London, 1931, p. 235; K.V. Rangaswami Aiyangar, *Aspects of the Social and Political System of Manusmriti*, pp. 156-157.

52. Baudhayana II. 9. 16, 7, S.B.E., vol. 14; Vasishtha XI, 48, S.B.E., vol. 14.

53. Manu IX, 138.

54. Manu IX, 137.

55. Manu IX, 106; Narada XII, 19, S.B.E., vol. 33.

56. Manu IX, 96; see also K.P. Jayaswal, *Manu and Yajnavalkya*, Calcutta, 1930, p. 225; T.P. Gopalakrishnan, *Hindu Marriage Law*, Allahabad, 1957, pp. 30-32.

son, for the sake of the increase of wealth, a blessed offspring of strength."[57] Marriage enabled a man to make himself complete by the association of his wife and his son.[58] His sacred obligations, i.e., the proper performance of his religious duties, faithful service to gods, his offspring, highest conjugal happiness, heavenly bliss for himself and his ancestors, depended on his wife alone,[59] as he was incompetent to perform the above mentioned acts without the help and presence of the latter.

8. *THE DISSOLUTION OF HINDU SASTRIC MARRIAGE*

It has been seen that a Hindu marriage, being a sacrament, once performed before the nuptial fire with the sacred texts, becomes irrevocable on the completion of the ceremony of taking seven steps by the couple.[60] There is no evidence as to the practice of divorce as such during the *Vedic* and post *Vedic* periods. It was a holy union of mind, body and soul of the spouses and, it was believed, that even death did not put an end to it, for the wife remained linked with her husband in soul after death in the next world.[61] It was the highest duty of husband and wife to remain united in marriage and be utterly faithful to each other.[62] It was ordained by the Creator that a husband could not release his wife by sale or repudiation.[63] The wife was required to be obedient to her husband under all circumstances. She was expected to worship him as God even if he was lacking in good qualities and virtue.[64]

According to Apastamba[65] if the solemn vow of marriage

57. Grihya-Sutra of Hiranyakesin, S.B.E., vol. 30, p. 190.

58. Manu IX, 45; see also Prof. Indra, *The Status of Women in Ancient India*, p. 86; Clarisse Bader, *Women in Ancient India*, p. 60; P. H. Prabhu, *Hindu Social Organisation*, pp. 150, 236; U.C. Sarkar, *Epochs in Hindu Legal History*, Hoshiarpur, 1958, p. 400.

59. Manu IX, 28; see also K.T. Bhashyam Aiyangar, *Women in Hindu Law*, Madras, 1928, p. 11.

60. Manu VIII, 227.

61. *Tekait Mon Mohini* v. *Basanta* (1901) 28 Cal. 751 at 758.

62. Manu IV, 101, 102; D.P. Vora, *Evolution of Morals in the Epics*, Bombay, 1959, pp. 40-48 (where instances of absolute fidelity are given).

63. Manu IX, 46; S.R. Sastri, *Women in Sacred Laws*, p. 91.

64. Manu V, 154.

65. Apastamba II, 10. 27. 6. S.B.E., vol. 2; Dwarka Nath Mitter, *The Position of Women in Hindu Law*, p. 278.

is transgressed both husband and wife certainly go to hell. Hindu marriage was regarded as an eternal and sacred bond which united the husband and wife for the performance of their religious sacrifices. Dissolution of marriage was thus not contemplated by the *sastra*, for it was un-*dharmic*, unrighteous and sinful.

9. *REMARRIAGE OF FEMALES*

It has been seen that the *sastra* did not countenance divorce. From this the question arises whether the remarriage of females was allowed ? The procedure of performing *sastric* nuptials was available only for virgins, and never for girls who had lost their virginity.[66] A girl was fit for being given in marriage only once as Manu has said, "Once is a maiden given in marriage and once does a man say, 'I will give', this is done only once."[67] The bride is free to be transferred from the father's house to that of the husband; but she is not allowed to leave her husband's home and go elsewhere, i.e., take another husband. This is supported by a hymn of the Atharvaveda, which reads, "Hence from the father's house, and not thence from the husband's house, I send the bride free. I make her softly fettered there so that she may live with her husband blessed in fortune and offspring."[68] This shows that no separation was allowed between husband and wife.

According to the *sastra* a woman was expected to lead a life of chastity and self-denial and was not to mention even the name of another man after the death of her husband.[69] She who remains virtuous and chaste after the death of her husband reaches heaven, although she may have no son.[70] On the contrary a woman who from a desire to have offspring

66. Manu VIII, 226.

67. Manu IX, 47.

68. Atharvaveda, XIV. 1. 18, *The Hymns of the Atharvaveda*, translated into English by R.T.H. Griffith, vol. II, Benaras, 1917, p. 163; Prof. Indra, *The Status of Women in Ancient India*, p. 83; P.H. Prabhu, *Hindu Social Organisation*, p. 169.

69. Manu V. 157; P.V. Kane, *History of Dharmasastra*, vol. II, part I, p. 583; P.N. Sen, *The General Principles of Hindu Jurisprudence*, pp. 276-277.

70. Manu V, 160; R.M. Das, *Women in Manu and his Seven Commentators*, pp. 224-225; T. Strange, *Hindu Law*, vol. I, London, 1830, p. 245.

violates her sacred duty towards her deceased husband, brings on herself disgrace in this world and loses her place in heaven.[71] "Nowhere is a second husband prescribed for a virtuous woman."[72] Thus the non-existence of nuptial ceremonies for a second marriage and the prohibition of remarriage of women are evidence against the recognition of divorce in the matrimonial system known to the *sastra*.

However, Narada, Parasara and Vasishtha authorise a woman to take another husband in five cases, i.e., when her husband is lost or dead, when he has become a religious ascetic, when he is impotent and when he has been expelled from caste.[73] A wife must wait for six years if her husband had disappeared, twelve years if he went to a foreign country for the purpose of studying. If he was heard of she should go to him.[74] According to Narada[75] if the husband had gone abroad a *Brahmana* wife should wait for eight years, or four years if she had no issue. A lesser number of years was prescribed for *Kshatriya* and *Vaisya* wives. After that period she was entitled to take another husband. Manu says that if the husband went abroad for sacred duty, the wife should wait for eight years, six years if he went for knowledge and fame, and three years if he went for pleasure or for another wife.[76] He does not mention what the wife should do after these years of waiting, but remarriage is obviously envisaged in such a case.

Narayana, Kulluka and Raghava following Vasishtha say that she should go to see her husband in the place where he might be expected to be present. But Nandana and Devala[77] are of the opinion that she could take another husband and in

71. Manu V, 161; Prof. Indra, *The Status of Women in Ancient India*, pp. 96-97; Ganganatha Jha, *Hindu Law in its Sources*, vol. I, Allahabad, 1930, pp. 515-516.

72. Manu V, 162; S.C. Bose, *The Hindoos As They Are*, Calcutta, 1883, pp. 244-251; N.K. Dutt, *Origin and Growth of Caste in India*, pp. 239-250.

73. Narada XII, 97; Parasara IV, 30; Vasishtha XVII, 74; see also P.H. Prabhu, *Hindu Social Organisation*, p. 191; H. Mehta, *The women under the Hindu Law of Marriage and Succession*, Bombay, 1943, pp. 17-18.

74. Gautama XVIII, 15-17, S.B.E., vol. 2.

75. Narada XII, 98-99, S.B.E., vol. 33.

76. Manu IX, 76; D.P. Vora, *Evolution of Morals in the Epics*, p. 79.

77. Devala, Book IV, ch. IV, section II, 151-153 in H.T. Colebrooke, *Digest of Hindu Law*, vol. II, Madras, 1874.

doing so there would be no sin at all.[78] It is argued on the authority of these texts that the second marriage of the wife presupposes the dissolution of the first.[79] It is also contended on the authority of the Atharva-Veda IX. 5, 27-28, that a widow could remarry on performing the *'Aja Panchoudana'* sacrifice. A second husband dwells in the same world with his re-wedded wife if she offers the *'Aja Panchoudana'* to the memory of her deceased husband. This argument is supported by the funeral hymn in the Rig-Veda X. 18. 8, which reads, "Rise woman, thou art lying by the side of one whose life is gone; come to the world of the living away from him, thy husband that is dead, and become the wife again of him who is willing to take thee by the hand and marry thee."[80]

However, this view did not find favour with Sir Gooroodas Banerjee,[81] who explained these texts on the ground that these rules either, like the practice of raising up issue by a kinsman on an appointed wife, relate to an earlier stage of Hindu society in which rapid multiplication of the race was regarded as an important object, or they merely show the existence of some difference of opinion among the Hindu sages on a point on which absolute unanimity of opinion can hardly be expected. The prevailing sentiment of Hindu society has always been repugnant to the second marriage of women. The true explanation seems to lie rather in the need of the *sastra* to recognise utilitarian practices. This is evident from the *Arthasastra* of Kautilya, whose provisions reflect customary law and usage. Kautilya[82] allows a woman to remarry under certain circumstances, e.g., where her husband had gone away on a long journey, or had become an ascetic or was dead.

78. R.M. Das, *Women in Manu and his Seven Commentators*, p. 198.

79. A.S. Altekar, *The Position of Women in Hindu Civilisation*, pp. 83-84; K. T. Bhashyam Aiyangar, *Women in Hindu Law*, p. 27; T.K. Tope, *Why Hindu Code?*, Poona, 1950, p. 26; Hon. Mr. Justice P.B. Gajendragadkar "*Hindu Code Bill*" (1951) 53 Bom. L.R., Journal, 77 at p. 99.

80. K.T. Bhashyam Aiyangar, *Women in Hindu Law*, p. 12; N. K. Dutt, *Origin and Growth of Caste in India*, pp. 72-73; A. S. Altekar, *The Position of Women in Hindu Civilisation*, p. 150.

81. G. Banerjee, *The Hindu Law of Marriage and Stridhana*, pp.207-208.

82. Kautilya III. 4, 24-31, *The Kautilya Arthasastra* translated by R.P. Kangle, Bombay, 1962; see also M.V. Krishna Rao, *Studies in Kautilya*, Delhi, 1958, p. 237.

She was expected to wait for certain periods of time depending upon whether she had children and was maintained by her husband's family. Remarriage of women in such cases could be attributed to custom and usage which were developing alongside the *sastra*. The texts authorising or presumed to be authorising a woman to take a second husband may alternatively be construed as cases of presumption of death—actual death and civil death—and could be seen by the orthodox as only apparent breaches of the *sastric* pattern of the indissolubility of marriage.

According to the commentaries and digests the above mentioned texts do not apply to the present (*Kali*)[83] age. The human race having degenerated from its original virtue and purity, the sages of Hindu law, for the benefit of human race declared that the remarriage of widows in the '*Kali*' age is forbidden. A.S. Altekar[84] on the authority of the *Aditya-purana*, Devanabhatta and Madhava, the commentator on Parasara, admits that widow-remarriage is no longer valid in the '*Kali*' age. Widow-remarriage in the present age was so much disapproved of that an extended meaning was given to the word 'widow' so as to include the betrothed girl whose prospective husband had died before the performance of the marriage ritual. If by mistake a man happened to marry such a girl, he was to perform a penance and abandon her. However, this practice did not find much approval in a society which continued to be guided by Manu's sensible opinion that no marital tie arises before the marriage ceremony is performed.

The stigma attached to the twice-married woman proves that widow-remarriage was not prevalent in orthodox Hindu society to which especially the *sastra* applied. She was called a *Punarbhu*, who might be of three kinds, namely, a 'widow' whose marriage had not been consumated, one who after

83. B. Bhattacharya, *The 'Kalivarjyas' or Prohibitions in the 'Kali' Age*, University of Calcutta, 1943, pp. 134 ff.; P.V. Kane, *The History of Dharmasastra*, vol II, part I, p. 620; T. Mitra, *The Law Relating to the Hindu Widow*, Calcutta, 1881, pp. 193-200; N.K. Dutt, *Origin and Growth of Caste in India*, p. 253; P.N. Sen, *The General Principles of Hindu Jurisprudence*, pp. 278-279.

84. A.S. Altekar, *The Position of Women in Hindu Civilisation*, p. 155; J.D.M. Derrett, *Hindu Law Past and Present*, pp. 112-113.

having left the husband of her youth and betaken herself to another, returns to the house of her former husband, and the woman, who on failure of brothers-in-law, is delivered by her relations to a *sapinda* (blood-relative) of the same caste.[85]

The *Punarbhu* was regarded as an inferior wife,[86] but her issue were legitimate,[87] though according to the quality of her marriage they occupied an inferior status,[88] as her son (*paunarbhava*) did not inherit his father's property as an heir but as a kinsman.[89] He was not fit for being invited to a *sraddha*[90] (a feast given to the *Brahmins* in the memory of one's ancestors). The husbands of remarried women were not to be associated with nor to be invited to the *sraddha*.[91] The daughters of the *Punarbhus* were to be avoided and regarded as girls of the lowest birth.[92] They were treated as equal to the "mothers of *Sudras*." (The mothers of *Sudras* were fourth-caste wives of a *Brahmana*, wedded for lust, and of low social status). The children of these women were not admitted to social meetings; they were considered as unfit for society.[93] Apastamba enumerates the twice-married woman among those who are unfit for being taken in marriage. He condemns remarriage of females altogether when he says, "If one has intercourse with a woman who had already another husband, then sin is incurred; in that case the son also is sinful."[94]

85. Narada XII, 46-48; Vasishtha XVII, 19-20; Ganganatha Jha, *Hindu Law in its Sources*, pp. 517-519.

86. Narada XII, 45.

87. Manu IX, 159.

88. Manu V, 162; N.K. Dutt, *Origin and Growth of Caste in India*, p. 239.

89. Manu IX, 160.

90. Gautama XV, 18, S.B.E., vol. 2; Manu III, 155; Yaj. I, 222, *Yajnavalkya Smriti* (with the commentary of Vijnanesvara called the Mitaksara), Book I, The Acharya translated by Srisa Chandra Vidyarnava, Allahabad, 1918; R.M. Das, *Women in Manu and his Seven Commentators*, p. 226.

91. Manu III, 166.

92. H.T. Colebrooke, *Digest of Hindu Law*, Madras, 1874, vol. II, Book IV, ch. IV, section III, 165.

93. H.T. Colebrooke, *Digest of Hindu Law*, vol. II, Book IV, ch. IV, section III, 162; see also G. Banerjee, *The Hindu Law of Marriage and Stridhana*, p. 209; D.P. Vora, *Evolution of Morals in the Epics*, pp. 80-81.

94. Apastamba II. 6. 3, 3-4, S.B.E., vol. 2.

According to Vatsyayana[95] who harmonises *kama* with *dharma* so that they may not clash in any way, there was no regular marriage for a widow, but if a woman who had lost her husband was of weak character and was unable to restrain her desires, she might unite herself to a man, who was a seeker after pleasure and was an excellent lover, and such a woman was called *punarbhu*. In the choice of such a lover it was best for her to follow the natural inclinations of her own heart. However, the connection with her was of a loose character. She was more independent than the wife wedded according to sacramental rites. She assumed the place of a mistress, patronised his wives, was generous to his servants and treated his friends with familiarity. She was expected to show greater knowledge of the arts than his wedded wives and to please the lover with the sixtyfour arts of love (*kamakalas*). She participated in sports, festivities, drinking parties, garden picnics and other amusements. Vatsyayana says that it was improper to establish sexual relations with the *punarbhu*, but such an act was not absolutely condemned, because pleasure was the guiding motive in all such connections. Thus the position of the *punarbhu* was quite distinct from that of the wedded wife who participated with her husband in all religious performances and had to live with decency. The inferior position accorded to the *punarbhu*, the imposition of social penalties upon her children, and sometimes upon her husband are evidence against the approval of widow-remarriage by orthodox Hindu society.

Divorce, in the sense of dissolution of marriage whereby the status of husband and wife ceases to exist as such, marital rights and duties are severed by law and the spouses are free to remarry, was not recognised at Hindu law by the *sastra*.[96] This is also supported by a hymn of the Atharva-Veda, which reads, "Be not divided, O husband and wife; live together all your lives, sporting with sons and grandsons, rejoicing in your

95. H.C. Chakladar, *Social Life in Ancient India*, Calcutta, 1954, pp. 127 ff. (a study in Vatsyayana's *Kama-Sutra*).

96. H.L. Seth, *Matrimonial Muddle in India*, Lahore, 1942, p. 23; Rajkumari Agarwala, "*Hindu Divorce Law—its History*" (1959) 2 M.L.J., Journal, p. 45; Ram Keshave Ranade, "*The Hindu Code* 1948", A.I.R. 1949, Journal, p. 12 at 13.

happy home."[97] According to Vatsyayana[98] even the *Gandharva* marriage (an approved form) when solemnised before the holy fire could not be dissolved. He treated this form of marriage as the best. In this respect he seems to be more humanitarian than religious. By marriage a girl normally became integrated into her husband's family. She formed part of the household, which consisted of his parents, brothers, unmarried sisters and sisters-in-law together with their children, all of whom enjoy commensality and worship jointly. Whether or not her marital relationship with her husband was happy, she could not be uprooted from the family by abandonment or supersession. Therefore, there was no divorce acknowledged by the *dharmasastra.*

However, a husband could abandon or supersede his wife under certain circumstances (see later the distinction between abandonment and supersession). Such an abandonment had to be just and reasonable otherwise a very humiliating punishment is prescribed for such an act by Apastamba[99] who says, "He who has unjustly forsaken his wife shall put on an ass's skin with the hair turned outside, and beg in seven houses saying, 'Give alms to him who forsook his wife.' That shall be his livelihood for 6 months." Similarly if a wife forsook her husband she had to perform a hard penance for twelve nights. According to Manu[100] a wife is punished for her sin of disloyalty to her husband in her next life by being born in the womb of a jackal and tormented by disease. Narada[101]

97. Atharvaveda XIV. 1. 21-22, *The Hymns of the Atharva-Veda*, translated by R.T.H. Griffith, vol. II, p. 164; Prof. Indra, *The Status of Women in Ancient India*, p. 83; P.V. Kane, *History of Dharmasastra*, vol. II, part I, p. 526.

98. *Vatsyayana* (translated by K. Rangaswami Iyengar), Book III, ch. V, 13, 30, pp. 131, 133.

99. Apastamba I. 10. 28, 19-20, S.B.E., vol. 2; Prof. Indra, *The Status of Women in Ancient India*, pp. 84-85; K.M. Kapadia, *Marriage and Family in India*, p. 100; P. H. Prabhu, *Hindu Social Organisation*, p. 276; S.C. Banerjee, *Dharma-Sutras. A Study in their Origin and Development*, Calcutta, 1962, pp. 163-164.

100. Manu IX, 30, S.B.E., vol. 25.

101. Narada XII, 95, S.B.E., vol. 33; Yaj. I, 76; N.K. Dutt, *Origin and Growth of Caste in India*, pp. 251-252; H. Cowell, *The Hindu Law*, Calcutta, 1870, p. 164.

enjoins that if a man leaves a wife who is obedient, of pleasant speech, skilful, virtuous and the mother of male issue, the king shall make him mindful of his duty by severe punishment. A person who leaves a blameless wife should be punished as a thief. Vasishtha[102] makes a sweeping remark when he states that though tained by sin, whether she be quarrelsome, or left the house or has suffered criminal force or has fallen into the hands of thieves, a wife cannot be abandoned.

She should be abandoned, however, if she yields herself to her husband's pupil, or to his teacher, or a man of degraded caste or attempts to kill her husband.[103] This shows that even unjust abandonment was not allowed by Hindu law, let alone the dissolution of marriage. Steele[104] as a result of his enquiries in the early British period understood 'abandonment' in the above case as equal to divorce, but it is submitted that this was incorrect. 'Abandonment' could be treated as relating to the worldly and/or the spiritual purposes of marriage. The former would be frustrated, where a wife was addicited to drink, was of bad conduct, was diseased, insane, guilty of adultery, had attempted to kill her husband or committed other heinous crime including procuring abortion.[105] The latter purpose of the marriage would be frustrated, if she was barren, bore daughters only and had reached the menopause.[106] Therefore, the husband would be justified in ceasing to cohabit with such a wife, but this 'abandonnent' never had the effect of divorce.

10. *THE DISTINCTION BETWEEN ABANDONMENT AND SUPERSESSION*

Since it might be apprehended that the right to abandon

102. Vasishtha XXVIII, 2-3, S.B.E. vol. 14; see also P.H. Prabhu, *Hindu Social Organisation*, p. 228.

103. Vasishtha XXI, 10-11, S.B.E., vol. 14.

104. A Steele, *The Law and Custom of Hindu Castes*, London, 1868, pp. 32, 171.

105. Mitak. on Yaj. I, 72, translated by J.R. Gharpure, *Yajnavalkya Smriti* (with the commentaries of the Mitakshara by Vijnanesvara and the Viramitrodaya by Mitramisra), Bombay, 1936, pp. 192-193.

106. Devala, Book IV, cf. I, section II, 62, H.T. Colebrooke, *A Digest of Hindu Law*, vol. II, Madras, 1874.

was tantamount to a right to divorce even under *sastric* law, the vocabulary needs to be examined. The Sanskrit word used for 'abandonment' is *tyaga*. Medhatithi[107] defines *tyaga* as giving up all intercourse with her and forbidding her to do household work. He says that for the wife going off in anger, caused by supersession, there are two optional alternatives in the shape of confinement or divorce. Here Jha's translation needs to be checked. Medhatithi[108] in fact says *tyaga* or *samnirodha*, abandonment or confinement in that order are alternatives. *Tyaga* denotes separation from conjugal intercourse as opposed to *Moksa*, which might be technical divorce.[109] It is not clear whether after being abandoned by her husband, a wife was free to marry again. Therefore, the word '*tyaga*' can denote several things. It implies supersession, e.g., where the husband abandoned an obedient, pleasant speaking, son-bearing and skilful wife.[110] It may imply a *divorcium a mensa et thoro*, where the wife became pregnant by another, or attempted to kill her husband, or committed heinous crime.[111] In such cases she was abandoned from marital intercourse and religious ceremonies. It may mean temporary separation, where a wife was abandoned for three months for the purpose of reforming her.[112] But abandonment in any case did not amount to dissolution of marriage whereby the status of the husband and wife ceased to exist as such and the marriage-tie was severed at law. Some coincidence with Christian teaching on divorce is visible here, but the point is not appropriate for further exploration here.

Manu says, "But she who shows aversion towards a mad man or an outcaste, a eunuch, one destitute of manly strength

107. Medhatithi on Manu VIII, 389, *Manu Smriti* translated by G. Jha, vol. IV, part II, Calcutta, 1926, p. 413.

108. Medhatithi on Manu VII, 80; see also S.K. Tewari, *Nullity of Marriage in Modern Hindu Law*, (unpublished) thesis, Ph.D., London, 1965, pp. 71-77.

109. K.P. Jayaswal, *Manu and Yajnavalkya*, Calcutta, 1930, p. 230; S. Venkataraman, "*Matrimonial Causes among Hindus*" (1962) 1 M.L.J., p. 1 ff.

110. Mitak. on Yaj. I, 76 translated by J.R. Gharpure, *Yajnavalkya-Smriti* Bombay, 1936, p. 199.

111. Mitak. on Yaj. I, 72, op. cit., pp. 192-193.

112. Medhatithi on Manu IX, 78.

or one afflicted with such diseases as punish crimes, shall neither be cast off nor deprived of her property."[113] G. Banerjee on the authority of Kulluka and Jagannatha[114] rightly states that what Manu excuses here is 'aversion', which means want of diligent attention, and not absolute abandonment.[115] Thus the text does not authorise even abandonment. This is supported by a popular verse which says that a husband could not release his wife by sale or repudiation.[116]

The object of 'abandonment' was to punish the wife for her misdeeds, e.g., a wife who had committed adultery was required to wear clothes smeared with clarified butter, and was to sleep on a mat of grass, or in a pit filled with cowdung, until her penance had been perforemd.[117] The 'abandonment' consists in not allowing her to participate in religious rites and conjugal matters, not casting her away onto the streets. She was to be kept apart in one room and provided with food and raiments. She was to wear dirty clothes and was treated with scorn. But after her periodical illness the sin was expiated and she was to be restored to her original position with her usual rights of a wife.[118] Similarly a wife who was disrespectful to her husband; was addicted to some evil passion; was a drunkard or diseased should be abandoned for three months after depriving her of her ornaments and furniture.[119] The object of this temporary punishment was to correct the wife and bring her to the right way. A husband should bear for one year with a wife who hated him. After that he should deprive her of her property and cease to cohabit with her.[120] Abandonment under the above circumstances is regarded as virtually legal

113. Manu IX, 79.

114. Book IV, ch. I, 57, 67, H.T. Colebrooke, *Digest of Hindu Law*; see also R.M. Das, *Women in Manu and his Seven Commentators*, p. 197.

115. G. Banerjee, *The Hindu Law of Marriage and Stridhana*, p. 214.

116. Manu IX, 46.

117. Vasishtha XXI, 8, S.B.E., vol. 14.

118. Gautama XXII, 35, S.B.E., vol. 2; Manu XI, 177, S.B.E., vol. 25; Narada XII, 91, S.B.E., vol. 33; Yaj. I, 70-72.

119. Manu IX, 78; see also R.M. Das, *Women in Manu and his Seven Commentators*, pp. 196-197.

120. Manu IX, 77, 81; Narada XII, 93.

dissolution of marriage.[121] This is not justifiable, for divorce as such did not exist at *sastric* Hindu law. Abandonment in the above cases is reasonable, because according to Manu,[122] a husband must be constantly worshipped as a god by a virtuous wife. The wife was expected to follow the same principle as her husband. By doing the above mentioned disgraceful acts, she was violating her sacred duty of obedience to her husband and was accordingly punishable.

Supersession (like 'abandonment') could be treated as relating to the worldly and/or the spiritual aspects of marriage. The former would be defeated and the wife would become unfit for the society of her husband, who might supersede her at any time, if she was addicted to spirituous liquour, was of bad conduct, rebellious, diseased, mischievous or wasteful.[123] Manu allows supersession of a barren wife in the eighth year, one all of whose children die in the tenth year, of her who is quarrelsome without delay.[124] Baudhayana allows supersession of a barren wife in the tenth year of marriage, bearing daughters only in the twelfth year, all of whose children die in the fifteenth year and uttering unpleasant wordst a once.[125] Kautilya allows supersession if a wife remains barren for eight years, if she bears still-born children for ten years and if she bears only females for twelve years. Then if he is desirous of having sons, he can marry again.[126]

Supersession under the above circumstances is justifiable. As the purpose of the Hindu *sastric* marriage is to perform

121. Kewal Motwani, *Manu Dharma Sastra—A Sociological and Historical Study*, Madras, 1958, p. 118. "After considering marriage as a highly ethical institution, Maun states, at great length, the grounds on which a legal dissolution is allowed."

122. Manu V, 154; Yaj. I, 77.

123. Manu IX, 80, Yaj. I, 73.

124. Manu IX, 81; R.M. Das, *Women in Manu and his Seven Commentators*, pp. 190-191; G. Banerjee, *The Hindu Law of Marriage and Stridhana*, p. 212.

125. Baudhayana II. 2, 6, S.B.E., vol. 14; S.C. Banerjee, *Dharma-Sutras—A Study in their Origin and Development*, pp. 163-164; P.V. Kane. *History of Dharmasastra*, vol. II, part I, pp.-552; Prof. Indra, *The Status of Women in Ancient India* p. 95; Clarisse Bader, *Women in Ancient India*, p. 60.

126. Kautilya III. 2, 38-40, *The Kautilya Arthasastra*, translated by R.P. Kangle, Bombay, 1963.

religious rites and beget male progeny, if either of the two is frustrated, a man is entitled to take another wife.[127] The above grounds defeat the religious aspect of marriage, because the delivery of the ancestors from hell after the death is considered to be brought about only by the continuation of the line through sons. The supersession had to be just and reasonable, and in the case of a sick wife who was virtuous and kind to her husband her consent had to be obtained.[128] However, in practice husbands could supersede their wives without their consent and even against their wishes merely on the ground that the wife was of a harsh and disagreeable nature.[129] Sometimes she was superseded even if she was virtuous and was the mother of male issue.[130] But in such a case she continued to occupy her status as a wife, and her marital rights remained unimpaired. She must be maintained properly and be given compensation as Vijananesvara comments, "Though superseded by another wife, she must be treated with courtesy, and receive gifts and respect as before."[131] In fact she had precedence over her husband's subsequent wife in the performance of religious sacrifices.[132] But if superseded wife goes out of her husband's home in anger, she must either be instantly confined or abandoned in the presence of the family.[133]

Both in abandonment and supersession the wife retained her status of a wife and had to be maintained. In the former she lost her conjugal, religious and household rights unless and until she was restored to her former position after the performance of the appropriate penance. Unjust abandonment was punishable. Prof. Indra[134] on the authority of Daksha Smriti,

127. Apastamba II. 5. 11, 12-13, S.B.E., vol. 2.

128. Manu IX, 82.

129. Manu IX, 81; see also A. S. Altekar, *The Position of Women in Hindu Civilisation*, pp. 106-107; K. M. Kapadia, *Marriage and Family in India*, pp. 98-99.

130. Yaj. I, 76.

131. Yaj. I, 74; Mitak. on Yaj. 74, *Yajnavalkya Smriti* translated by J. R. Gharpure, vol. II, part I, Bombay, 1936, p. 196; see also G. Banerjee, *The Hindu Law of Marriage and Stridhana*, p. 211.

132. Yaj. I, 88.

133. Manu IX, 83.

134. Prof. Indra, *The Status of Women in Ancient India*, p. 94.

IV, 45 asserts that the wife even though she be fallen should not be abandoned, and a man violating this principle is born as a woman in his next life and bears the agony of barrenness. Thus according to the *sastra* a Hindu marriage being a sacrament cannot be dissolved, because the wife is a gift from gods which cannot be revoked by the act of human beings.

11. *DIVORCE UNDER CUSTOM OR USAGE*

The position under the *sastra* has been indicated briefly. How then is it possible to claim that Hindus in India are familiar with divorce ? The answer lies in the field of custom. The *sastra* itself recognised custom as a source of law. The acts productive of merit which form part of the customs of daily life, as they have been settled by the agreement of those who know the law, have authority.[135] The time-honoured institutions of each country, caste and family should be preserved intact.[136] The laws of countries, castes and families, which are not opposed to the sacred law, have also authority.[137] The Veda, the sacred tradition, the customs of virtuous men, and one's own pleasure are means of defining the sacred law.[138] When it is impossible to act up to the precepts of sacred law, it becomes necessary to adopt a method founded on reasoning, because custom decides everything and overrules the sacred law.[139] Customs prevalent in a country must be acknowledged as authoritative.[140] There is evidence that the *smritis* themselves represented the existing practices.[141] Thus custom is transcendent law according to the sages so far as it is consistent with the *sastric* principles . The Vedas, the *smritis* and the practices of good men are the sources of law.[142]

135. Apastamba I.1, 1-2, S.B.E., vol. 2.
136. Bṛihaspati II, 28, S.B.E., vol. 33.
137. Gautama XI, 20, S.B.E., vol. 2.
138. Manu II, 12, S.B.E., vol. 25.
139. Narada I, 40, S.B.E., vol. 33.
140. Vasishtha I, 10, S.B.E., vol. 14.
141. U. C. Sarkar, "*Hindu Law: its Character and Evolution*" (1965) vol. XVI, The Law Review, Panjab University, 1 at pp. 9-11.
142. Baudhayana I. I. I, 1-4, S.B.E., vol. 14; see also N. C. Sen-Gupta, *Sources of Law and Society in Ancient India*, Calcutta, 1914, pp. 64 ff.; A. S. Nataraja Ayyar, *Mimamsa Jurisprudence*, Allahabad, 1952, pp. 48-62.

The right of dissolution of marriage recognised by custom has been preserved by S. 29 (2) of the Hindu Marriage Act, 1955[143]. The writers belonging to high castes attribute this to the low cultural level and high degree of illiteracy of tribes rendering the enforcement of the provisions of the Act both inexpedient and difficult.[144] According to O'Malley[145] divorce is opposed to the sacramental idea of marriage, but is permitted by many low castes, on such grounds as the unchastity of the wife or her failure to bear sons. Even among them, however, it is regarded as a concession to a husband rather than as a right. Divorce or deviations from the ordinary Hindu law are to be found only among the aboriginal tribes and the lower classes of Aryans; they are to be met with among the higher castes of Aryans only where (as in Southern India) they are surrounded by non-Aryans or have been influenced by non-Hindu communities.[146] However, this view popular to higher caste written is not correct for divorce is known in communities which are not not necessarily low, e.g., in the states of Maharashtra and some parts of the Punjab.[147] divorce is practised custom even by *Brahmins*.

Widows can validly remarry under the custom of 'Karewa' or 'Darewa'. The most usual form of 'Darewa' is when a widow marries the brother of her deceased husband.[148] The origin of this custom can be traced from the time of the Rig-Veda.[149] The second marriage is contracted under the form

143. *Chellappan* v. *Madhavi*, A.I.R. 1961 Ker. 311F.B.; *Chinuprasad* v. *Jani*, "*Hindu Marriage Act and Divorce*", A.I.R. 1964, Journal, p. 116.

144. S. Venkataraman, "*The Hindu Marriage Act* 1955" (1955) 2 M.L.J., Journal, 33 at p. 34.

145. L.S.S. O'Malley, *Indian Caste Customs*, Cambridge U.P., 1932, p. 94.

146. G. Banerjee, *The Hindu Law of Marriage and Stridhana*, p. 280; see also L. S. Mehta, "*Some Implications of The Hindu Code Bill* 1948", A.I.R. 1950, Journal, 26 at p. 27; Paras Diwan, "*Divorce Law of Hindus, contemplated reform and a few suggestions*", A.I.R. 1953, Journal, 7 at p. 9.

147. H. A. Rose, *A Compendium of the Punjab Customary Law*, Lahore, 1911, pp. 53-58.

148. H. A. Rose, *op. cit.*, p. 42; J.C. Ghose, *The Principles of Hindu Law*, Calcutta, 1906, pp. 696-698.

149. N. K. Dutt, *Origin and Growth of Caste in India*, pp. 72-73.

known as *Chaddar Andazi*.[150] The fact, that dissolution of marriage and remarriage of females are recognised by customary law, is no evidence that people governed by such customs are of low culture or of low morality. On the contrary it rather militates against it, for public morality is better served by a good system of divorce than by ineffective orthodoxy. Moreover, the courts do not recognise a custom which is contrary to reason, morality and public policy.

Among the Khasas in the Himalaya districts of Uttar Pradesh, marriage is not a sacrament, but a secular transaction. The main features are the transfer of dominion over the woman for consideration and her actual or constructive appropriation as a wife. No stigma is attached to divorce and widow-remarriage. Whether a wife divorces her husband for just cause, e.g., leprosy or impotency, apostacy, etc., or without such a cause, the second husband is in all cases required to refund the marriage expenses.[151] The marriage can also be dissolved by mutual consent of the spouses among the Khasas and the Patwas[152] of Madhya Pradesh. Widow-remarriage is also frequently practised.[153]

In the Assam valley, among some agricultural classes, the interchange of pan-leaf constitutes the ceremony of marriage, and tearing of the pan-leaf by the husband and the wife indicates its dissolution.[154] Second marriage is contracted in the forms of 'Sagai' and 'Shugna' in northern India.[155] Among the Lingayat of south Canara the remarriage of a wife deserted (i.e., divorced) by her husband is valid. The remarriage is called *Serai Udiki*. The ceremony consists in tying a *tali*

150. *Nathu* v. *Ram* (1905) Punjab Record 29.

151. L. D. Joshi, *Khasa Family Law*, Allahabad, 1929, pp. 2, 162; a very interesting example of the working of this rule is given by Jim Corbett in *My India*, O.U.P., 1954, pp. 59-62.

152. *Smt. Premanabai* v. *Channolal*, A.I.R. 1963 Madh. Pr. 57.

153. Bhagwant Rao Dubey, "*Widow Re-marriage in Madhya Pradesh*", *Man in India* (1965) vol. 45, p. 50 (a quarterly anthropological Journal); see also Ram Keshav Ranade, "*Widow-Remarriage* (whether *an approved form or an unapproved form*)" A.I.R. 1950, Journal, p. 59.

154. E. T. Dalton, *Descriptive Ethnology of Bengal*, Calcutta, 1872, p. 86.

155. *Hurry Churn* v. *Nimai* (1884) 10 Cal. 138; *Kally* v. *Dukhee* (1880) 5 Cal. 692.

(necklace) and giving a new cloth to the woman.[156] This could only happen if the original bond of matrimony were severed.

Among the lower castes women can remarry under certain circumstances, e.g., where the husband is impotent or where there are constant quarrels between the spouses, and the husband with the consent of his wife breaks her neck ornament and tears her saree and gives her a *chor chitti*, i.e. a deed of releasement.[157] After this the wife is free to contract a second marriage, which is called the *Pat* in the Maharashtra and *Natra* in Gujarat.[158]

According to the custom prevailing in Manipur divorce or *Khainaba* is permissible even amongst the Hindus. There is no condition attached to it, and it can be obtained at the pleasure of either spouse, even on a slight pretext. The remarriage of a divorced woman is alo recognised.[159] The caste system is still practised by the orthodox Hindus in India. Particular communities governed in their social relations by their castes recognise the authority of the Panchayats (i.e. important and influential members of the caste) to dissolve the marriage. The proceedings of the Panchayats are informal and their judgements are not recorded.[160] Therefore, there is lack of material and knowledge on the working of divorce under caste rules. The courts do not recognise the authority of the caste Panchayat to dissolve a marriage without the consent of both parties.[161] However, if such divorce is obtained by custom, its existence has to be proved by the party alleging it.[162]

156. *Virasangappa* v. *Rudrappa* (1885) 8 Mad. 440 (Manu and Narada cited at p. 450). As to the status of Lingayats, see Honourable Mr. Justice P. B. Gajendragadkar, "*Hindu Code Bill*", (1951) 53 Bom. L. R. 77 at p. 88.

157. Golapchandra Sarkar Sastri, *A Treatise on Hindu Law*, p. 169.

158. *Rahi* v. *Govind* (1876) I Bom. 97; J. S. Siromani, *Commentary on the Hindu Law*, Calcutta, 1885, p. 83. (It seems that *Natra* is capable of being confused with concubinage. See *Laxmansingh* v. *Kesharbai*, A.I.R. 1966 Madh. Pr. 166 at p. 169).

159. *Puyam* v. *Moiranthem*, A.I.R. 1956 Manipur 18.

160. See also J.D.M., Derrett, "*Divorce by Caste Custom*" (1963) 65 Bom. L. R., Journal, p. 161 at 163.

161. *Kishenlal* v. *Prabhu*, A.I.R. 1963 Raj. 95; see also *Pramanbai* v. *Channolal* A.I.R. 1963 Madh. Pr. 57.

162. *Balli* v. *Rapetti* (1957) 2 An. W. R. 308.

As it has been shown (above at p. 33) S. 29 (2) of the Hindu Marriage Act, 1955 does not disturb the position which a customary divorce occupied before the enactment. For the operation of this section it must be proved as a fact that such customary dissolution of marriage was effected.[163] In Andhra Pradesh in the Shepherd's community, divorce in accordance with custom is prevalent. Where such divorce is obtained it is not necessary for the parties to have again to go before the court under S. 10 or 13 of the Hindu Marriage Act, 1955 and obtain sanction of the court to render the divorce valid.[164]

From all that has been said earlier it must be concluded that divorce as such was not recognised by the *sasrta*. Marriage being a sacrament once solemnised with the sacred rites before the nuptial fire was irrevocable, and was believed to exist even after the death of the husband. So a widow was not allowed to remarry, and it was not until the passing of the Hindu Widow's Remarriage Act, 1856 that the harshness of this *sastric* principle was abolished by legalising the remarriage of widow. It is the most fashionable view of Indian writers belonging to the high castes that dissolution of marriage was actually practised by the aborigines and lower communities of non-Aryan origin, or some communities who have been influenced by non-Hindus. It is submitted that this is not correct. In view of the relics of Mahenjodaro the contribution of non-Aryans to Hindu culture cannot be calculated with certainty. As we have seen before there has been a mixture of the *sastric* principles and the practice of the people. This is testified to by the Arthasastra of Kautilaya and other customs. Customary divorce is practised by many communities which are by no means completely tribal or low. Such customs have been rightly preserved by the Hindu Marriage Act, 1955, which recognises a utilitarian concept of law.

12. *LEGISLATIVE MEASURES*

The Native Converts' Marriage Dissolution Act, 1866 provided an indirect way of divorce for converts to Christianity.

163. *Edamma* v. *Hussainappa*, A.I.R. 1965 Andh. Pr. 455; *Kamala* v. *Kumaran*, A.I.R. 1958 Bom. 12.

164. *Are Lachiah* v. *Are Raja* (1963) 1 An. W.R. 295.

Under this Act when one of the spouses adopts Christianity and the other refuses to live with the convert on that ground for a period of six months, the latter may apply to the court to order the Hindu spouse for restitution of conjugal rights or alternatively to dissolve the marriage.

Under the Indian Divorce Act, 1869, the Indian Christians could get divorce on the following grounds. Under Section 10 any husband could petition for divorce on the ground that his wife has, since the solemnisation of the marriage, been guilty of adultery. Similarly a petition could be presented for divorce by a wife on the ground that her husband has exchanged his Christian religion for that of some other, and had married another woman; or has been guilty of incestuous adultery; or of bigamy with adultery; or of marriage with another woman with adultery; or of rape, sodomy or bestiality; or of adultery coupled with such cruelty as without adultery would have entitled her to a divorce a *mensa at thoro*; or of adultery coupled with desertion, without reasonable excuse for two years or upwards.

The Indian Divorce Act, 1869, applicable to Christians, was also made available to Hindus marrying under the Special Marriage Act, 1872. This was repealed and replaced by the Special Marriage Act, 1954, which provides under S. 27 that either spouse could petition for divorce on the ground that the other has committed adultery; or has been guilty of desertion for three years; or is undergoing a sentence of imprisonment for seven years or more for an offence as defined in the Indian Penal Code (Act XLV of 1860) provided that divorce shall not be granted on this ground, unless the respondent has prior to the presentation of the petition undergone at least three years imprisonment out of the said period of seven years; or has treated the petitioner with cruely; or has been incurably of unsound mind for a continuous period of not less than three years;or has for a period of not less than three years immediately preceding the presentation of the petition, been suffering from venereal disease in a communicable form, the disease not having been contracted from the petitioner; or has not been heard of as being alive for a period of seven years or more; or has not resumed cohabitation for a period of two years or upwards after the passing of a decree for judicial separation against the respondent; or has failed to comply with a decree for restitution of conjugal rights for a period of two years or upwards after the passing of the decree against the respondent ; and by the wife on the ground that her husband has been guilty of rape, sodomy , or bestiality. Section 28 provides for divorce by mutual consent.

Drastic changes were effected in the personal laws of the Hindus by the Hindu Marriage Act 1955. The introduction of divorce was an innovation for a proportion of Hindus and not all, because by S. 29 (2) of the same Act any right recognised by custom or conferred by any special enactment, such as the Travancore Nayar Act (2 of 1100), to obtain the dissolution of Hindu marriage, whether solemnised before or after the commencement of the Hindu Marriage Act, 1955 has been saved. The motive behind this enactment was to open the way towards a progressive society and to recognise the independence of women. It abolished polygamy and introduced divorce and judicial separation, which are based on the principles borrowed from the (English) Matrimonial Causes Act 1950 (as modified by the (English) Matrimonial Causes Act, 1965).

Under S. 13 (1) of the Hindu Marriage Act, 1955 divorce is available on the following grounds, namely, that the other spouse is living in adultery; or has ceased to be a Hindu by conversion to another religion; or has been incurably of unsound mind for a continuous period of not less than three years immediately preceding the presentation of the petition; or has, for a period of not less than three years immediately preceding the presentation of the petition, been suffering from a virulent and incurable form of leprosy; or has, for a period of not less than three years immediately preceding the presentation of the petition, been suffering from veneral disease in a communicable form; or has renounced the world by entering any religious order; or has not been heard of as being alive for a period of seven years or more by those persons who would naturally have heard of it, had that party been alive; or has not resumed cohabitation for a space of two years or upwards after the passing of a decree for judicial separation against that party; or has failed to comply with a decree for restitution of conjugal rights for a period of two years or upwards after the passing of the decree.

The following additional grounds are provided for a wife petitioner. In the case of any marriage solemnised before the commencement of this Act, that the husband had married again before such commencement or that any other wife of the husband married before such commencement was alive at the time of the solemnisation of the marriage provided that in either case the other wife is alive at the time of the petition; or that the husband has been guilty of rape, sodomy or bestiality.

The Act is based mainly on the provisions of the Matrimonial Cause Act, 1950, whereby under Section 1 (I) either spouse may petition for divorce on the ground that the other has since the celebration of the marriage committed adultery; or has deserted the petitioner without cause for a period of at least three years immediately preceding the presentation of the petition; or has treated the petitioner with cruelty; or is incurably of unsound mind and has been continuously under care and treatment for a period of at least five years immediately preceding the presentation of the petition; and by the wife on the ground that her husband has, since the celebration of the marriage, been guilty of rape, sodomy or bestiality.

Under Section 14 either spouse can petition for a decree of judicial separation on the same grounds as are available for divorce, or on the ground of failure to comply with a decree for restitution of conjugal rights, or on any ground on which a decree for divorce *a mensa et thoro* might have been pronounced before the Matrimonial Cause Act, 1857.

Kenya followed the Indian example by passing the Hindu Marriage and Divorce Ordinance, 1960 for Hindus domiciled there. Under Section 10 (i), either party can petition for divorce on the ground that the respondent has since the celebration of marriage committed adultery; or has deserted the petitioner without cause for a period of at least three years immediately preceding the presentation of the petition; or has since the celebration of the marriage treated the petitioner with cruelty; or is incurably of unsound mind and has been continuously under care and treatment for a period of at least five years immediately preceding the petition; or has ceased to be a Hindu by reason of conversion to another religion ; or has renounced the world by entering a religious order and has remained in such order apart from the world for a period of at least three years immediately prceding the persentation of the petition; or a decree of judicial separation has been in force between the parties for a period of at least two years immediately preceding the presentation of the petition, and the parties have not cohabited since the date of the decree.

A wife can petition on the additional ground that her husband has since the celebration of the marriage, been guilty of rape, sodomy or bestiality; or in the case of a marriage solemnised before the commencement of the ordinance, at the time of the marriage was already married; or married again before such commencement, the other wife being in either case alive at the date of the presentation of the petition.

Uganda passed the Hindu Marriage and Divorce Ordinance, 1961. Under Section 9 (2) in addition to the grounds for divorce mentioned in the Divorce Ordinance, Matrimonial Causes, Chapter 112, a petition for divorce may be presented by either party to a marriage on the ground that the respondent has ceased to be a Hindu by reason of conversion to another religion; or has renounced the world by entering a religious order and has remained in such order apart from the world for a period of at least three years immediately preceding the presentation of the petition; and by the wife, in the case of a marriage solemnised before the commencement of this Ordinance, on the ground that her husband at the time of marriage was already married; or married again before the commencement of this Ordinance, the other wife being in either case alive at the date of the presentation of the petition.

The Divorce Ordinance (1904) Section 5 (1)[165] provides that a husband may petition for the dissolution of his marriage on the ground that since the solemnisation thereof his wife has been guilty of adultery. Under Section 5 (2), a wife may petition for the dissolution of her marriage on the ground that since the solemnisation thereof her husband has changed his profession of Christianity for the profession of some other religion, and gone through a form of marriage with another

165. *Laws of Uganda*, Cap. 112.

woman; or has been guilty of incestuous adultery or of bigamy with adultery;; or of marriage with another woman with adultery; or of rape, sodomy, or bestiality; or adultery coupled with cruelty; or adultery coupled with desertion, without reasonable excuse, for two years or upwards.

In 1923 Tanganyika had passed the Marriage, Divorce and Succession (Non Christian Asiatics) Ordinance (Laws of Tanganyika, Cap. 112). This, in brief, gave the High Court jurisdiction to hear and determine all matrinonial suits and suits arising out of marriages which were valid marriages within the Ordinance, and authorised the court to apply the 'law of the religion', in matters of succession, the law of the religion including caste custom in the case of Hindus, and being specifically open to be determined by the court by any means which it thought fit, whether evidence on the subject were legal evidence or not. Under Section 8, text books on Hindu law, such as those of Mulla and Mayne, will be used, and the Indian cases upon which they rely.[166]

Kenya Ordinance, 1960 is similar to the (English) Matrimonial Causes Act, 1950 in this, that adultery is a ground for divorce. Both of these differ from the Hindu Marriage Act, 1955, under which 'living in adultery' forms a ground for divorce, but a single act of sexual intercourse by the husband or wife with some one who is not his or her spouse gives the other party a ground for judicial separation. Uganda differs from all of these because in the case of a wife petitioner, adultery has to be incestuous or coupled with bigamy; or coupled with marriage with another woman; or coupled with cruelty, or coupled with desertion without reasonable excuse for two years or upwards in order to provide a ground for divorce. The provision for presumption of death does not appear in the Kenya or Uganda ordinances.

The Kenya and Uganda ordinances are more in accord with the (English) Matrimonial Causes Act, 1950 than with the Hindu Marriage Act, 1955. This is evident in the provisions and phraseology of the former. Yet the prohibition of second marriage of the husband is common to both the East

166. J.D.M. Derrett, "*Comments, Recent Legislation.*" (1962), vol. II Am. Jour. Comp. Law, p. 396.

African ordinances and the Hindu Marriage Act, 1955, and so are the grounds for renunciation of the world and conversion to another religion. However, the provisions for venereal disease and leprosy do not occur in the Kenya or Uganda statutes. The provision of care and treatment for unsoundness of mind does not appear in the Hindu Marriage Act, 1955, because the large number of population makes it impracticable that such mental patients are properly looked after in the mental hospitals. Here poverty is one of the causes. But care and treatment is provided for both in the (English) Matrimonial Causes Act, 1950 and the Kenya Ordinance, 1960, S. 10 (2). Failure to resume cohabitation for a period of two years or upwards after a decree of judicial separation has been granted does not appear as a ground for divorce under the Uganda Ordinance. The Kenya and Uganda Ordinacnes differ from each other as they do from the Hindu Marriage Act, 1955 and the (English) Matrimonial Causes Act, 1950.

Though the provisions of the English and Hindu statutes have been adopted by the Kenya and Uganda ordinances, the result of the application may not be the same in every case, e.g., the economic, social, educational and cultural outlook of the Hindus in East Africa is different from those in India and from the English. However, the concept of divorce was unfamiliar to the Hindus there as it was in India and was first introduced by the legislature and divorce laws were enacted on the western notion of marriage and divorce. This is claimed by many vocal critics to have destroyed the purely sacramental nature of the Hindu marriage and has turned it into a civil contract, which like any other contract can be terminated by the parties on the prescribed grounds. This is a superficial view. Society has its own notions of what marriage is. Conventionally these are contained within the juridical concept of "sacrament". It may be more true to say that remedies have been provided for those to whom their sacrament is no longer meaningful.

Chapter III

THE HISTORY OF DIVORCE IN ENGLAND

1. *BACKGROUND TO STATUTORY DIVORCE*

The Anglo-Saxon law appears to have recognised divorce either by mutual consent or on the ground of the wife's unfaithfulness or by desertion.[1] According to the view of the eminent Dr. Stephen Lushington[2] and Sir John Stoddart[3] even the church courts, at least for a short period between 1550-1602, may have granted a divorce *a vinculo matrimonii*, i.e., dissolution of a valid marriage by lawful authority, conferring the right of remarriage with a new partner, during the life-time of the former partner, on each of the divorced persons. This has to be distinguished from divorce *a mensa et thoro*, i.e., separation from bed and board, which corresponds to modern judicial separation, whereby the legal status of the husband and wife remains intact, and the parties are not entitled to remarry.[4] In the light of Salk. Rep,[5] a divorce for adultery was anciently *a vinculo matrimonii*; therefore, in the beginning of the reign of Queen Elizabeth I, the opinion of the Church of England was that after a divorce for adultery the parties might marry again. This is consistent with the bond required by Canon 107 of 1603 against remarriage after a decree of divorce and is also justifiable on the ground that if the ecclesiastical courts had no jurisdiction to grant divorce *a vinculo matrimonii*, the proviso in the Bigamy Act, 1604, to the effect that the Act should not

1. W. S. Holdsworth, *History of English Law*, vol. II, London, 1956, p. 90.

2. Evidence given before the Select Committee of the H. L. to consider Lord Brougham's Bill to amend the jurisdiction of the judicial committee of the P. C., presented in 1844. Questions 217-242. Appendix to Report of Divorce Law Commission, 1853.

3. Evidence as in note 2 above, Questions 809 et seq.

4. K. E. Kirk, *Marriage and Divorce*, London, 1948, pp. 34-36; William Blackstone, *Commentaries on the Laws of England*, Oxford Ed., Bk. I, Ch. 15, pp. 440-442.

5. 3 Salk. 138 = 90 E. R. 738.

extend to any person divorced by a decree in the ecclesiastical courts, cannot be accounted for.[6]

The church had complete jurisdiction over the law of marriage and divorce, which was exercised through the ecclesiastical courts, which applied canon law.[7] There are conflicting views as to whether before the Reformation, the English church had a system of ecclesiastical law, familiar to England alone, which was binding on the English church courts; or whether the general Romano-canonical law, which was prevalent in Europe at that time, applied with minor exceptions in the English ecclesiastical courts. F. W. Maitland stated that in all probability large portions of the canon law of Rome were regarded by the courts Christian in this country as absolutely binding statute laws. He went so far as to say that there was no English law of marriage.[8] Roman Canon Law or the *Jus Commune* of the church was the really operative law in the church courts of England as elsewhere, and it was of great authority.[9]

Before the Reformation in England, the law administrated by the English ecclesiastical authorities was kept more or less uniform with that administered in corresponding continental courts because of the common ultimate appeal to the Pope.[10] However, in England the authority of the Canon law was at all times much restricted, being considered, in many points, repugnant to the laws of England, or incompatible with the jurisdiction of the courts of common law.[11] It is rightly stated by Prof. T. E. James[12] that Roman civil law was pervading in respect of matrimonial causes throughout civilised Europe

6. R. H. Graveson and F. R. Crane, ed., *A Century of Family Law*, London, 1957, pp. 315-316.

7. W. S. Holdsworth, *History of English Law*, vol. I, pp. 622-623; Julius Hirschfeld, "*The Law of Divorce in England and Germany*" (1897) 13 L.Q.R. 395 at p. 397.

8. F. W. Maitland, *Roman Canon Law in the Church of England*, London, 1898, pp. 2, 39.

9. A. Ogle, *The Canon Law in Medieval England*, London, 1912, pp. 14-15, 53.

10. J. Jackson, *The Formation and Annulment of Marriage*, London, 1951,

until about the fifth or sixth centuries, when ecclesiastical law came into its own. The canon law so far as marriage was concerned, accepted the basic principles of Roman law until the Council of Trent. The present matrimonial law in England is a compound mainly of three systems, the Roman law, the Canon law and English enactments from 1857-1950 as amended and consolidated by the (English) Matrimonial Causes Act, 1965.

In *R.* v. *Millis,*[13] Tindal, C. J., said, "That the canon law of Europe does not, and never did, as a body of laws, form part of the law of England, has been long settled and established law. Lord Hale defines the extent to which it is limited very accurately. He says, 'the rule by which they proceed is the canon law, but not in its full latitude, and only so far as it stands uncorrected either by contrary Acts of Parliament or the common law and custom of England; for there are diverse canons made in ancient times, and decretals of the Pope, that never were admitted here in England' ". This was approved in *R.* v. *St. Giles-in-the-Fields,*[14] where it was held that the marriage of a man with the sister of his deceased wife is prohibited and void by statute. (See the Deceased Wife's Sister's Marriage Act, 1907). The same question, i.e., whether the husband's marriage with his deceased wife's sister is valid, came up before the Indian court in *V.H. Lopez* v. *E.J. Lopez,*[15] where the remarks of the English judges in the above cases were approved by Cunningham, J.

The Canon law emphasised the indissolubility of marriage and prior to the Reformation in England, its sacramental aspect. The harshness of the doctrine of the indissolubility of marriage was greatly modified by the growth of the canon law of nullity, which in practice was restricted by evidential and financial considerations.[16]

13. *R.* v. *Millis* (1843-44) 10 Cl. and Fin. 534 at 680 =8 E.R. 844 at 898.

14. *R.* v. *St. Giles-in-the-Fields* (1847) 11 Q.B. 173 at 189=116 E.R. 441 at 447.

15. *V. H. Lopez* v. *E. J. Lopez* (1885) 12 cal. 706 F. B.; *Bishop of Exeter* v. *Marshall* (1867) L.R. 3 H.L. 17 at 35 (The opinion of Tindal, C.J., was again approved) ; see also J.A. Saldanha, *Civil Ecclesiastical Law* (applicable to Christians in British India), Trichinopoly, 1935. pp. 89-102.

16. Prof. T. E. James in *A Century of Family Law*, p. 25.

The Ecclesiastical courts in Europe had no power to pronounce a divorce *a vinculo matrimonii*, if there had been a valid marriage. After the early seventeenth century they only gave decrees of divorce *a mensa et thoro*. However as we have seen, after the Reformation[17] the ecclesiastical courts in England appeared to have claimed power to dissolve marriage on the ground of adultery. This is shown by the case of the Marquis of Northampton, who in 1542, having obtained a decree of divorce in the ecclesiastical courts on the ground of his wife's adultery and subsequently remarried, obtained recognition in 1552 of the validity of his remarriage by a Court of Bishops presided over by the Archbishop; and the parliament, on his petition, passed an Act pronouncing him to be 'separate, divorced, and at libertie by the laws of God to marrye.' This Act was shortly repealed and the opinion was over-ruled in 1602 in Fuliambe's Case,[18] when Archbishop Bancroft sitting in the Star Chamber held that a decree of divorce pronounced by the ecclesiastical courts did not dissolve the marriage.[19]

After the Restoration divorce *a vinculo matrimonii* could be obtained on the ground of adultery only by petitioning parliament by private bill. The party deserving divorce had first to obtain a decree of separation *a mensa et thoro* from the ecclesiastical courts; secondly, to institute an action in the civil courts, and obtain damages from the one who had wronged him, and thirdly, to obtain an Act of Parliament to sever the marriage bond.[20] This procedure was highly expensive with the consequence that divorce was uncommon and restricted to the very rich.[21] This difficulty led to a series of statutes.

In 1857 the first Matrimonial Causes Act was passed to

17. Archbishops Commission's Report, *The Canon Laws of the Church of England*, London, 1947, pp. 45-68.

18. *Rye* v. *Fuliambe*, Moore's Reports 683 = 72 E.R. 838.

19. Raydon, *Practice and Law of Divorce*, London, 1964, p. 3.

20. C. Gasquoine Hartley, *Divorce* (today and tomorrow), London, 1921, pp. 47-48.

21. W. S. Holdsworth, *History of English Law*, vol. I, pp. 622-623; Dom Peter Flood, *The Dissolution of Marriage*, London, 1962, p. 70; R. H. Graveson and F. R. Crane, ed., *A Century of Family Law*, p. 5; O. R. McGregor, *Divorce in England*, London, 1957, p. 10.

give effect to the recommendations of the Royal Commission, which had been appointed in 1850 to enquire into the law relating to matrimonial offences. Matrimonial Causes Act, 1857 had the following provisions. A secular court of divorce was created to exercise the former jurisdiction of the ecclesiastical courts, which came to an end. The Act for the first time permitted divorce *a vinculo matrimonii* by judicial process. Divorce *a mensa et thoro* was replaced by a decree of judicial separation, grounds for which were adultery, or cruelty or desertion without cause for two years or unnatural offences.

A divorce *a vinculo matrimonii* could be granted to a husband on the ground of his wife's adultery, but to a wife only if her husband's adultery was aggravated in certain ways, i.e., he had been guilty of incestuous adultery, or adultery with bigamy, or adultery with cruelty, or adultery with desertion for two years, or unnatural offences (rape, sodomy, bestiality). Connivance, collusion and condonation were absolute bars to a petition for divorce of either type, i.e., divorce *a vinculo matrimonii* and *a mensa et thoro*. The petitioner's own adultery, delay, cruelty, desertion, conduct conducing to adultery were discretionary bars. The husband could claim damages from a co-respondent (instead of bringing a common law action). This strange[22] distinction between the position of the husband and that of the wife remained until the passing of the (English) Matrimonial Causes Act, 1923, which brought the husband and wife onto an equal footing by permitting the latter to petition on the grounds of adultery alone.

The (English) Matrimonial Causes Act, 1937 further extended the grounds for divorce, A divorce or judicial separation could be obtained for cruelty, or desertion without cause for three years, or incurable unsoundness of mind, where the respondent had been detained continuously under care and treatment for five years. These grounds were in addition to adultery which was already a ground. Modern grounds for divorce are now contained in S. I of the (English) Matrimonial Causes Act, 1950 as consolidated by S. I of the (English) Matrimonial Causes Act, 1965.

22. O. R. McGregor, *Divorce in England*, pp. 20-21 (comments on the distinction); L. J. Blom-Cooper, "*A Century of Divorce*" (1958) 25, The Solicitor, at p. 19.

2. *THE CONCEPTS OF HINDU AND CHRISTIAN MARRIAGE*

As in Hindu law so in Canon law and theology, marriage is a sacrament, and, therefore, indissoluble during the joint lives of husband and wife.[23] A sacrament is a rite ordained as an outward and visible sign of an inward and spiritual grace, specially instituted directly by Christ or by the Church.[24] It can also be defined as a mystery. The marriage mystery is in the first place celebrated by the mutual consent of a man and a woman (there being no impediment), but is not considered by the church a true marriage unless they confirm their consent in the presence of a priest and, having joined hands, promise to be faithful to each other till death.[25] The mutual surrender of man and woman, and the mutual acceptance of that surrender, sufficiently constitute the sacrament.[26] It is a spiritual union, constituted by the will of the parties, which the physical consummation confirms and perfects.[27] The union between man and wife is representative of the union between Christ and the Church. It is a union in virtue of which Christ is bound to the soul by ties of love so close that conjugal affection alone affords a term of comparison.[28] Marriage is properly a discharge from parental control; husband and wife pass away from their own families to form in their union a new family. It is the teaching of the Gospel, that not the woman alone, but also the man, "shall leave his father and mother, and shall cleave to his wife; and the two shall become one flesh." This entire union of man and woman effected by marriage is indissoluble except by death.[29]

23. Sir Lewis Dibdin and Sir Charles E. H. Chadwyck Healey, *English Church Law and Divorce*, London, 1912,-pp. 46-47.

24. Funk and Wagnalls, *A Standard Dictionary of the English Language* New York, 1895, vol. II.

25. James Hastings, *Encyclopedia of Religion and Ethics*, New York, 1918, vol. 10, p. 903.

26. T. A. Lacey, *Marriage in Church and State*, London, 1947, p. 39.

27. S. B. Kitchin, *A History of Divorce*, London, 1912, pp. 62-64.

28. George Hayward Joyce, *Christian Marriage* , London, 1948, pp. 147-148.

29. T. A. Lacey, *Marriage in Church and State*, pp. 7, 14.

Marriage is an institution deriving its origin from God and not from any human legislation and must be deemed a divine or religious contract, even when celebrated according to a secular form. It is an ethical, religious and legal institution and present matrimonial laws have resulted out of a long and bitter struggle between the Church and the State. The former considered marriage as a sacrament, while the State by various legislations treated it as any other contract and prescribed a civil form, obligatory upon all citizens. By the Common Law of England an important principle arising from the marriage contract was established from the earliest times, based on the maxim that husband and wife were one person in law. The wife's existence was regarded as having merged in that of her husband, and she was held to be incapable of holding separate property or of performing many legal acts.[30] This is similar to the concept of Hindu *sastric* law according to which a wife's personality merges into that of her husband as a river mingles with the ocean,[31] a concept which persisted although at Hindu law the wife retained a separate proprietary right.

Christian marriage was similar to Hindu *sastric* marriage in that it was a sacrament, and, therefore, divorce was not allowed, although judicial separation (divorce *a mensa et thoro*) could be obtained under certain circumstances. This is equivalent to the Hindu 'abandonment' (*tyaga*). The nature of the union is different, because Hindu *sastric* law regarded the marriage as subsisting even after the death of the husband. That is why a Hindu widow was not allowed to remarry. On the other hand a Christian marriage was indissoluble during the joint lives of the husband and wife.

There is ample evidence in both ancient and modern society to prove the statement that procreation of children is regarded as a fundamental purpose of marriage.[32] Though progeny was the aim of Hindu marriage it laid more stress

30. J. T. Hammick, *The Marriage Law of England*, London, 1887, pp. 2-3.

31. Manu IX, 22, S.B.E., vol. 25.

32. Raphael Powell, "*The Concept of Marriage in Ancient and Modern Law*" (1950) vol. III, Current Legal Problems, p. 46; L. Shelford, *The Law of Marriage and Divorce*, pp. 1-17.

on the procreation of male children, as sons were supposed to enable a man to clear off one of his natal spiritual debts, and were the means of obtaining heaven. That is why a Hindu was allowed to remarry in case his wife failed to bless him with a son. For a Hindu marriage was a religious necessity, because it enabled him to perform sacrifices to gods, which he was incompetent to perform without the company and help of his wife.

A brief survey of the history of English matrimonial law, as we have seen, shows that from the religious point of view an English marriage like a Hindu marriage was also a sacrament and, therefore, indissoluble. The English law proceeded on the basis that the stability of the marriage must be maintained so far as possible and it is only in the last resort, when the marriage has utterly broken down, that divorce should be granted. India seems to have followed the same pattern. But the grounds for divorce as they exist in India are more rigid than they are in present England. A comparison of the two systems will be made in the following chapters.

CHAPTER IV

ADULTERY

1. *ADULTERY AS A MATRIMONIAL FAULT*

In English law[1] and the relevant provisions of the Kenya[2] and Uganda[3] Ordinances a husband or wife may petition for divorce on the ground that the respondent has since the celebration of the marriage committed adultery. S. 13 (1) (i) of the Hindu Marriage Act, 1955 makes "Living in adultery" a ground for divorce but a single act of sexual intercourse under the same Act[4] with a person other than his or her spouse provides a ground for judicial separation. If, however, the parties fail to resume cohabitation for a period of two years or upwards after the passing of such a decree, either party can petition for divorce.[5] As the draftsman of the Hindu Code has borrowed exclusively from the English Matrimonial Causes Acts, English case law in so far as it is relevant, has a strong persuasive authority in the Indian courts.

The meaning of adultery is nowhere defined in the above enactments and rightly so, because proof of adultery is a question of evidence, which varies from one country to another and from one society to another. In Murray's dictionary[6] the old French 'avouterie' appears. In the fourteenth century French, 'adultere' was being derived afresh from Latin 'adulterium' and gradually superseded the popular 'avoutire' and 'avouterie'; under the same influence the English 'avoutrie' was progres-

1. S. 1 (1) (a) of the (English) Matrimonial Causes Act, 1950.
2. S. 10 (1) (a) of the Hindu Marriage and Divorce Ordinance, 1960 (Kenya).
3. S. 5 (1) of the Divorce Ordinance (15 of 1904) Matrimonial Causes, *Laws of Uganda*, Cap. 112.
4. S. 10 (1) (f) of the Hindu Marriage Act, 1955.
5. S. 13 (1) (viii) of the Hindu Marriage Act, 1955, as amended by the Hindu Marriage Amendment Act. 1964 (44 of 1964).
6. James A. H. Murray, *A New English Dictionary on Historical Principles*, Oxford, 1888; *The Shorter English Dictionary on Historical Principles*, Oxford, 1933.

sively refashioned into 'advoutrie', 'adoutrie', 'adoultrie', 'adoultry', 'adultry' and 'adultery', ending in a direct English translation of 'adulterium', practically a distinct word from 'avoutrie', though connected with it by intermediate forms. It is not only the meaning of the word in English law but also in Hindu law with which we are concerned. It was held in the recent case of *Chanda* v. *Nandu*[7] that the word 'adultery' like the word 'adulteration' is derived from a Latin root through French, which originally meant "mixing, degrading or counterfeiting". It is defined as the sexual intercourse of two persons, one of whom is married to a third person. It is called double adultery where both are married and single where only one is married.[8] It is in this wide sense that 'adultery' in S. 13 (1) (i) of the Hindu Marriage Act, 1955 was understood in the above case of *Chanda* v. *Nandu*.

Adultery consists of a breach by either sex of the marriage vows of fidelity to the spouse and violation of the marriage bed, though extended meanings have been given by theologians who applied this term to unchastity and to marriages of which they disapproved.[9] In Canon or Ecclesiastical law adultery means sexual connection between a man and a woman, of whom one is married to a third person. In all the authorities, adultery is defined as 'the sin of incontinence between two married persons, or it may be when only one of them is married.'[10] It was immaterial whether the offender was male or female. Hence adultery had a wider scope than at common law, as it was committed by a married man having connection with a single woman. The spiritual courts never described the conduct of a single person who had intercourse with another as adultery. It is a violation of the marriage bed, so the true test of whether the sexual intercourse amounted to adultery is whether the woman who took part in an act of sexual inter-

7. *Chanda* v. *Nandu*, A.I.R. 1965 Madh. Pr. 268.

8. Funk and Wagnalls, *A Standard Dictionary of the English Language*, New-York, 1895.

9. *The Shorter Oxford English Dictionary on Historical Principles*; H. C. Wyld, *The Universal Dictionary of the English Language*, London, 1932.

10. *Babineau* v. *B.* (1924) 4 D.L.R. 951 at 952; Sir Thomas Tomlins, *The Law-Dictionary*, London, 1820, Earl Jowitt, *The Dictionary of English Law*, London, 1959; *American and English Encyclopedia of Law*, second edition, vol. I, p. 747.

course was dishonouring or defiling her own marriage bed, or that of the man with whom the intercourse took place.[11]

The essence of the offence consists, not in the moral turpitude of the act of sexual intercourse, but in the voluntary surrender to another person of the reproductive organs of the guilty person and any submission of those organs to the service or enjoyment of any person other than the husband or the wife comes within the definition of 'adultery'.[12] This is correct so far as the act of sexual intercourse is concerned, but the learned judge went further and said, "The fact that it has been held that anything short of actual intercourse, no matter how indecent or improper the act may be, does not constitute adultery, really tends to strengthen my view that it is not the moral turpitude that is involved but the invasion of the reproductive function. So long as nothing takes place which can by any possibility affect that function, there can be no adultery, so that unless and until there is actual sexual intercourse, there can be no adultery. Sexual intercourse is adulterous because, in the case of the woman, it involves the possibility of introducing into the family of the husband a false strain of blood. Any act on the part of the wife which does that would, therefore be adulterous."[13]

The stress laid on "the reproductive powers" would lead to the somewhat surprising inference that, in order to constitute the offence of adultery, there must be not only the act of sexual intercourse but also the interference with the reproductive faculties. This would presuppose the existence of an ability to procreate in both the parties, and unless the sexual intercourse leads to conception there could be no adultery. Adultery involves the surrender of the reproductive powers or the organs of generation, whether capable of actual generation or not. It is the physical contact between the sexual organs of the offending man and woman plus the moral turpitude which amount to adultery. Karminski, J., regards adultery as fornication so far as the physical contact is involved, "Adultery, of course, is fornication, but fornication when a party to the

11. Karminski, J., in *Abson* v. *A.* (1952) p. 55 at 64.
12. Orde, J., in *Oxford* v. *O.* (1921) 49 Ont. L. R. 15 at 22.
13. Orde, J., supra, at p. 23.

fornication is married, and the physical act so far as I know is the same in both adultery and fornication."[14]

In English law adultery is a matrimonial offence against sexual faithfulness which the spouses owe to each other. This includes the physical act of sexual intercourse as well as the breach of trust of the guilty party. The offence lies in enjoying the illicit sexual intercourse and not in interfering with the reproductive potentialities of the woman, for the former may not necessarily lead to conception. The offence is complete with a single act of sexual intercourse as was said by Lord Chelmsford, "It must be borne in mind that the offence of adultery is complete in a single instance of guilty connection with a married woman. It is the first act which constitutes the crime, and though the adulterous intercourse between the parties should continue for years, there is not a fresh adultery upon every repetition of the guilty acts, although all and each of them may furnish proof of the adultery itself."[15]

For the purpose of divorce in English law, adultery has been defined as the consensual sexual intercourse between a married person and a person of the opposite sex, not the other spouse, while the marriage subsists.[16] It is in this sense that the word 'adultery' was construed under the Hindu Marriage Act, 1955.[17] The order of words in this definition varies slightly from author to author, but the content is almost the same. It can be more accurately defined by changing it to: "Adultery is a voluntary act of sexual intercourse between a married person and a person of the opposite sex, who is not the other spouse, while the marriage subsists, the guilty spouse being sane at the relevant time." This will allow for the defence of insanity.

14. Karminski, J., in *Sapsford* v. *S.* (1954) P. 394 at 400.

15. Lord Chelmsford in *Gipps* v. *G.* (1864) 11 H. L. Cas. 1 at 28; *Conradi* v. *C.* (1868) L.R. 1 P. & D. 514 at 522 (the commission of an isolated act of adultery is sufficient).

16. Latey on *Divorce*, 14th. Ed., 1952, p. 74; Raydon, *Practice* and *Law of Divorce*, 9th. Ed., London , 1964, p. 146; Halsbury's *Laws of England*, 3rd. Ed., vol. 12, p. 235; D. Tolstoy, *The Law and Practice of Divorce*, London, 1963, p. 27.

17. *Gitabai* v. *Fattoo*, A.I.R. 1966 Madh. Pr. 130; *Subbarama* v. *Saraswathi*, A.I.R. 1967 Mad. 85 at p. 89.

2. *MENS REA IN ADULTERY*

The dictionary meaning of 'voluntary' is 'depending on the exercise of free will'. An act is voluntary when it proceeds from the exercise of free will—volition. This volition may be manifested by the physical movement of the person concerned. Therefore, a voluntary act requires both the mental and physical elements of volition or will. It follows from this that force or fraud can render the act involuntary. In order to constitute the offence of adultery the man and woman involved in the sexual intercourse must consent to the act. The absence of consent or willingness on the part of the party concerned will render his or her act innocent.

The test of consent was well defined by Lord Merrivale in the following words,[18] "The question was whether the respondent had committed adultery, i.e., to have willingly yielded herself to the embraces of some man other than her husband". In this case the wife had been raped by a man unknown, and it was held that she was not guilty of adultery. Similarly in *Long* v. *L.*[19] a woman who was found to be weak both physically and mentally, and who asserted that she was not a consenting party to the sexual intercourse, was held not guilty of adultery.

As lack of consent renders the sexual intercourse involuntary, those who are disqualified by age from giving consent, cannot be guilty of adultery; a girl aged 12 years, who had sexual intercourse with a married man was held not guilty of adultery.[20] However the involuntary act of the innocent party does not render the guilty one free from blame. In *Coffey* v. *C.*[21] a respondent, who had been convicted, under S. 4 of the Criminal Law Amendment Act, 1885 of an attempt to have unlawful and carnal knowledge of a girl under the age of 13 years, was found to have been guilty of rape. His wife was

18 *Clarkson* v. *C.* (1930) 143 L. T. 775.

19. *Long* v. *L.* (1890) 15 P.D. 218. In *Coleman* v. *C.* (1866) L.R. 1 p. 81, where a husband had by threats and personal violence coerced the wife into leading a life of prostitution against her will and desire, the marriage was dissolved not withstanding her adultery.

20. *Bernett* v. *B.* (1957) 1 All E.R. 388.

21. *Coffey* v. *C.* (1898) p. 169.

granted a decree on the ground of rape. He had also been guilty of adultery with another woman on a different occasion.

Since volition is a necessary element in the matrimonial offence of adultery, it would seem that a man who is forced against his will under threat of injury to have sexual intercourse with an unwilling woman, is not guilty of rape or of adultery. However, in the absence of force or threat a man cannot plead that sexual intercourse was thrust upon him, e.g., when a husband admitted intercourse with his maid servant but pleaded that she had forced herself into his bed against his wishes, his plea was rejected as highly improbable.[22] When a male co-respondent pleaded that he was seduced by the respondent his defence was rejected.[23]

If the consent of the woman is obtained by fraud either as to the relationship between the parties or the nature of the act, it is regarded as no consent at all, and the act amounts to rape and not adultery. A man had sexual intercourse with a girl of 19 years under the pretence that he was treating her medically and performing a surgical operation; it was held that the act amounted to rape.[24] In order to constitute the offence of adultery, the guilty spouse must perform the act of sexual intercourse voluntarily.

Once the act of intercourse is established, the presumption is that it took place voluntarily, and the burden of proof falls on the party who alleges that it took place involuntarily, if a wife alleges rape the onus is on her to prove that that was so.[25] In *Clarke* v. *C.*[26] the wife admitted sexual intercourse but claimed that she had been raped, but her story was not believed by the court. There is dictum to the effect that, if free consent is vitiated through drunkenness, the sexual intercourse will not amount to adultery. Where a wife alleged that sexual intercourse took place when she was drugged or intoxicated, Hill, J., expressed the opinion that, if she did not know what had taken place and was not a consenting party,

22. *Storey* v. *S.* (1887) 12 P.D. 196.

23. *Morton* v. *M.* (1937) p. 151 at 153.

24. *R.* v. *Flettery* (1877) 2 Q.B. 196. This was followed in *R.* v. Williams (1923) 1 K.B. 340 (a similar case).

25. *Redpath* v. *R.* (1950) 1 All E. R. 600 (C.A.).

26. *Clarke* v. *C.* (1954) The Times, June 3rd. (C.A.).

he would imagine that it would not amount to adultery at all.[27] In *Gower* v. *G.*[28] the husband employed an agent to obtain proof of his wife's adultery. The agent planned an excursion for the purpose of bringing about the adultery. He made the wife and the co-respondent intoxicated and, when they were insensible, put them to bed together. This story was believed by the court, and it was held that the husband could not obtain a divorce on the ground of such adultery.

It was held to be an act of rape, when the accused rendered a woman insensible by giving her liquor, intending to excite her and, when she became quite drunk, had sexual intercourse with her.[29] Similarly if the woman consents, while she is under the influence of terror, the act amounts to rape; where a father had established a reign of terror over his family and his terrified daughter, remained passive, while he had sexual intercourse with her, he was held guilty of rape.[30] Free and willing consent is of the essence of voluntary intercourse.

3. *THE OTHER PARTY*

In order to constitute the offence of adultery, the sexual intercourse must take place between a man and a woman, at least one of whom must be married, and they must not be married to each other. If both are married, it is called double adultery. If both of them are unmarried, they have committed fornication.

A divorced woman is treated like a single woman for the purpose of adultery. As the marriage bond between her and her former husband has been dissolved, she cannot commit adultery, if she has sexual intercourse with a single man. In *Chorlton* v. *C.*[31] a wife obtained a maintenance order on the ground of her husband's desertion. Later the marriage was dissolved on the ground that the husband had committed adultery. After this the husband alleged that the wife had committed adultery with a named man, and pleaded that she was

27. *Prior* v. *P.* (1929) 73 Sol. Jour. 441; Latey on *Divorce*, p. 74.
28. *Gover* v. *G.* (1872) L.R. 2 P. & M. 428 at 429.
29. *R.* v. *Camplin* (1845) 1 Den. 89 = 169 E.R. 163.
30. *R.* v. *Jones* (1861) 4 L.T. 154.
31. *Chorlton* v. C. (1952) p. 169.

not entitled to maintenance. The husband's application for the discharge of the order was dismissed by the justices, who found that, although there had been opportunity for sexual intercourse to take place, there was no evidence of guilty affection. On appeal, Lord Merriman, P., said, "I am not prepared to accede to the view that a husband can prove adultery against his ex-wife because of sexual intercourse which she, as a woman who has obtained a divorce, has had with a person of the opposite sex, without proving that that person is a married man at the material time. It is for that reason that we have not thought it necessary to consider the weight of evidence which was adduced to show that sexual intercourse took place between these persons."

It is otherwise, if the divorced woman is found to have had sexual intercourse with a married man. In the words of Karminski, J., "The true test as to whether the sexual intercourse amounted to adultery is this : when the woman took part in an act of sexual intercourse with the married man was she then dishonouring or defiling her own marriage bed or that of the man with whom the intercourse took place ? (This has been shown earlier at p. 53). Clearly so far as the woman was concerned, she could not be defiling or dishonouring her own marriage bed, because as a single woman she had no marriage bed and no married home; but so far as the man was concerned, he was a married man, and if she had sexual intercourse with him she was committing adultery, because she was defiling or dishonouring the marriage bed of that man and his wife."[32]

In order to form a ground for divorce adultery must have been committed during the subsistence of the marriage.[33] In *Coleman* v. *C.*[34] the petitioner, when she married, was the divorced wife of an *American.* She sued her second husband on the ground of his adultery, which was proved. She herself had been divorced for adultery by her previous husband. Lord Denning, construing S. 4 (2) proviso of the (English) Matrimonial Causes Act, 1950, held that the only relevant adultery is adultery during the marriage.

32. Karminski, J., in *Abson* v. *A.* (1952) p. 169.
33. S. 4 (2) proviso of the (English) Matrimonial Causes Act, 1950.
34. *Coleman* v. *C.* (1955) 3 All E. R. 617 (C.A.).

4. *INSANITY IN ADULTERY*

The parties involved in the act of sexual intercourse must understand the nature and legality of their act. So insanity is a defence to adultery. In *S*.v. *S*.,[35] decided eight years ago, a husband had sexual intercourse with the intervener, who was a mental patient at the relevant time. There was evidence that, at the time of the intercourse, she would have known that she was in the process of sexual intercourse but she would have been incapable by reason of her mental illness of a full understanding that such conduct was unlawful or morally wrong. It was held that insanity within the M'Naghten rules[36] was a defence to a charge of adultery against the insane person. Since the intervener did not know at the relevant time what she was doing was legally or morally wrong, she could not be held guilty of adultery.

In *Yarrow* v. *Y*.,[37] decided at the end of the last century, the defence of insanity failed, because there was evidence that at the time the defendant committed various acts of adultery, she was capable of understanding the nature and quality of her actions. But the court left open the question whether such insanity as would entitle the defendant to an acquittal on an indictment for a criminal offence would constitute a valid answer to a suit for divorce on the ground of adultery.

In *Hanbury* v. *H*.[38] Sir Charles Butt, P., in his charge to the jury said that, quite apart from mania produced by drink, there might be a case in which insanity would be a defence and there are other cases in which it might not be....It is for them to find insanity or sanity at particular times and whether the accused was capable of understanding the nature and consequences of his acts. The fact that in this particular case the jury held that the person concerned was capable of such under-

35. *S*. v. *S*. (1962) p. 133.

36. The application of M' Naghten rules to matrimonial law has been heavily criticised. This will be dealt with under the chapter of cruelty.

37. *Yarrow* v. *Y*. (1892) p. 92.

38. *Hanbury* v. *H*. (1892) p. 222 at 223-224; see also P.R.H. Webb, "*Insanity as a Defence in Proceedings for Divorce and Judicial Separation*" (1966) 6 Medicine, Science and the Law 102 at pp. 103-104.

standing does not affect the legal principle; had they found otherwise, insanity would have been a good defence.

Insanity is a defence in American law. In *Laudo* v. *L.*,[39] a wife, insane from dementia praecox, had illicit relations with men other than her husband; she was held not to have committed adultery giving him the right to divorce her, the element of intent being lacking. It was found that, at the time of the commission of the adulterous acts, she was mentally incapable of understanding the nature, quality, effect, and consequences thereof and this was a complete defence to the action for divorce. Nothing could be more unjust than to permit a husband to cast his wife away, because of a misfortune which, without her will, might befall her, as, for example, where she is the victim of rape and the like; adultery to justify divorce must be voluntary.[40]

Now that insanity is no longer a defence to a charge of cruelty, it might be argued that it should no longer be permitted as a defence to adultery. But this view is not justifiable as the test in cruelty is twofold, the conduct of the respondent as well as its effect on the injured spouse are of the essence. The need for physical protection from the danger arising out of the conduct of the guilty party is the primary concern, whereas this is not so in a case of adultery. Consent being an essential element in adultery, its lack on the part of the woman can turn the act of sexual intercourse into rape. Consequently people who are disqualified from giving free consent cannot be held guilty of adultery. In *Barnett* v. *B.*,[41] it was held that a girl aged 12 years who commits an act of sexual intercourse cannot be guilty of adultery. The most important word in the definition of adultery is 'consensual', which means 'by consent'. The law throughout its development has had a high regard for consent and consent can only be given by those eligible to give it. Mr. Commissioner, Temple-Morris said in this case, "In my view she cannot be guilty of adultery. To make such a decision would be against sound sense,

39. *Laudo* v. *L.* (1919) 177 N.Y.S. 396.

40. Bishop on *Marriage and Divorce,* 2nd Ed., vol. I, cited in *Laudo* v. *L.* (1919) 177 N.Y.S., at p. 399; see also H. Tarlo, "*Intention and Insanity in Divorce Law*" (1963) 37 Aust. L.J. 3, pp. 12-19.

41. *Barnett* v. *B.* (1957) 1 All E.R. 388 at 390.

decency and morality. I go so far as to say this, that to find a girl of 12 years guilty of adultery would be highly against public interest. It is most undesirable that a young girl of 12 years of age, in these circumstances, should live the rest of her life branded as an adulteress, when she had no legal voice or acquiescence in the criminal deed, which was perpetrated on her."

The same rule should apply when consent is vitiated by insanity; if a woman suffering from schizophrenia has sexual intercourse with a man in the honest belief that the man is her husband, it would be unjust to brand such a woman an adulteress and permit her husband to divorce her for adultery.

5. *CONTRAST BETWEEN ENGLISH LAW AND HINDU LAW*

The Law of India differs remarkably from English Law in making adultery a criminal offence, whereas the latter regards it only as a matrimonial offence. Under the Indian Penal Code[42] only a man can be guilty of adultery and only when he has sexual intercourse with the wife of another. This does not include an unmarried, widowed or divorced woman. This restricted meaning however is not given to 'adultery' for the purpose of Hindu matrimonial causes, under which both the husband and the wife can be held guilty of adultery. The definition of adultery in matrimonial causes is presumed to be the same as in English law, but there is no discussion of the questions raised in Indian case law comparable to that in England.

In English law the ground for divorce is adultery, but in Hindu law in India it is "living in adultery." A husband or wife can present a petition for judicial separation if he or she has, after the solemnisation of the marriage, had sexual intercourse with any person other than his or her spouse.[43] A single act of adultery suffices under this clause.[44] Here the actual words used are 'sexual intercourse' and not 'adultery'. In 'sexual intercourse' the physical act is the same as in

42. S. 497 of the Indian Penal Code.

43. S. 10 (1) (f) of the Hindu Marriage Act, 1955.

44. *Bhagvan* v. *Amar*, A.I.R. 1962 Punj. 144; *Gitabai* v. *Fattoo*, A.I.R. 1966 Madh. Pr. 130.

'adultery' but it does not necessarily follow that the other essential elements of adultery have to be established. There is, as yet, no case in which this question has been raised. If 'sexual intercourse' in this context means the physical act only it will create hardships, putting a woman who is raped in the same category as those who wickedly and deliberately commit the act of adultery. P. V. Deolalkar[45] equates the words 'sexual intercourse' with adultery, and so limits them to 'consensual intercourse'. This would exclude adultery suffered under force, fraud or threat. But words in a statute are normally given their ordinary dictionary meaning, according to which 'sexual intercourse' simply means 'connexion between the sexes.'[46] Non-resumption of cohabitation for a period of two years or upwards after the passing of a decree of judicial separation forms a ground for divorce.[47] The purpose behind this provision is obviously to give the parties time to be reconciled and prevent the marriage from being destroyed by a single lapse from morality.

6. *LIVING IN ADULTERY*

The phrase 'living in adultery' occurs in S. 488 of the Indian Code of Criminal Procedure, 1898 which makes the fact that the wife is living in adultery a defence to her claim for maintenance against her husband, so that in interpreting the phrase, recourse may be had to its interpretation in cases under that section. In *Re Fulchand Maganlal*[48] the husband relied upon the evidence that he had no access to his wife at any time during which a son who was born to his wife could have begotten, and contended that she was not entitled to maintenance. It was held that 'living in adultery' refers to

45. P. V. Deolalkar, *The Hindu Marriage Act.* 1955, Nasik City, 1959, pp. 76-77.

46. J.D.M. Derrett, *Introduction to Modern Hindu Law*, p. 219.

47. S. 13 (1) (VIII) of the Hindu Marriage Act, 1955.

48. *Re Fulchand Maganlal*, A.I.R. 1928 Bom. 59; *Gantapalli* v.*G.* (1897) 20 Mad. 470 F. B. (The words point to a continuous course, of conduct, not to isolated acts of immorality); *Patala* v. *P.* (1907) 30 Mad. 332 (one act of adultery was held insufficient to amount to living in adultery) ; *Subramania* v. *Ponnakashiammal*, A.I.R. 1958 Mys. 41 (two acts of adultery insufficient).

a course of conduct or at least something more than a single lapse from virtue. There might have been only a single act of adultery, so the wife was not 'living in adultery'. In *Lakashmi* v. *Andiammal*[49] where the only evidence offered was that the wife was expecting a baby of which the husband could not be the father, and had more than one lover, it was held that this did not constitute 'living in adultery'. In *Durghatia* v. *Ayodhya*[50] it was held that even the fact that a child had been conceived in adultery will not suffice in itself to hold that the mother lived in adultery. A plaintiff who alleges that the defendant 'lives in adultery' has to prove a course of conduct over some period with repetition of adultery, with the same or more than one person. Between an individual lapse and life as a common prostitute, there are gradations of increasing impurity; where exactly the occasional lapse deepens into a 'life in adultery' is a question of fact depending upon the repetition and brazeness of the conduct, the signs of remorse and readiness to turn back; but it certainly begins at a stage beyond the first lapse.

'Living in adultery' under the Hindu Marriage Act, 1955 has wide meaning and applies to various types of relationships, e.g., it covers the case of 'living in adultery' with a prostitute, concubine or a harlot. The distinction between a concubine and a harlot is in that the former is affected to one man only, although in an irregular union. In India or in Europe the word 'concubine' has long had a definite meaning. The person denoted by it had and still has, where it remains applicable, a recognised status below that of a wife and above that of a harlot.[51] Harlots solicit to immorality, and a prostitute is a woman who surrenders her body for a monetary consideration to someone who is not in law entitled to have sexual intercourse with her.[52] A mistress does not come in the same category as a prostitute, for the relationship in the former case is of more permanent and decent nature, but in all these cases the

49. *Lakashmi* v. *Andiammal*, A.I.R. 1938 Mad. 66.
50. *Durghatia* v. *Ayodhya*, A.I.R. 1953 V.P. 28.
51. *Bai Nagubai* v. *Bai Monghibai*, (1926) 50 Bom. 604 at 610.
52. *Emperor* v. *Lalya* (1929) 31 Bom. L.R. 521; *Narasamma* v. *Dharmaraju* (1955) 1 An. W.R. 584.
53. *Mahalingam* v. *Amsavalli* (1956) 2 M.L.J. 289.

woman, if married, is said to be 'living in adultery', for the parties habitually assume and exercise towards each other rights and privileges which belong to the matrimonial relation.[53] For the purpose of 'living in adultery' it is not essential that such living should be in the house of the adulterer.[54]

The fact, that the wife, after giving birth to an illegitimate child, had stopped the adulterous association and had been living with her parents, leading a chaste and respectable life, is sufficient to free her from the offence of 'living in adultery.'[55] In *Rajani* v. *Prabhakar*,[56] a husband petitioned for divorce on the ground that the wife was living in adultery. After a period of about fifteen months, during which the petitioner's wife was shown to have lived in adultery, there was a period of over two years, about which there was no evidence to show that she lived in adultery. It was held that this did not fall within the purview of 'living in adultery' under S. 13 Sub-s. (1) Cl. (1) of the Hindu Marriage Act, 1955, but the petitioner had made out a case for judicial separation under S. 10, according to which a single act of adultery is sufficient. The expression is in the present tense 'is living in adultery', so if a spouse was living in adultery sometime in the past, but had abandoned the adulterous connections for some time extending to the filing of the petition, it would not be possible to invoke this section, for the purpose of which it must be shown that the period during which the spouse was living an adulterous life was so related, from the point of proximity of time, to the filing of the petition that it could be reasonably inferred that the petitioner had a fair ground to believe that, when the petition was filed, she was living in adultery.

It has been seen that the birth of an illegitimate child does not necessarily prove that the woman concerned is living in adultery. However, such evidence can be used to prove sexual intercourse as a ground for judicial separation. In *Vedavalli* v. *Ramaswamy*[57] the wife petitioned for judicial sepa-

54. *Kista* v. *Amirthammal*, A.I.R. 1938 Mad. 833.

55. *Kallu* v. *Kaunsilia* (1904) 26 All. 326; followed in *Jatindra* v. *Gouri*, A.I.R. 1925 Cal. 794 (the birth of an illegitimate child does not necessarily prove that the mother had been living in adultery).

56. *Rajani* v. *Prabhakar*, A.I.R. 1958 Bom. 264 at 267.

57. *Vedavalli* v. *Ramaswamy*, A.I.R. 1964 Mys. 280; see also *Vira Reddy* v. *Kistamma*, A.I.R. 1969 Mad. 235.

ration, alleging that her husband had had sexual intercourse with his niece. Her evidence clearly disclosed that her husband was on terms of indelicate familiarity and illicit intimacy with his spinster niece, who was living with the spouses in the matrimonial home. This illicit connection led to the pregnancy of the niece. Entry in the admission register of the hospital, where she gave birth to a child, denoted the uncle as her husband. It was held that the evidence was sufficient to establish the accusation that the husband had sexual intercourse with the niece as required by S. 10 (1) (f) of the Hindu Marriage Act, 1955.

In *Avinash* v. *Chandra*[58] it was laid down that stray acts of adultery on the part of the wife, in the absence of proof of her living in adultery, do not form a ground for dissolution of marriage, though they might entitle the husband to judicial separation. The Madras Hindu (Bigamy Prevention and Divorce) Act, 1949 gave a husband the right to petition for dissolution of his marriage on the ground that his wife was the concubine of any other man or was leading the life of a prostitute. This situation is now covered by S. 13 (1) (i) of the Hindu Marriage Act, 1955, under which living in adultery is a ground for divorce, while single or occasional lapses from virtue are remedied by a decree of judicial separation.[59]

Circumstances which lead to the presumption of adultery are enumerated in the recent case of *Samuel* v. *Roshni*,[60] where it was laid down that adultery can be inferred from the fact that the respondent wife shared a bed or bedroom for the night with a person of the opposite sex other than her husband, and there is evidence of illicit affection or undue familiarity between them coupled with an opportunity to commit adultery. In India it is not usual for a young man and a woman to live together in a house when they are neither related nor married to each other. Society being very much more conservative here than elsewhere, it would not be unreasonable to infer adultery from the facts that the respondent and the co-

58. *Avinash* v. *Chaudra*, A.I.R. 1964 All. 486; reversed in A.I.R. 1967 S.C. 581.

59. *Mahalingam* v. *Amsavalli* (1956) 2 M.L.J. 289.

60. *Samuel* v. *Roshni*, A.I.R. 1960 Madh. Pr. 142 (Special Bench).

respondent stayed in one house together for a long time, that the respondent had refused to go back to her husband, that the respondent and the co-respondent had not the courage to come into the witness-box to deny the charge of adultery, that they had ample opportunity to commit adultery while alone in the house, and their stay together cannot be accounted for on any other reasonable innocent hypothesis. In the instant case, the respondent stayed in the house of the co-respondent for over three years alone with him. This was held to be sufficient evidence that adultery had been committed.

A similar conclusion was reached in *Gibbs* v. *G.*,[61] where the wife was living alone with the co-respondent at the latter's bungalow. When the husband came to fetch her back she refused to return. This coupled with the ample opportunity afforded by being alone in the bungalow was held sufficient to lead to the conclusion that adultery had been committed.

In *Bhagwan* v. *Amar.*[62] a husband sought a decree of divorce on the ground of adultery committed by the wife with the co-respondent and with unknown persons. He alleged that his wife as a result of her adulterous conduct was expelled from the Education Department, where she was a teacher. Following *Rajani* v. *Prabhakar* (discussed earlier at p. 64) it was held that it must be shown that up to the date of petition the offending party is living in the matrimonial offence of adultery. Living in adultery means a continuous course of adulterous life as distinguished from one or two lapses from virtue.

The Royal Commission on Marriage and Divorce in England[63] considered whether a single act of adultery should continue to be a ground for divorce or the law should be changed so as to require a course of conduct consisting of several acts of adultery. It was argued that this would introduce the element of compulsion. The Royal Commission recommended that there should be no alteration in the existing law of adultery in England but India seems to have adopted the other alternative

61. *Gibbs* v. *G.*, A.I.R. 1933 All. 427 (a case under the Indian Divorce Act, 1869).

62. *Bhagwan* v. *Amar*, A.I.R. 1962 Punj. 144.

63. Report 1951-1955 (1956) Cmd. 9678, p. 37.

in making 'living in adultery' a ground for divorce. The motive was to give both parties opportunities for reconciliation; a single act of adultery can be condoned or a guilty party can give up an adulterous association before it deepens into 'living in adultery'. Where a single act of adultery is relied on, there is the difficulty of obtaining evidence, for such acts are usually done secretly. The possibility of reconciliation and maintenance of morality are clearly envisaged by the Hindu Marriage Act, 1955.

7. *APPLICATION OF ENGLISH LAW TO HINDU SOCIETY*

In English law nothing short of actual sexual intercourse will amount to adultery. Kissing[64], amorous letters,[65] manual satisfaction,[66] attempt at sexual intercourse without penetration and masturbation of the co-respondent with the help of the wife,[67] indecent advances to a woman,[68] allowing sexual liberaties to men for money, but without sexual intercourse[69] and the fact of the husband being seen in bed with the co-respondent but without intercourse[70] have been held insufficient to found a charge of adultery. The same is not necessarily true in Hindu law, although the Hindu Marriage Act, 1955 is based on English law and the English case law has a strong persuasive authority in Indian courts. Having regard to the social customs, manners, way of living and the Hindu notion of morality, an Indian court may come to a conclusion altogether different from an English court, while applying the same principle of law. This difference can be illustrated by reference to a few cases.

In *Devyani* v. *Kantilal*[71] a Hindu wife petitioned for divorce on the ground that her husband was living in adultery. The facts were that according to the wife, she and her husband

64. *Hamerton* v. *H.* (1828) 2 Hag. Ecc. 8 at 14.
65. *Chalmers* v. *C.* (1930) 46 T.L.R. 269-270.
66. *Sapsford* v. *S.* (1954) p. 394.
67. *Dennis* v. *D.* (1955) p. 153.
68. *Lewis* v. *L.* (1956) p. 205.
69. *Moffatt* v. *M.* (1961) 105 Sol. Jour. 889.
70. *Christian* v. *C.* (1962) 106 Sol. Jour. 430 (C.A.)
71. *Devyani* v. *Kantilal*, A.I.R. 1963 Bom. 98.

were living in Karim Building and, soon after she left him, he started to live with the woman charged with adultery and was so living at the time of the petition. When the wife questioned him about the relation with the woman he gave her a beating and said that the woman was his wife. The wife then left him and went to stay with her parents. According to the husband and the woman charged, the allegations were untrue. They admitted that the husband was living in the woman's house as a paying guest; he took his meals there but slept in the lobby except during the rains, when he had to come inside. The woman asserted that at no time had she any adulterous intercourse with the petitioner's husband. The husband contended that the woman was a friend of the petitioner and whenever he visited the woman at her husband's place, he went along with the petitioner and never alone. Notwithstanding this, it was held that the husband was living in adultery with the woman, since there had been reasonable opportunities for sexual intercourse. Indian mentality seems to assumes that opportunity is enough to ground the presumption of intercourse, apparently without proof of guilty attachment.

In *England* -v. *E.*[72] there was abundant evidence that the couple concerned had ample opportunity of having sexual intercourse. But the English court refused to find adultery proved. The facts were that a man spent the night in the room of a married woman. It was admitted that they were attracted to each other, that they had planned to get married, if their respective spouses would divorce them. Some months before the night in question the man had been a constant visitor to the wife's room, often in the late evening. It was held that adultery had not been committed. The court accepted the evidence that the man had spent the night in a chair only to look after the wife when she was ill; although the possibility of adultery had on occasions been discussed between them, they had agreed that there should be no sexual intercourse until they could marry.

The evidence in *Christian* v. *C.*[73] was even stronger. A wife petitioned for divorce on the ground of her husband's

72. *England* v. *E.* (1953) p. 16.
73. *Christian* v. *C.* (1962) 106 Sol. Jour. 430 (C.A.).

adultery. The facts were that the husband had become very friendly with the intervener and had written her a number of amorous letters. On one occasion he was seen in bed with her. He admitted this but stated that he had not at any time had sexual intercourse with her. It was held that adultery was not established.

Decisions like in the two cases last mentioned are unlikely to be reached in Indian courts where social customs do not generally permit the same familiarity between men and women as is tolerated in England. Undue familiarity and even amorous letters have been held sufficient to prove adultery in India. It was pointed out in *Subbarama* v. *Saraswathi*[74] that English decisions provide a very useful guide for basic principles but they must not be extended any further as the moral, social and cultural outlook of the Hindus is markedly different from the English. There is no sphere in which it is more unsafe to draw generalisations from the facts of foreign judicial precedents than the sphere of matrimonial law. In *Rajalingam* v. *Lingayya*[75] the husband petitioned for divorce on the ground that the wife was living in adultery. He produced photographs of his wife and the co-respondent in a compromising pose. This was held sufficient to prove that the wife was living in adultery, despite evidence that such photographs could be produced by trickery.

The burden of proof of a matrimonial offence both at Hindu, and English law is not as heavy as in a criminal case, but the fault must be proved beyond reasonable doubt.[76] Normally adultery can only be proved by circumstantial evidence as direct evidence is rarely forthcoming. Even if direct evidence is produced, the courts tend to look upon it with suspicion, as it is highly improbable that any person can be a witness to such acts which are generally performed with utmost secrecy.[77] In *Nokhi* v. *Tehru*[78] the wife sought divorce on the ground

74. *Subbarama* v. *Saraswathi*, A.I.R. 1967 Mad. 85.

75. *Rajalingam* v. *Lingayya*, A.I.R. 1964 Andh. Pr. 308.

76. *Preston-Jones* v. *P.-J.* (1951) A.C. 391; *Dassi* v. *Dhani Ram*, A.I.R. 1969 Punj. 25; J.A. Coutts, "*The Standrad of Proof of Adultery*" (1949) 65 L.Q.R. 22; J.A. Andrews, "*Evidence of Adultery*" (1961) 77 L.Q.R. 390.

77. *Pattayee* v. *Manickam*, A.I.R. 1967 Mad. 254.

78. *Nokhi* v. *Tehru*, A.I.R. 1957 Him. Pr. 65.

of her husband's living in adultery. The evidence showed that he had cohabited with the other woman for several years and had two children born to her. At the time of the petition they were living under the same roof. From this it was rightly inferred that they were living in adultery. The same decision would no doubt be reached on the same facts in England. But the same could not be said of *Tribat* v. *Bimla*,[79] where the husband alleged that his wife was unchaste and leading an adulterous life; one Kartar used to visit her and she had been absent from her house for about six days continuously without explanation. He had seen her at the fair in the company of two military men, sitting together and eating sweets. This was held to be sufficient to prove that the wife had been living in adultery. Such an evidence would hardly lead to the inference of adultery in England, where women are more independent and social customs quite different. In *Varadarajulu* v. *Baby*[80] a husband petitioned for divorce on the ground that his wife was living in adultery. He adduced evidence that she had been living in illicit intimacy continuously with several men and produced a photograph of the wife and her paramour. There was evidence as to entry by police showing that when the alleged paramour was under lock-up, the respondent had gone to see him stating herself to be his wife. In this case the evidence was clearly strong enough to come to the conclusion that the wife was living in adultery.

Since proof of 'adultery' or 'living in adultery' is a question of evidence the Legislature has intentionally left these phrases undefined.[81] The social stautus of the parties, their relationship to each other and the type of association have to be taken into account, for social conduct differs among Indians of the professional classes from that which is normal among people living in a village, whose livelihood depends directly or indirectly upon agriculture.

79. *Tribat* v. *Bimla*, A.I.R. 1959 J. & K.

80. *Varadarajulu* v. *Baby*, A.I.R. 1965 Mad. 29.

81. *Chanda* V. *Nandu* A.I.R. 1965 Madh. Pr. 268. at p. 269.

CHAPTER V

DESERTION

1. *THE INGREDIENTS OF DESERTION*

To be a ground for divorce under the English law[1] and Hindu law in Kenya[3] desertion must be without cause for a period of at least three years immediately preceding the presentation of the petition. It has three essential ingredients, disruption of cohabitation, absence of just or reasonable cause and their combination throughout the three years immediately preceding the presentation of the petition. Hindu law in India is different in that a decree for judicial separation can be granted to either party on the ground that the other spouse has deserted the petitioner for a continuous period of not less than two years immediately preceding the presentation of the petition.[3] The explanation to this section describes 'desertion' as desertion of the petitioner by the other party to the marriage without reasonable cause and without the consent or against the wish of such party; it includes the wilful neglect of the petitioner by the other party to the marriage.

The elements of desertion are substantially the same as in English law[4]. But what amounts to just or reasonable cause in English law, may not do so in Hindu law, owing to the different customs of Hindu society. Whereas in English law desertion is a ground for divorce, in Hindu law it can only result in a decree of judicial separation but if the parties fail to resume cohabitation for a period of two years or upwards after the passing of such a decree, either party can petition for the dissolution of the marriage.[5] It was held in *Waryam* v.

1. S. 1 (1) (b) of the (English) Matrimonial Causes Act, 1950.
2. S. 10 (1) (b) of the (Kenya) Hindu Marriage and Divorce Ordinance, 1960.
3. S. 10 (1) (a) of the Hindu Marriage Act, 1955; *Sitabai* v. *Ramchandra*, A.I.R. 1958 Bom. 116.
4. *Bipinchandra* v. *Prabhavati*, A.I.R. 1957 S.C. 176.
5. S. 13 (1) (viii) of the Hindu Marriage Act, 1955 as amended by the Hindu Marriage Amendment Act, 1964.

Pritpal[6] that a decree for dissolution of marriage could not be granted at the instance of the spouse against whom judicial separation had been decreed and the remedy was not available to persons, who had been found guilty of matrimonial lapses. But since the Hindu Marriage Amendment Act, 1964, either party to the marriage can petition for divorce on the ground that there has been no resumption of cohabitation for a period of two years or upwards, after the passing of a decree for judicial separation in a proceeding to which they were parties. The object of this provision was to give ample time for the parties to reconcile their differences and to discourage divorce.

"There is a difficulty in defining desertion and cases may arise in which it would be very difficult to say whether the facts proved would fall within the meaning of the statute. Without attempting to lay down a precise definition of 'desertion,' I think it undoubtedly must mean a wilful absenting himself by the husband; and that such absence and cessation of cohabitation must be in spite of the wish of the wife. She must not be a consenting party."[7] "It is essential to the constitution of desertion that there should be a voluntary abandonment by the husband of the society of the wife against her will."[8] Lopes, L. J., conveyed the same idea when he said, "A husband deserts his wife if he wilfully absents himself from the society of his wife in spite of her wish."[9]

The stress in the above definitions is on the 'voluntary abandonment or cessation of cohabitation' of one spouse against the will of the other. The guilty spouse must separate with the deliberate and wilful intention of bringing the cohabitation to an end. Thus there will be no desertion if the husband is compelled to separate, e.g., when he is imprisoned[10] or is unable to join the other because of a political situation over which they have no control. In *Kobus* v. *K.*[11] the husband

6. *Waryam* v. *Pritpal*, A.I.R. 1961 Punj. 320.

7. Sir Cresswell Cresswell in *Thompson* v. T. (1858) 8 Sw. and Tr. 231 = 164 E. R. 706 at 707.

8. Sir James Hannen in Townsend v. *T.* (1873) L.R. 3 p. & M. 129 at 130.

9. Lopes, L. J., in *Reg.* v. *Leresche* (1891) 2 Q.B. 418 at 420.

10. *Townsend* v. *T.* (1873) L.R. 3 P. & M. 129.

11. *Kobus* v. *K.* (1958) The Times, Dec. 11; *Kaye* v. *K.* (1953) The

escaped and came to England, while the wife remained in Poland. He wrote to her asking her to join him in England, since it was not safe for him to return to Poland. He made no attempt to get her out of Poland. His petition for divorce on the ground of desertion was dismissed because the wife had not deserted him, but was compelled by circumstances to live apart. Taking into account the risk to the wife involved in leaving Poland, it seemed to the court difficult to hold that in remaining in a country where people were said to be enslaved, she was guilty of desertion.

Lord Penzance defined desertion in the following words, "No one can desert who does not actively and wilfully bring to an end an existing state of cohabitation..If the state of cohabitation has already ceased to exist, whether by the adverse act of the husband or wife, or even by the mutual consent of both, 'desertion' in my judgement, becomes from that moment impossible to either, at least until their common life and home have been resumed."[12]

This is not entirely correct, for it presupposes an existing state of cohabitation and common life in the matrimonial home. This is too wide, for although in the overwhelming majority of cases desertion in fact takes place between parties who are enjoying a state of cohabitation, there are cases where the behaviour of a spouse separated under agreement could amount to desertion. In fact the parties need never have cohabited at all,[13] and in certain circumstances even refusal to start cohabitation can constitute desertion.[14]

Lord Penzance's statement was held to be inapplicable in cases where there is already a *de facto* separation between the spouses.[15] This original separation may be consensual[16]

Times, April 1 (a similar case, where the husband and his wife were kept apart by compulsion).

12. Lord Penzance in *Fitgerald* v. F. (1869) L. R. 1 P. & D. 694 at p. 697.

13. *De Laubenque* v. *D.L.* (1899) p. 42; *Venugopal* v. *Lakshmi*, A.I.R. 1963 Mad. 288. (The fact that the wife has not lived with the husband or the marriage was not consummated cannot make any difference).

14. *Shaw* v. *S.* (1939) p. 269.

15. *Thomas* v. *T.* (1945) 62 T.L.R. 166.

16. *Pardy* v. *P.* (1939) p. 288, 302.

or under compulsion, and the desertion starts to run from the time the guilty party forms the intention to live separate and apart permanently.[17] In *Foster* v. *F.*[18] the wife petitioned under the Indian Divorce Act, 1869, for divorce on the grounds of adultery and desertion. It was contended on behalf of the husband that desertion has not been proved, reliance being placed on *Fitzgerald* v. *F.*[19] because the husband had not actually and wilfully brought the cohabitation to an end. But ten years previously there had been earlier divorce cross petitions which had been dismissed and the husband had rejected subsequent efforts at reconciliation made by and on behalf of the wife. Desertion is abandonment against the will of the spouse charging it and the facts of the case came within the concept of desertion.

In *Pulford* v. *P.*[20] it was established that the conduct of the party charged must be looked at. If he or she has not recognised the duty of cohabitation in the married state, desertion has arisen. There may be a complete renunciation of that conjugal duty and an intention to put an end to cohabitation, though there is no matrimonial home, and cohabitation as an existing state of things has been suspended by circumstances not under the control of the party. In the words of Jeune, P., "Desertion means the cessation of cohabitation brought about by the fault or act of one of the parties. Therefore, the conduct of the parties must be considered."[21] 'Cohabitation' means living together as husband and wife and performing the rights and duties which flow out of that relationship. It consists in the wife rendering wifely duties to her husband and the husband cherishing and supporting his wife as a husband should. Cohabitation does not not necessarily imply that the parties must be living physically under the same roof.[22] The party who intends to bring the cohabitation to an end and whose conduct in reality causes its termination commits the act of

17. *Beekam* v. *B.* (1948) p. 302 (C.A.).

18. *Foster* v. *F.*, A.I.R. 1937 Oudh. 116, 119; see also A.G. Roy, *Commentary on Hindu Law*, Patna, 1960, p. 86.

19. *Fitzgerald* v. *F.* (1869) L.R. 1 p. & D. 694.

20. *Pulford* v. *P.* (1923) p. 18.

21. Jeune, P., in *Frowd* v. *F.* (1.904) p. 177.

22. *Bradshaw* v. *B.* (1897) p. 24.

desertion. Desertion is a question of intention and the conduct of the deserting spouse shows his intention,[23] Desertion is not a specific act, but a course of conduct continuing over a considerable period.[24] As these cases were followed by the Supreme Court of India in *Bipinchandra* v. *Prabhavati*,[25] Hindu law appears to be identical with English law so far as the above principles have been adopted.

Desertion requires two elements on the part of the deserting spouse, namely the fact of separation and an intention to desert, and there will be no desertion unless both these elements coincide in points of time. A *de facto* separation may take place without there being an *animus deserendi*, but if that *animus* supervenes, desertion will begin from that moment unless, of course, there is consent on the part of the other spouse.[26] The separation must also be unjustified in the sense that the deserting spouse must leave without reasonable cause, otherwise his or her act will not amount to desertion.[27]

(i) *The Fact of Separation*

There can be no desertion unless there is separation between the spouses. This separation can be actual, as when one partly leaves the matrimonial home and lives apart from the other, or it can be implied, as when the parties live under the same roof, but their joint married life has ceased to exist as such. Where the parties are living as two household units under the same roof, this may or may not amount to *de facto* separation, depending upon the facts. The true test of whether the separation amounts to desertion is whether there has been a renunciation of conjugal duties.

There may be no matrimonial home, and yet no forfeiture of the rights of the spouses. Desertion is not the withdrawal from a place, but from a state of things. The law does not deal with the mere matter of place. What it seeks to enforce is the recognition and discharge of the common obli-

23. *Sickert* v. *S.* (1899) p. 278.

24. Day J. in *Wilkinson* v. W. (1894) 58 J.P. 415 at 416.

25. *Bipinchandra* v. *Prabhavati*, A.I.R. 1957 S. C. 176, 187.

26. *Pardy* v. *P.* (1939) p. 288, 302 (C.A.); *Williams* v. *W.* (1939) p. 365, 368 (C.A.).

27. *Frowd* v. *F.* (1904) p. 177, 179.

gations of the married state.[28] The implication of dersertion is the rejection of all the obligations of marriage.[29] The mere fact, that one of the spouses has renounced some of the marital obligations or refused to perform isolated duties, will not suffice for the purpose of desertion, e.g., refusal by a husband or wife to have sexual intercourse, however, wilful and unjustified does not of itself amount to desertion.[30] But the position is different if the refusal is used as an excuse for desertion or it is accompanied by other circumstances, e.g., where the spouses are living separate and apart.[31] The situation is similar in Hindu law. In *Bhagawanti* v. *Sadhu*[32] it was held that mere refuse of matrimonial bed by the wife is no desertion; the Hindu religion regards abstinence from sexual intercourse as a virtue.

There may be desertion, although husband and wife are living in the same dwelling, if there is such a forsaking and abandonment by one spouse of the other that the court can say that the spouses were living separate and apart from one another.[33] Desertion can exist while the parties are living under the same roof. The husband who shuts himself in one or two rooms of his house, and ceases to have anything to do with his wife, is living separately and apart from her as effectively as if they were separated by the outer door of a flat.[34]

If it is impossible for the deserting spouse to find accomosation elsewhere, he or she may be forced by circumstances to live under the same roof as the other. *Prima facie* in such a case the parties are living together, as in *Bull* v. *B.*[35] where the wife refused to converse with her husband, to have sexual intercourse with him, to sit in the same room or at the same table with him, to go out with him, or to allow him to have his own friends to the house, cooked his meals, though he

28. Sir Henry Duke in *Pulford* v. *P.* (1923) p. 18 at 21-22.
29. *Perry* v. *P.* (1952) p. 203 at 215 (C.A.).
30. *Weatherley* v. *W.* (1947) A.C. 628 H.L.; J. Ridley, "*The Refusal of Sexual Intercourse and the Law of Desertion*" (1948) 64 L.Q.R. 243; P. M. Bromley, *Family Law*, London, 1962, pp. 100-103.
31. *Hutchinson* v. *H.* (1963) 1 All E.R. 1.
32. *Bhagwanti* v. *Sadhu*, *A.I.R.* 1961 Punj. 181.
33. *Hopes* v. *H.* (1949) p. 227 at 234 (C.A.).
34. *Hopes* v. *H.*, supra, at p. 235.
35. *Bull* v. *B.* (1953) p. 224, 226, 228 (C.A.).

bought his own rations, and occasionally mended his clothes for him, it was held that this did not amount to desertion and her previous period of desertion had been interrupted by these acts. But the presumption from living under the same roof can be rebutted, as appears from *Bartram* v. *B.*[36] where a wife, who had deserted her husband for some years, went to live under the same roof as her husband, only because there was no other accomodation within reach of her work. She refused to sleep with her husband, never went to his rooms or mended his clothes; she cooked for him and went out with him, and at times she even sat at the same table as her husband for meals. But it was held that there was desertion, and her previous period of desertion continued.

The test of desertion is whether the spouses have ceased to be one household unit and have split into two households.[37] But the withdrawal from cohabitation must be complete and there cannot be desertion, if the parties continue to perform even some of their marital obligations. The mere fact that the husband pays for the maintenance of his wife and children, when there is an implied separation, will not prevent the circumstances from amounting to *de facto* separation. Thus in *Smith* v. *S.*[38] where a married couple lived for years in different parts of the same house, after the husband had withdrawn from cohabitation with his wife and ceased to have anything to do with her at all except to leave small sums of money from time to time at a place where she could pick them up, it was held that he was in desertion.

In *Hopes* v. *H.*[39] a man, his wife and two daughters formed one household, sharing the same living room, kitchen, stairs, passages and offices, although the spouses always occupied separate bedrooms, and the wife behaved in such a way towards her husband as to indicate that she wished him to leave the

36. *Bartram* v. *B.* (1950) p. 1 (C.A.); a similar conclusion was reached in *Watson* v. *Tuckwell* (1947) 63 T.L.R. 634.

37. *Hopes* v. *H.* (1949) p. 227, 231, 236 (C.A.); *Littlewood* v. *L.* (1943) p. 11 (where the parties were of disagreeable nature, and the matrimonial services had not completely ceased; held no desertion).

38. *Smith* v. *S.* (1940) p. 49; *Shilston* v. *S.* (1945) 174 L.T. 105; *Macdonald* v. *M.* (1859) 4 Sw. & Tr. 242 = 164 E.R. 1508.

39. *Hopes* v. *H.* (1949) p. 227.

house and not return. It was held that there was no *de facto* separation to found desertion by the wife. Gross neglect or chronic discord is not a ground for divorce.

This case was followed in *Naylor* v. *N.*[40] where, after a quarrel, the wife, cast off her wedding-ring and indicated to the husband her intention of no longer being a wife to him. Thereafter, although the parties continued to live in the matrimonial home, they led entirely separate lives; they occupied separate bedrooms, had no sexual intercourse and the wife performed no wifely duties for the husband. The Divisional Court held that in the circumstances there was desertion. Similarly in *Walker* v. *W.*[41] the parties lived in the same house, but the wife withdrew into a separate bedroom, which she kept locked. She performed no household duties for the husband, who had to do his own washing, mending and ironing. As his wife would do no cooking for him, the husband had his meals out as often as possible and only cooked for himself on Sunday mornings, always at a time when the wife was not using the kitchen herself. When the parties wished to communicate with one another, they did so by written notes. On these facts it was held that the parties were not living together in one household, and the wife had deserted the husband. That separation can exist while the spouses are living under the same roof has been repeatedly laid down.

If the test of splitting the matrimonial home into two household units, as expounded by Lord Denning in *Hopes* v. *H.*[42] is applied to *Wanbon* v. *W.*,[43] that decision is incorrect. Here the wife withdrew from the husband's bedroom and refused to have marital intercourse with him. She refused to cook for him, make his bed, mend his clothes or perform any wifely services. She never addressed a word to the husband, except to find fault with him. On these facts the learned judge, Pilcher, J., granted the husband a decree on the ground of desertion, although the evidence was that the husband and wife

40. *Naylor* v. *N.* (1962) p. 253.

41. *Walker* v. *W.* (1952) 2 All E. R. 138 (C.A.); *Baker* v. *B.* (1952) 2 All E.R. 248 (C.A.); *Angal* v. *A.* (1946) 2 All E.R. 635; *Shilston* v. *S.* (1945) 174 L.T. 105; *Wilkes* v. *W.* (1943) p. 41; *Smith* v. *S.* (1940) p. 49.

42. *Hopes* v. *H.* (1949) p. 227.

43. *Wanbon* v. *W.* (1946) 2 All E.R. 366.

continued to live under the same roof. The correctness of this case was doubted by Lord Denning, who said, "I find myself in agreement with all the decisions of the Divorce Division except perhaps *Wanbom* v. *W.*, where the parties were said to be still in one household. If that means that, although living at arm's length, they were still sharing the same living room, eating at the same table and sitting by the same fire, then I cannot agree with the finding of desertion".[44]

The line between desertion, which is a ground for divorce, and gross neglect or chronic discord, which is not, is a very fine one. This line is drawn at the point where the parties live separately and apart, when the line dividing neglect or discord from desertion is crossed, then they are no longer residing with one another or cohabiting with one another.

The phrases 'not residing with one another,' 'living separately and apart', or 'living apart' or 'not cohabiting with one another', mean the same thing, and there is no sensible distinction between them. They all express the fact of separation. The confusion arising out of these phrases was the cause of the misconceived decision in *Evans* v. *E.*[45] the husband had bolted the doors of the house against the wife; she re-entered through the window, and afterwards lived against her husband's will in rooms different from those occupied by him. She had her meals separately, paid him no rent and performed no domestic or wifely services for him. The Justices found that he had deserted her, (a finding fully justified according to well established principles) and ordered him to pay maintenance for the wife and children. But when the wife sought to enforce the order, the Divisional Court by a majority held it was unenforceable, because, although the husband had deserted her and was still deserting her, she was still 'residing with' him. This is self contradictory. How can anyone say that, at one and the same time, a wife is residing with her husband and that he has deserted her ? She may be residing at her husband's house but she is not residing with him.

The correct view was expressed in *Thomas* v. *T.*,[46] the husband had driven his wife out of the house and she obtained

44. Lord Denning in *Hopes* v. *H.* (1949) p. 227 at 235, 237.
45. *Evans* v. *E.* (1948) 1 K. B. 175.
46. *Thomas* v. *T.* (1948) 2 K.B. 294.

a maintenance order on the ground of his desertion. She afterwards returned to the house and lived in rooms entirely separate from those occupied by the husband, a situation indistinguishable from *Evans* v. *E.*[47] The Divisional Court held that she was entitled to enforce her maintenance order, because she had not resumed cohabitation with her husband. The husband had deserted her and was still in desertion; she was not cohabiting with him.

If *Evans* v. *E.* were right, Mrs. Thomas would still be residing with her husband. Indeed there is no reason why Mrs. Thomas should be able to enforce her order and Mrs. Evans should not. If Mrs.. Evans, instead of getting back straight through the window, had stayed away a few nights, so as to be able to say she had been 'living apart' from her husband, she would apparently have been able to enforce her order just as Mrs. Thomas did; but because she had nowhere else to go, she could not. Such a result is clearly wrong, as was pointed by Lord Denning at the end of his judgement in *Hopes* v. *H.*; "relieved of *Wanbon* v. *W.* and *Evans* v. *E.*, the law becomes consistent on this subject". In both the cases the spouses were living separate and apart as two distinct household units, although in the same house, and there was sufficient separation to amount to desertion. Thus *Evans* v. *E.*[48] was wrongly decided.

(ii) *The Intention to Desert*

The fact of separation will not amount to desertion, unless it co-exists with the intention of remaining permanently separated on the part of the guilty spouse.[49] Hindu law in India has developed in the same direction. Following English authorities,[50] it was held in *Kuppanna* v. *Palaniammal*[51] that

47. *Evans* v. *E.* (1948) 1 K.B. 175.

48. Commented upon in (1948) 64 L.Q.R., pp. 8, 16.

49. *Williams* v. *W.* (1939) p. 365, 368 (C.A.); *Pardy* v. *P.* (1939) p. 288, 302 (C.A.); P.M. Bromley, *Family Law*, p. 103; D. Tolstoy, *The Law and Practice of Divorce*, London, 1963, pp. 41-42.

50. *Williams* v. *W.* (1939) p. 365 (C.A.); *Pardy* v. *P.* (1939) p. 288 (C.A.); Latey on *Divorce* 14th Ed., p. 104; Raydon on *Divorce*, 5th Ed., p. 101.

the two elements required to be present on the side of the deserting spouse to constitute desertion are the *factum* of separation, and the *animus deserendi* or intention to bring the cohabitation permanently to an end. There is, therefore, the possibility of a *de facto* separation without the *animus* to desert, in which case it cannot be held that the spouse charged with desertion is guilty of desertion. The fact of separation without intention to desert permanently does not constitute desertion. In *Bipinchandra* v. *Prabhavati*[52] the wife left her husband's house in shame, not having the courage to face the husband, after his discovery of her reprehensible conduct but this did not render her a deserter, for when she left, she had no intention to bring the matrimonial cohabitation permanently to an end, nor did she form this intention subsequently.

The permanence of the intention turns *de facto* separation into desertion. A temporary separation for business or health reasons will not raise a presumption of *animus deserendi*, In *Clark* v. *C.*,[53] the wife was receiving treatment in a mental hospital. She was not fit to run a home or look after the husband. The husband had not provided a home for her nor was he able to provide anyone to look after her. It was held that she was not in desertion. This principle was extended in *G.* v. *G.*[54] to the case where the wife lived temporarily separate and apart from her husband not for the sake of her own health but for the protection of her child's health. There was no evidence that the wife had declared, unequivocally and for all time, that she would not live with her husband again. She had manifested no *animus* to bring the cohabitation permanently to an end, and consequently there was no desertion. If, however, the wife had taken advantage of these circumstances, which necessitated temporary separation and had declared that she would at no time live with the husband again,

51. *Kuppanna* v. *Palauiammal*, A.I.R. 1955 Mad. 471 (a case under the Madras Hindu Bigamy Prevention and Divorce Act, 1949).

52. *Bipinchandra* v. *Prabhavati*, A.I.R. 1957 S.C. 176, 182. (The authorities of Raydon on *Divorce* and *Halsbury's Laws of England*, 3rd Ed., vol. 12, pp. 241-243, were there cited).

53. *Clark* v. *C.* (1956) 1 All E.R. 823.

54. *G.* v. *G.* (1964) 1 All E.R. 129 (this will be fully dealt with in relation to 'just cause').

then an *animus deserendi* on the part of the wife might well have been inferred.

However, a justified temporary separation can change its character to desertion, if the spouse obliged to separate envinces his or her intention to bring the cohabitation permanently to an end. In *Lilley* v. *L.*[55] the wife, who suffered from neurosis, was living apart from her husband. She was held guilty of desertion, for her attitude went far beyond saying "I cannot return to you at present." She added in effect, "and I never will."

Similarly in *Tomlinson* v. *T.*[56] a wife was held guilty of desertion. She left the matrimonial home not merely because she felt she must get medical aid and go into hospital, as in fact occurred, but because she intended to leave her husband for good. But in another case it was held that there was no *animus deserendi* on the part of the wife, who was subject to delusions; she accused her husband of associating with other women, attempting to murder her and assaulting her; she left the matrimonial home and never returned. After three years the husband petitioned for divorce on the ground of desertion. It was held that as the wife was suffering from paranoid psychoses and was acting under a delusion as to the husband's violent intentions, she had no mental capacity to form an intention to desert.[57]

Where there is a *de facto* separation, desertion becomes operative from the time the guilty party forms the intention to live permanently separate and apart, unless there is consent by the other spouse. The same applies to Hindu law, e.g., if there is a de *facto* separation in existence, the essential question is whether the act can be attributed to *an animus deserendi.* Where a wife went to her father's house with the knowledge and consent of her husband and at one stage expressed her

55. *Lilley* v. *L.* (1960) p. 158, 183; a similar conclusion was reached in *Keeley* v. *K.* (1952) 2 T.L.R. 756.

56. *Tomlinson* v. *T.* (1958) The Times, May 14; a similar conclusion was reached in *Keeley* v. *K.* (1952) 2 T.L.R. 756; *More* v. *M.* (1950) p. 168; *Pulford* v. *P.* (1923) p. 18-23 (where the cohabitation was suspended while the wife was in the asylum. The husband intended and put an end to the cohabitation; he was held guilty of desertion).

57. *Perry* v. *P.* (1964) 1 W.L.R. 91; see also George S. Gulick and William S. Anderson, *American Jurisprudence*, vol. 17, New York, 1957, p. 317

desire to rejoin her husband but later deliberately stayed away, in spite of the fact that the husband offered to take her back, it was held that her deliberate act of staying on, after her husband had called back, amounted to desertion.[58] But in *Suryaprakasa* v. *Venkata*[59] the wife was taken away by her father from the husband's house with the consent of the husband. It was held that there was nothing in the attendant circumstances to warrant an inference that the wife desired to reside away from her husband or that her separate living was attributable to an *animus deserendi* but she might become guilty of desertion later, if she indicated an intention to live away from him permanently.

On the authority of Halsbury's Laws of England, 3rd Ed., p. 241, it was held in *Manglabai* v. *Deorao*[60] that the essence of desertion is the intentional permanent forsaking and abandonment of one spouse by the other against the former's consent. The abandonment must be intentional and deliberate. The mere fact that the husband wrote a letter in anger to the wife or her parents saying that he would have nothing to do with her is no evidence of desertion by the husband.[61] Following the principle laid down by Lord Penzance in *Fitzgerald* v. *F.*[62] to the effect that desertion means abandonment, and implies an active withdrawal from cohabitation that exists, it was held in *Kako* v. *Ajit*[63] that the gist of the matrimonial offence of desertion consists in the intention of the deserting spouse never to return to the marital home. While the decision is correct on facts it is doubtful whether the statement of Lord Penzance was rightly applied, because there was no active withdrawal from the existing cohabitation as the parties were already living separate and apart. The situation where there is no existing cohabitation has been dealt with earlier in this chapter.

Both at Hindu law[64] and English law desertion commences

58. *Jivubai* v. *Ningappa*, A.I.R. 1963 Mys. 3.
59. *Suryaprakasa* v. *Venkata*, A.I.R. 1961 Andh. Pr. 404.
60. *Manglabai* v. *Deorao*, A.I.R. Madh. Pr. 193, 195.
61. *Rukman* v. *Faquir* , A.I.R. 1960 Punj. 493.
62. *Fitzgerald* v. *F.* (1869) L. R. 1 p. & D. 694 at p. 697.
63. *Kako* v. *Ajit*, A.I.R. 1960 Punj. 328.
64. *Ram* v. *Dev*, A.I.R. 1950 E. Punj. 317 (citing Raydon on *Divorce*, 1949, pp. 99-101, 103, *Pulford* v. *P.* [1923] p. 18).

from the time when the fact of separation and *animus derserendi* coincide. The fact that the *de facto* separation exists under compulsion is immaterial. In *Beekan* v. *B.*[65] the spouses were compelled by the enemy, during the war time, to live in separate camps; it was held that there was no desertion, until the wife manifested her intention to desert her husband for good and marry a Norwegian, with whom she had formed an attachment. Desertion commenced when the *animus deserendi* supervened . On the contrary there was no intention to desert permanently and consequently no desertion in *Kaye* v. *K.*[66] where the separation was under compulsion. For all practical purposes it was never possible for the wife to leave Poland, and come to England nor was the husband able to join her there. The husband's petition for divorce on the ground of desertion was dismissed, for he had failed to prove that the wife had the intention to desert. The letters from the wife had made it clear that she would have lived with her husband, had he gone to Cracow.

The same principle applies where the compulsory separation takes place as the result of imprisonment of one of the spouses. Thus in *Townsend* v. *T.*[67] a husband having committed several thefts, separated from his wife with her knowledge and consent, for the purpose of avoiding arrest. He was afterwards arrested and imprisoned, and having committed other thefts after his release, he was on subsequent occasions again imprisoned. While in prison and in the intervals between his imprisonments, he kept up a correspondence with his wife and made repeated endeavours to induce her to return to cohabitation. She refused, and the cohabitation was never resumed. The wife's petition for divorce on the ground of adultery coupled with desertion was dismissed. It was held that there was no desertion, as the separation on the part of the husband was involuntary. Sir James Hannen in the

65. *Beekan* v. *B.* (1948) p. 302 (C.A.); *Szajna* v. *S.* (1954) The Times, June 19 (the wife being loyal to her country; the husband was not unreasonable in fearing to return to Poland; held she was guilty of desertion as her duty to her husband came before any loyalty which she might owe to her country).

66. *Kaye* v. *K.* (1953) The Times, April 1.

67. *Townsend* v. *T.* (1873) L.R. 3 P. & M. 129.

course of his judgement said that there had never been a voluntary abandonment by the husband of the society of his wife against her will. He never voluntarily absented himself from her, but was prevented from rejoining her either by his imprisonment or by her refusal to resume cohabitation. If he had been living in adultery with another woman, his persistence in such a connection would have been the strongest evidence of an intention to abandon his wife; but the relapses of the husband into a criminal course of life do not in themselves afford such evidence. There was no *animus deserendi* on the part of the husband and the *de facto* separation in itself could not amount to desertion.

However, the *animus deserendi* was found in *Drew* v. *D.*[68] where the husband, when leaving his wife, stated to her that he was going to Ireland for a week's shooting. In fact he went to Australia to escape arrest on a charge of embezzlement. He also had adulterous relations with different women. Subsequently he was brought back and sentenced to ten years' penal servitude. It was held that the circumstances under which the respondent left his wife constituted desertion, and that the desertion would continue, notwithstanding the fact that he was brought back to this country in custody and prevented by his imprisonment from returning to his wife. Once time has begun to run, compulsory separation will not interrupt it.

2. *CONSTRUCTIVE DESERTION*

As has been seen desertion is not the withdrawal from a place but from a state of things,[69] so that the spouse leaving the matrimonial home is not necessarily the deserting party. Where one spouse acts in such a wilful, unreasonable and unjustifiable way that the other is driven out by his behaviour, the former becomes guilty of constructive desertion, although it is the latter who leaves the matrimonial home physically and locationally, e.g., where a husband carries on an adulterous association with other women to the disgust of his wife, which results in her leaving the matrimonial home. There

68. *Drew* v. *D.* (1888) 13 P.D. 97.
69. *Pulford* v. *P.* (1923) p. 18, 21.

is no substantial difference between a husband who forcibly turns his wife out with the intention of bringing the marital cohabitation permanently to an end and one, who with like intention, obliges her to leave by his act or words.[70] In constructive desertion there is expulsive conduct,[71] which has to be ascertained in the light of the presumption that a man intends the natural and probable consequences of his acts.[72]

As English law has a great persuasive authority in India, the position is practically the same at Hindu law. The concept of constructive desertion was well defined in *T. Rangaswami* v. *T. Aravindammal*.[73] It was held that in certain circumstances the deserting spouse may not be the person who actually leaves the matrimonial home. The actual parting may be due to the deserting spouse making continued joint life impossible and thus compelling the deserted spouse to leave the matrimonial home. In such cases abandoning of the matrimonial home is not the act of the spouse who leaves but the spouse who causes the departure. The test is not the abandoning of the matrimonial home but the fact that the other party has caused such abandonment by his actions, since he must be taken to intend the consequences of such actions. If it is a natural consequence of the behaviour of one spouse that the other will leave the matrimonial home, the offending spouse must be presumed to have intended that this should happen.

Following the English case, *Pulford* v. *P.*,[74] it was held in *Leela* v. *Manohar*[75] that the question of desertion cannot be decided by merely inquiring which party left the matrimonial home first. The husband may live there but make it impossible for his wife to live there and, if in that state of things the wife leaves the matrimonial home, it is the husband who is guilty of desertion. The court has to look at the conduct of both spouses and the party whose conduct in reality brings the cohabitation permanently to an end commits the action of desertion.

70. *Graves* v. *G.* (1864) 3 Sw. & Tr. 350; *Sickert* v. *S.* (1899) p. 278.
71. *Buchler* v. *B.* (1947) p. 25, 29-30 (C.A.).
72. *Edwards* v. *E.* (1948) p. 268 (C.A.).
73. *T. Rangaswami* v. *T. Aravindammal*, A.I.R. 1957 Mad. 243.
74. *Pulford* v. *P.* (1923) p. 18.

As in simple desertion, there must be an intention to bring the cohabitation to an end.[76] As in English law so in Hindu law, a mere wish to expel, even if it exists, without acts equivalent to expulsion, is insufficient to constitute constructive desertion.[77] The intention to drive away the other spouse can be inferred from the conduct of the guilty party, or it may be established independently of such conduct, e.g., in *Boyd* v. *B.*[78] a husband was convicted of incest and served a term of imprisonment. Upon his release the wife condoned the offence and resumed cohabitation. He was subsequently convicted of an indecent assault upon a girl of 13 years. Upon his second release he offered to come back to the wife, who declined his offer and petitioned for divorce on the ground of desertion. It was held that the husband was not guilty of constructive desertion, for there was no clear intention on his part to drive the wife away. The man was a sexual pervert, who was unable to control himself.

In this case the husband was held to have had no *animus deserendi* irrespective of his bad conduct. It is submitted that this was wrong. The conduct of the husband proved his intention. A husband who subjects his wife to a long series of acts of insults and cruelty which ultimately causes her to leave the matrimonial home with her children cannot be heard to say that he had no intention to drive her out.[79] The presumption that a person must be taken to intend the natural consequences of his acts is also applicable to a case where the husband's conduct is directed towards a third person which he must know will affect his wife indirectly.[80]

The conduct of the husband in *Boyd* v. *B.*[81] was so

75. *Leela* v. *Manohar*, A.I.R. 1959 Madh. Pr. 349.
76. *Hosegood* v. *H.* (1950) 66, part I, T.L.R. 735 (C.A.).
77. *Perumal* v. *Sithalakshmi*, A.I.R. 1956 Mad. 415 (where an exhaustive study of English case law was made, and assistance was drawn from Latey on *Divorce*, 14th Ed., pp. 104-105; D. Tolstoy, *The Law and Practice of Divorce*, 2nd Ed., pp. 34-35; Raydon on *Divorce*, 4th Ed., pp. 101-102; Sir Henry Rattigan, *Law of Divorce* (applicable to Christians in India), 2nd Ed., p. 139).
78. *Boyd* v. *B.* (1938) 4 All E. R. 181.
79. *Thomas* v. *T.* (1924) p. 194 (C.A.).
80. *Edwards* v. *E.* (1948) p. 268 (C.A.).
81. *Boyd* v. *B.* (1938) 4 All E. R. 181.

heinous in relation to his daughter that the wife was fully justified in living separate and apart from him. The point is clarified in *W.* v. *W.*,[82] where the facts were similar. The husband was guilty of incest with his daughter and was sentenced to a term of imprisonment. On his release he sought reconciliation with his wife. At first she seemed willing to receive him but later she wrote him a letter telling him not to come to her house any more, because of what he had done to the second daughter. Then the wife got a separation order with a non-cohabitation clause, on the ground of her husband's constructive desertion. On appeal by the husband it was held that the husband's offences against the two daughters, even in the absence of repetition or persistence by him, constituted such cruel conduct as justified the wife in bringing the cohabitation to an end; there had been constructive desertion. It was expressly stated that *Boyd* v. *B.* was wrongly decided.

This can be compared with the situation in an Indian case where the expulsive conduct directed at the wife by the relations of the husband, to which he took no objection, was imputed to the husband himself. In *Ram* v. *Dev*,[83] a wife, who was living with her husband and his family, alleged that the husband's father made improper overtures to her. The father-in-law asked her to massage him; on another occasion he asked her to remove her veil and show her face to him. She complained to her husband, who resented the allegation; she was ill-treated and beaten. Later she was sent away to her parents' house. The husband never wrote to her in spite of the fact that she sent several letters including a registered one. She had tried to bring about reconciliation, but failed. She insisted that her husband should live separately from his parents, to which he was not agreeable. It was held that the wife was justified in living apart from the husband on account of the conduct of the husband and his father. The husband was consequently in desertion.

If a husband brings a concubine into the matrmonial home, in consequence of which the wife leaves, he must be presumed to have intended to drive the wife out and conse-

82. *W.* v. *W.* (1961) 2 All E. R. 626.
83. *Ram* v. *Dev.*, A.I.R. 1950 E. Punj. 317.

quently he is in desertion. In *Stree* v. *S.*[84] the husband brought a concubine into the house where his wife was living with him and she left him. Relying on *Sickert* v. *S.*[85] and *Dickinson* v. *D.*,[86] it was held that such conduct as that of the husband amounted to desertion.

A man's intention must be distinguished from his desire. Thus he may wish his wife to remain with him but if he brutally ill-treats her in such a way that, as a reasonable person, he must know that she will consequently leave him, the inference is that he must intend her to leave, even though he may want or desire her to stay. This is the inferential or objective test. According to *Lang* v. *L.*[87] *prima facie* a man must be presumed to intend the natural consequences of his acts, though it is always open to him to rebut this presumption if he can.[88] In practice it seems impossible to rebut this presumption, according to *dicta* in some cases,[89] although it is not an irrebuttable presumption of law; if a woman, whose husband is carrying on an adulterous association, withdraws from cohabitation and refuses to resume it unless he gives up the connection, what evidence will be necessary to rebut the presumption that the husband intended her to put an end to the matrimonial consortium ?

The conduct which drives the other spouse away must be grave and weighty. The test is the same as that applied to find out whether a spouse has just cause for leaving the other in a case of simple desertion. The conduct expelling a

84. *Stree* v. *S.*, A.I.R. 1935 Mad. 541, Sp. Ben. (A case under the Indian Divorce Act, 1869).

85. *Sickert* v. *S.* (1899) p. 278.

86. *Dickinson* v. *D.* (1889) 62 L.T. 330.

87. *Lang* v. *L.* (1955) A. C. 402; *Waters* v. *W.* (1956) p. 344; *Ingram* v. *I.* (1956) p. 390; see also A.L. Goodhart, "*Constructive Desertion*" (1955) 71 L.Q.R. 32; A.L. Goodhart, "*Cruelty, Desertion and Insanity in Matrimonial Law*" (1963) 79 L.Q.R. 98, pp. 110-116.

88. *Hosegood* v. *H.* (1950) 66 T.L.R. 735, 738-739 (C.A.).

89. Lord Green M. R. in *Buchler* v. *B.* (1947) P. 25, 30 (C.A.); Gorell Barnes, J., in *Sickert* v. *S.* (1899) p. 278 at p. 284; Royal Commission on divorce recommended by a majority that this presumption should be irrebuttable (1956), Cmd. 9678; see also Lord Denning, "*Presumptions and Burdens*" (1945) 61 L.Q.R. 379, 381.

spouse from the matrimonial home must exceed in gravity such behaviour, vexatious and trying though it may be, as every spouse bargains to endure when accepting the other for better or for worse. "It may no doubt be galling, or in some sense of the word, humiliating for a wife to find that the husband prefers the company of his men friends, his club, his newspaper, his games, his hobbies or indeed his own society, to association with her and a husband may have similar grievances against his wife. But this is what may be called the reasonable wear and tear of married life and if it were a ground for divorce a heavy toll would be levied on the institution of matrimony.[90]

Lord Porter meant the same thing when he said, "A husband's irritating habits may so get on the wife's nerves that she leaves as a direct consequence of them but she would not be justified in doing so. Such irritating idiosyncrasies are part of the lottery in which every spouse engages on marrying and taking the partner of the marriage "for better, for worse". The course of conduct must be grave and convincing."[91] The mere fact that the wife is a slut does not justify the husband in leaving, and the wife is not in constructive desertion.[92] The same is true at Hindu law. In *Narayan* v. *Prabhadevi*[93] a husband petitioned for a decree of judicial separation on the ground of desertion alleging that the wife quarrelled and disobeyed his mother and made his life unhappy by frequently picking petty quarrels with his mother. The court, followed a dictum of Lord Porter in *Lang* v. *L.*[94] to the effect that, though a husband's irritating habits may so get on the wife's nerves that she leaves as a direct consequence of them, she would not be justified in doing so. Such irritating idiosyncrasies are part of the lottery in which every spouse engages on marrying, taking the other partner of the marriage "for better, for worse". It was held that the husband was not entitled to a decree of judicial separation; the wife was not in desertion, because she had offered to come and live with the husband and he refused

90. Asquith, L.J., in *Buchler* v. *B.* (1947) p. 25, 47 (C.A.).
91. Lord Porter in *Lang*. v. *L.* (1955) A.C. 402, 418.
92. *Bartholomew* v. *B.* (1952) 2 All E.R. 1035 (C.A.).
93. *Narayan* v. *Prabhadevi*, A.I.R. 1964 Madh. Pr. 28.
94. *Lang* v. *L.* (1955) A.C. 412, 418.

to have her on the above pretexts. Having accepted her in marriage before the nuptial fire, he has to make allowance for her irritating idiosyncrasies. Her conduct was not equivalant to dismissal from the consortium. On the other hand the husband was in constructive desertion in not taking her back.

Conduct driving the petitioner out need not amount to a matrimonial offence, but it must be grave and weighty.[95] In *Saunders* v. *S.*[96] the wife left the husband and made a complaint against him, alleging desertion and wilful neglect to maintain. The wife's case was that he opened her letters; he had done nothing to protect her, when his father abused her; he was unduly hard on her at the birth of the child, making her work long hours in the shop they owned; he kept her short of money, showed a lack of consideration in the burden that she was bearing in the shop and at home; he had done nothing to help her when the child was ill. The justices found that the husband had shown a considerable degree of callousness and lack of consideration for the wife's feelings; he had deserted her, and they made a maintenance order. The appeal by the husband was dismissed; it was held that both in cruelty and constructive desertion the test was whether the conduct of the guilty spouse was grave and weighty.

Divorce law in Kenya has also developed on somewhat similar lines, e.g., in *Hella Kaufmann* v. *H. K.*,[97] following *Buchler* v. *B.*,[98] it was held that the essential element of desertion must be an intention to bring the cohabitation to an end. The husband's behaviour may be so bad that his wife leaves him, but the court must be satisfied that the conduct of the husband is such as to show a clear intention on his part to drive the wife away. Similarly in *Sheila McKeller* v. *John McKeller*,[99] following *Buchler* v. *B.*, it was held that mere neglect by the husband and use of abusive language do not entitle the wife to leave the matrimonial home and the husband was not in constructive desertion.

95. *Buchler* v. *B.* (1947) p. 25 (C.A.).
96. *Saunders* v. *S.* (1965) 2 W.L.R. 32.
97. *Hella Kaufmaun* v. *H.K.* (1949) 23 (2) K.L.R. 52.
98. *Buchler* v. *B.* (1947) p. 25 (C.A.).
99. *Sheila McKeller* v. *John McKeller* (1956) 29 K.L.R. 101.

Where the case sought to be made is in the nature of cruelty, it is not possible to build up a case of constructive desertion by what is really a case of unproved cruelty.[100] In *Timmins* v. *T.*,[101] a wife's allegations of cruelty were not proved, yet the Court of Appeal by a majority held that the same facts were just cause for separation from her husband. Hodson, L. J., dissenting, stated that cruelty does not shade off into just cause. Similarly in *Skull* v. *S.*[102] Lord Merriman, P., stated that the same conduct as fell short of cruelty could not be dressed up as constructive desertion. *Skull* v. *S.* was followed in the Indian case, *Abraham* v. *A.*[103], where it was laid down that conduct which for one reason or another falls short of cruelty, may nevertheless, afford good cause for leaving, but the same evidence as has been given in an unproved case of cruelty cannot be relied on to establish constructive desertion.

In a recent case[104] a wife brought proceedings before the justices alleging persistent cruelty and desertion. The allegations included physical violence sufficient to constitute a threat of injury to 'limb' and other conduct by the husband which caused her to attempt suicide. The justices found that persistent cruelty was not proved but that there had been constructive desertion by the husband. On appeal the Divisional Court held that there must be a rehearing, because, among other factors, in the circumstances, the two findings were inconsistent and the finding of constructive desertion raised the suspicion that a wrong test had been applied, the right one being whether the husband was guilty of such grave and weighty misconduct that he must have known that the wife, if she acted like a reasonable woman, would in all probability withdraw permanently from cohabitation.

Timmins v. *T.*[105] is inconsistent with *Barker* v. *B.*,[106] where

100. *Pike* v. *P.* (1954) p. 81, 87 (C.A.).
101. *Timmins* v. *T.* (1953) 2 All E. R. 187 (C.A.).
102. *Skull* v. *S.* (1954) p. 458.
103. *Abraham* v. *A.*, A.I.R. 1959 Ker. 75, 79.
104. *Griffiths* v. *G.* (1964) 3 All E. R. 929.
105. *Timmins* v. *T.* (1953) 2 All E.R. 187 (C.A.)
106. *Barker* v. *B.* (1949) p. 219, 226; see also *Bright* v. (1954) p. 270; *Hill* v. *H.* (1954) P. 291; Lionel Rosan, "*Cruelty and Constructive Desertion*" (1954) 17 M.L.R. 432.

Hodson, J., said. "It is not open to any court to say 'this is not cruelty, but is so near it that it amounts to grave and weighty matter justifying separation'." The same learned judge reiterated this argument in *Pike* v. *P.*[107] where Denning, L. J., stated that separation could be justified by conduct different from cruelty but not by conduct less than cruelty. If the conduct complained of is too trivial to amount to cruelty, it cannot be sufficiently grave and weighty to amount to constructive desertion. In *Young* v. *Y.*[108] an attempt was made to reconcile *Pike* v. *P.*[109] and *Timmins* v. *T.*[110] on the ground that in the latter the husband's dictatorial and overbearing conduct was not due to any desire to injure or distress his wife and for that reason, and that reason only, it was not cruelty. Where the gravity of the conduct itself is in question, irrespective of its motive or its effects, the standard is the same for good cause for separation as well as for cruelty.

This seems to create an exception rather than make reconciliation because the judgement gives reasons why the same grave and weighty conduct does not amount to cruelty, and does not lay down that conduct less than cruelty will suffice for constructive desertion, which was the principle on which *Timmins* v. *T.* was decided. However, reconciliation is possible where the conduct causing the separation is different from cruelty, such as habitual drunkenness[111] or any adulterous association[112] but not where the conduct is in the nature or form of cruelty. Conversely, if the conduct of a spouse amounts to constructive desertion, it can be held to constitute cruelty, as Lord Merriman, P., held in the following words, "If the ill-treatment consisting of deliberately inducing belief in an adulterous association is, in appropriate circumstances, held sufficient to justify the allegation that the wife has positively been expelled from the home, I can see no reason why the

107. *Pika* v. *P.* (1954) p. 81, 87-88 (C.A.).
108. *Young* v. *Y.* (1962) 3 All E.R. 120.
109. *Pike* v. *P.* (1954) p. 81 (C.A.).
110. *Timmins* v. *T.* (1953) 2 All E.R. 187 (C.A.).
111. *Hall* v. *H.* (1962) 3 All E.R. 518 (C.A.).
112. *Pizzala* v. *P.* (1896) 12 T.L.R. 451; *Dickinson* v. *D.* (1889) 62 L.T. 330. This was applied under the Indian Divorce Act, 1869, in *Stree* v. *S.*, A.I.R. 1935 Mad. 541 (Sp. Ben.).

same conduct should not be held to constitute the offence of persistent cruelty."[113]

At Hindu law in *Putal* v. *Gopi*[114] a wife, who had been beaten occasionally by her husband, went to her father's house, whereupon the husband launched a criminal prosecution against the father, alleging that he enticed away the wife for immoral purposes and to procure her remarriage. The father was acquitted. This was clear case of cruelty, as was rightly held. Kanhaiya Singh, J., in the course of his judgement said that even if the conduct of the husband did not amount to cruelty, the behaviour of the husband was such that the wife would be fully justified to withdraw from cohabitation. The distinction between cruelty and expulsive conduct which amounts to constructive desertion does not seem to have been drawn. This distinction is important because if a wife's petition on the ground of cruelty is dismissed on the ground that the conduct complained of is not sufficiently grave and weighty to amount to cruelty, she is estopped from bringing a fresh petition on the same facts alleging constructive desertion or from pleading them as just cause for leaving her husband in any future proceedings instituted by him.[115]

Constructive desertion can be established where the conduct complained of is different from cruelty, provided always that such conduct is grave and weighty, e.g., if a husband deliberately induces his wife to believe that he is carrying on an adulterous association, and his wife leaves the matrimonial home in consequence.[116] Such a belief must be held bonafide and must be induced by the conduct of the guilty spouse.[117] Further the deserted spouse must have reasonable grounds for the belief and the mere fact that the husband was told by his mother that the wife had committed adultery will not suffice.[118]

In *Cox* v. *C.*[119] the husband overheard a conversation between his wife and his sister, in which the wife stated that a man at her place of employment had shown affection for her

113. *Walker* v. *W.* (1962) p. 42.
114. *Putal* v. *Gopi*, A.I.R. 1963 Pat. 93.
115. *Bright* v. *B.* (1954) p. 270; *Hill* v. *H.* (1954) p. 291.
116. *Baker* v. *B.* (1954) p. 33; *Glenister* v. *G.* (1945) p. 30, 38.
117. *Beer* v. *B.* (1948) p. 10.
118. *Elliot* v. *E.* (1956) p. 160 (C.A.); *Wood* v. *W.* (1947) p. 103.
119. *Cox* v. *C.* (1958) 1 All E.R. 569.

and that, while waiting for the works truck to take her and the other employees home, she had embraced him in the daytime to an extent which produced sexual excitement. After hearing this conversation, the husband withdrew from cohabitation. On a complaint by the wife that he had deserted her, the husband alleged that he honestly and reasonably believed that she had committed adultery. It was held that he was guilty of desertion, as he had no evidence of opportunity for his wife to commit adultery and his belief in her adultery was not founded on reasonable grounds.

However, an Indian court might come to a different conclusion in similar circumstances, having regard to differences in the notion of morality and social customs prevalent in Hindu society, where any suspicious association between a man and a woman may lead to a presumption of adultery, e.g., in *Rajalingam* v. *Lingayya*,[120] a husband petitioned for divorce on the ground that his wife was 'living in adultery'. In evidence he produced photographs in which his wife and the co-respondent were shown sitting in a compromising manner. This, coupled with other oral evidence, was held sufficient to prove not only one act of adultery but continuous 'living in adultery' and consequently the husband got a decree of divorce.

In England, if one spouse discovers that the other has committed adultery or has reasonable belief that adultery has been committed, the innocent spouse may be justified in leaving the matrimonial home and subsequently alleging constructive desertion, even though the adultery was not persisted in nor continued.[121] This view is unlikely to recommend itself in India, where divorce is disliked. A spouse is more likely to condone an isolated lapse from virtue than to break up the marriage. At English law such a belief will amount to just cause for leaving even though it is a mistaken one[122] but this ceases to be so when the husband's suspicion continues after a court of competent jurisdiction has found that the wife has not committed adultery.[123]

120. *Rajalingam* v. *Lingayya*, A.I.R. 1964 Andh. Pr. 308.

121. *Kemp* v. *K.* (1961) 2 All E.R. 764; *Everitt* v. *E.* (1949) p. 374.

122. *Williams* v. *W.* (1943) 2 All E.R. 746, 752 (C.A.).

123. *Allen* v. *A.* (1951) 1 All E.R. 724 (C.A.); H.K. Bevan, "*Belief in the other Spouse's Adultery*" (1957) 73 L.Q.R. 225.

Habitual drunkenness amounts to constructive desertion only if its consequences are so grave and weighty that it is practically impossible for the innocent spouse to continue married life, even though there may be no intent to injure on the part of the guilty spouse. The conduct justifying separation must be in "excess of that which any spouse bargains to endure."[124] But the neurotic condition of the husband, and nothing more, is not sufficient ground for the wife to withdraw from cohabitation and consequently the husband is not in constructive desertion.[125] The test is whether the conduct of the guilty spouse is sufficiently grave and weighty to amount to constructive desertion.

3. *WITHOUT THE CONSENT OR AGAINST THE WISH OF THE OTHER SPOUSE*

In order to complete the offence of desertion two elements within the control of the deserted spouse are necessary; absence of consent on his or her part, and absence of conduct giving reasonable cause to the spouse in desertion. To be in desertion a spouse must be living separate and apart without the consent of the other, as there is no desertion if the separation is consensual;[126] divorce by mutual consent is not allowed.[127]

In *Spence* v. *S.*[128] there were serious quarrels accompanied by physical contests between the parties. A fortnight before the wife left, she had, to the knowledge of the husband, made open and active preparations for departure, and the divison of their household property had been discussed. On a petition for divorce on the ground of desertion by the wife, it was held that the separation did not amount to desertion, since the departure of the wife was with the complete consent and approval of the husband.

The position is the same at Hindu law. In *Rajalakshmi*

124. *Hall* v. *H.* (1962) 3 All E.R. 518 (C.A.); *Beer* v. *B.* (1906) 96 L.T.R. 704.

125. *Leng.* v. *L.* (1946) 2 All E.R. 590.

126. *Pardy* v. *P.* (1939) p. 288, 302; *Williams* v. *W.* (1939) p. 365, 369 (C.A.).

127. *Emmanvel* v. *E.* (1946) p. 115, 116.

128. *Spence* v. *S.* (1939) 1 All E.R. 52, 58.

v. *Jambulinga*[129] where the wife left her husband with his consent and there was no evidence that she formed the intention to desert permanently at any subsequent stage, it was held, following *Pardy* v. *P.*,[130] that there was no desertion, the separation being consensual. In *Perumal* v. *Sithalakshmi*,[131] it was pointed out by Ramaswami, J., that assistance has to be derived from the English case law on desertion under the Matrimonial Causes Acts and the matrimonial offence of abandonment under the Indian Divorce Act, 1869, In the instant case the wife left the husband's house with all her clothes with the intention to live permanently with her parents and this action was approved by the husband, (a situation similar to that in *Spence* v. *S.*, supra) and he never called her back. There was evidence that the husband was trying to get rid of the wife, because of some congenital defect in her leg, and was planning to remarry. It was held that the wife did not leave her husband's house or continue to stay at her parents' place without his consent or against his will but with his permission. Under the circumstances the wife was not staying apart from the husband without his consent; consequently there was no desertion.

In *Kantilal* v. *Indumati*[132] it was laid down that the party seeking to prove desertion must give evidence of conduct on his part, showing unmistakably that such desertion was against his will. It is not enough to show that he was unwilling that his wife should go and stay away from him. It is further necessary for him to prove that he had expressed his wishes by calling his wife back or otherwise giving her to understand that her absence was against his wish. While the decision is correct on the facts it goes too far in requiring the petitioner to prove that he had expressly declared his wishes by recalling his wife for, although the deserted spouse is required to show willingness to receive the deserting one and resume married life on

129. *Rajalakshmi* v. *Jambulinga*, A.I.R. 1956 Mad. 195.

130. *Pardy* v. *P.* (1939) 3 All E.R. 779, 782-783.

131. *Perumal* v. *Sithalakshmi*, A.I.R. 1956 Mad. 415, 416. (Passages with approval were cited from Latey on *Divorce*, 14th. Ed., pp. 104-105; D. Tolstoy, *Law and Practice of Divorce*, 2nd. Ed., pp. 34-35; Raydon on *Divorce*, 4th. Ed., pp. 101-102; Sir Henry Rattigan, *Law of Divorce* (applicable to Christians in India), 2nd. Ed., p. 139).

132. *Kantilal* v. *Indumati*, A.I.R. 1956 Saur. 115.

such conditions as are reasonable, he is not bound by law to call back the deserting party.[133]

There is no desertion if the parties live separate and apart under a separation agreement but, if the consent to separation is withdrawn, desertion will commence from the time of the repudiation of the agreement, and acquiescence in the repudiation does not amount to acquiescence in desertion.[134] However, if the party not in breach stands on the agreement and refuses to accept the other's repudiation, desertion will not begin.[135]

In English law a judicial separation[136] and a separation order[137] with non-cohabitation, as distinct from a maintenance order,[138] which merely regulates the financial position of the spouses and therefore, does not preclude desertion, discharge the parties from their marital duty of cohabitation and stop desertion from arising or running. In *Gibson* v. *G.*[139] a maintenance agreement without a separation clause was entered into by the parties. Trouble arose between the parties when the wife's father came to stay with them. The wife left the husband, who was only too glad to see her go; each of them was heartily glad to get rid of the other. Subsequently, on the wife's petition charging the husband with cruelty and desertion, it was held that the separation was not by consent. Likewise at Hindu law a separation deed is a conclusive answer to a claim for desertion without reasonable cause but a mere financial agreement to pay maintenance does not preclude desertion. Relying on *Crabtree* v. *C.*,[140] it was held in *Kako*

133. *Rajalakshmi* v. *Jambulinga*, A.I.R. 1956 Mad. 195.

134. *Pardy* v. *P.* (1939) p. 288 (C.A.).

135. *Clark* v. *C.* (1939) p. 257.

136. S. 14 (2) of the (English) Matrimonial Causes Act, 1950.

137. Summary Jurisdiction (Married Women) Act, 1895, S. 5 and Licensing Act, 1902, S. 5 (2); *Harriman* v. *H.* (1909) p. 123.

138. *Crabtree* v. *C.* (1953) 2 All E.R. 56 (C.A.) (a maintenance agreement which defined the duration of the husband's financial liability does not amount to a stipulation that the wife agreed to the husband's living apart from her); see also *Bosley* v. *B.* (1958) 2 All E.R. 167 (C.A.); Blom-Cooper, "*Separation Agreements and Grounds for Divorce*" (1956) 19 M.L.R. 638; P.W. Young, "*Separately and Apart*" (1964) 5 Australian Lawyer 145.

139. *Gibson* v. *G.* (1956) The Times, 18 July (C.A.).

140. *Crabtree* v. *C.* (1953) 2 All E.R. 56 (C.A.).

v. *Ajit*[141] that the payment of maintenance allowance does not put an end to desertion, which remains 'continuing', because the agreement to make this payment does not bind the parties to live separately. But where there is a formal separation deed entered into by the parties to a marriage, as long as the deed stands, it is impossible to maintain that the husband has deserted his wife without reasonable cause, particularly when no attempt is made to set aside the deed.[142] If a Hindu woman is living separate and apart from her husband under a decree granted under the Hindu Women's Right to Separate Residence and Maintenance Act, 1946, she is not in desertion.[143]

The consent can be tacit or oral[144] or it may be embodied in a deed of separation.[145] In any case it must be real and what apparently is a clear consent may not be so when all the circumstances of the case are studied closely. Thus there was held to be no consent on the part of the wife, who suffered, not unjustly, from a deep sense of grievance because of the conduct of her husband and told him shortly after the separation that she did not want to see him again and wanted a divorce.[146] Similarly it has been held that a wife, who said to her husband, "Go if you like, and when you are sick of her, come back to me", and made him swear upon the Bible that he would return to her, had not truly consented to his leaving her.[147]

In the recent case of *Phair* v. *P.*[148] the wife told the husband to get out of the matrimonial home, and the husband left. The husband admitted that he wanted to leave, because he felt that he and his wife were quite unsuited to each other. The judge dismissed the husband's undefended petition on the ground that parting was consensual. The husband appealed and it was held by the Court of Appeal that it was the wife's

141. *Kako* v. *Ajit*, A.I.R. 1960 Punj. 328.

142. *Rozario* v. *R.*, A.I.R. 1941 Bom. 372 (relying on *Hyman* v. *H.* (1929) A.C. 601, H.L.).

143. *Kuppanna* v. *Palaniammal*, A.I.R. 1955 Mad. 471.

144. *Graeff* v. *G.* (1928) 93 J.P. 48.

145. *Piper* v. *P.* (1902) p. 198.

146. *Bevan* v. *B.* (1955) 1 W.L.R. 1142.

147. *Haviland* v. *H.* (1863) 32 L.J.P.M. & A. 65.

148. *Phair* v. *P.* (1963) 107 Sol. Jour. 554 (C.A.).

act which was the immediate cause of the separation. The mere fact that the wife was glad to see the back of the husband did not amount to consent. The parties did not come to an agreement to live separate and apart, for agreement necessarily implies choice. Here the husband was told to go without being given any choice.

In order to be effective consent must be voluntarily and freely given. Thus a wife who had been forced by her husband to sign a separation agreement, without legal advice, when she was under great mental stress due to her husband's threats, her own ill-health and destitution, was held not to have genuinely consented to living apart from him.[149] Likewise there is no consent, if the wife is fraudulently persuaded to live apart on the pretext that the separation is to be temporary.[150]

'Consent' is strictly construed in English law. The parties must not agree or concur to separation. Consent is distinguished from mere desire, as the desire of the deserted spouse that the deserting spouse should resume conjugal relations is not an element of desertion. A deserted wife may be thankful that her husband has gone; he may nevertheless have deserted her. Desertion is evidenced by the intention of the absent husband, not by the acquiscence of the wife in his absence or even the desire of the wife for his absence. 'Against the consent' must be read in the context "if she were a party to his leaving and consented to it.[151]

The real test is whether the separation is really due to the conduct of the deserting spouse. Thus during a quarrel with her husband, a wife confessed adultery. Following her confession she decided to leave the matrimonial home and actually left it a fortnight later. The husband was not displeased by her leaving. Thereafter, the parties corresponded regularly met at weekends and had sexual intercourse on a number of occasions. Eventually they ceased to communicate with each other. On the husband's appeal from the dismissal of his petition for divorce on the ground of desertion, it was held that

149. *Holroyd* v. *H.* (1920) 36 T.L.R. 479; see also P. M. Bromley, *Family Law*, p. 104.

150. *Harrison* v. *H.* (1910)54 Sol. Jour. 619; *Lepre* v. *L.* (1963) 2 All E.R. 49, 58.

151. *Harriman* v. *H.* (1909) p. 123, 148 (C.A.).

the original separation was not consensual. The husband did not consent to his wife's behaviour and no blame could attach to him because he let his adulterous wife leave him. The fact that the husband was glad that she went did not change the quality of her act. Consequently the wife was in desertion.

But the Court of Appeal held that this desertion had been terminated by the husband's course of conduct consisting in regular visits to and intercourse with the wife (which also condoned the adultery). This had made the separation consensual and there was no desertion.[152] This can be compared with a decision (noticed above at p. 81) at Hindu law, where a wife left her husband's place out of shame, not having the courage to face him, after he had discovered her reprehensible conduct. The evidence showed that she had no intention to leave him permanently and had tried to bring about a reconciliation on a number of occasions. It was held by the Supreme Court[153] of India that she was not guilty of desertion. Here the wife left merely to hide her feelings of shame, whereas in *Pizzey* v. *P.*[154] she went with the deliberate intention of deserting her husband a fortnight after the confession of adultery, during which time she must have given deliberate thoughts to the action she was going to take, and she was rightly found guilty of desertion at this stage.

According to one English view once desertion has started through the fault of the deserting spouse, it is no longer necessary for the deserted spouse to show that during the material period he actually wanted the other spouse to come back.[155] It is not incumbent on the deserted spouse to show that he was at all times during the three years next preceding the petition ready and willing to receive the deserting one.[156] Lord Denning conveyed the same idea when he said, "English law, unlike Scots law, does not require a petitioner to prove that she was throughout the statutory period of desertion "willing to adhere" to her husband."[157]

152. *Pizzey* v. *P.* (1961) p. 101 (C.A.).
153. *Bipinchandra* v. *Prabhavati*, A.I.R. 1957 S.C. 176.
154. *Pizzey* v. *P.* (1961) p. 101 (C.A.).
155. *Church* v. *C.* (1952) p. 313.
156. *Sifton* v. *S.* (1939) p. 221.
157. Beigan v. B. (1956) p. 313 (C.A.)

The decision in *Beigan* v. *B.*[158] held not only that the deserted spouse is not disentitled to relief if he or she is merely thankful that the other has left in the circumstances but also that the conduct of the deserted spouse is irrelevant, unless it affects the mind of the deserting party in relation to desertion. L.J. Denning said, "If a wife locks the door against her husband, it does not automatically terminate his desertion. It depends upon whether it has any effect on him by preventing him from seeking a reconciliation."

Here Hindu law parts company with the current trend of English law. Following the statement of English law in 12 Halsbury's Laws of England, 3rd Ed., p. 244, as applied in *Bipinchandra* v. *Prabhavati*,[159] it was held in *Suryprakasa* v. *Venkata*[160] that the petitioner must prove that he was always willing to fulfil his own marital obligations, and that the respondent left against his will. In this respect it follows the older view, expressed by Lord Macmillian in *Pratt* v. *P.*,[161] to the effect that, in fulfilling its duty of determining whether on the evidence a case of desertion without cause has been proved, the court ought not to leave out of account the attitude of mind of the petitioner. The difference is due to the fact that Indian courts have followed the older English authorities. This trend is not likely to be persisted in after *Baigan* v. *B.* (supra) and *Gibson* v. *G.*[162] have been fully studied in India.

Under the Indian Divorce Act, 1869, desertion must be against the will of the innocent spouse. A petitioner will not succeed, if he himself is guilty of matrimonial misconduct.[163] Similarly where a wife left her husband because of his intemperate habits and drunkenness for which he was convicted and later the husband left her for another woman, she petitioned

158. *Beigan* v. *B.*, supra.

159. *Bipinchandra* v. *Prabhavati* A.I.R. 1957 S. C. at p. 189.

160. *Suryaprakasa* v. *Venkata*, A.I.R. 1961 Andh. Pr. 404, 407; see also *Rajalakshmi* v. *Jambulinga*, A.I.R. 1956 Mad. 195, 197, where each party stood on his dignity; the husband wanted the offer to return to be made by his father-in-law, the wife wanted her husband to take her back; it was held that though the husband was not bound in law to ask or invite his wife to end the separation, he had failed to prove that she had formed the 'animns deserendi.'

161. *Pratt* v. *P.* (1939) A.C. 417, 420, H.L.

162. *Gibson* v. *G.* (1956) The Times, 18 July (C.A.).

163. *Hill* v. *H.* , A.I.R. 1923 Bom. 284.

for divorce on the ground of desertion and it was held that the desertion was not against her will.[164]

Hindu law requires that it must be shown by the wife that she was obliged to leave her husband's home because of his conduct and against her own wishes. It further requires that in order to succeed a petitioner must come into court with clean hands, i.e., free from his own matrimonial misconduct. In *Mato* v. *Sadhu*[165] a wife demanded sexual intercourse from her husband with the threat that, if she did not get it, she would receive it from other men. The husband refused. She left him and petitioned for a decree of judicial separation on the ground, *inter alia*, of desertion, alleging that his refusal led to her adultery with one or more persons. Relying on *Hill* v. *H.*,[166] Latey on Divorce, 14th Ed., p. 182, and *Otaway* v. *O.*,[167] it was held that she was not entitled to any relief because, *inter alia*, of her own promiscuous behaviour. *Otaway* v. *O.*, it should be noted, is a very old case and the view there taken must be modified, in view of social considerations which make it contrary to public policy to insist on the maintenance of a union which has utterly broken down.[168]

The proper test at English law is whether the deserted spouse's conduct had any actual effect on the mind of the deserter. If the intention permanently to break up the matrimonial home is established, either by the wrongdoer's own declarations or because his conduct has been such as to lead to the conclusion that he must have intended that result, he is guilty of desertion, and he continues to be so, notwithstanding that the other spouse has been guilty of a matrimonial offence (e.g., adultery) which is proved to have had no influence on his intention.[169] Conversely where a husband deserts

164. *Glancy* v. *G.*, A.I.R. 1915 Low. Bur. 71.

165. *Mato* v. *Sadhu*, A.I.R. 1961 Punj. 152.

166. *Hill* v. *H.*, A.I.R. 1923 Bom. 284.

167. *Otaway* v. *O.* (1888) 13 P.D. 141; see also *Teja* v. *Sarjit*, A.I.R. 1962 Punj. 195. The wife left her husband's house because she had reasonable ground to suspect that her husband was carrying on with his sister-in-law with whom he was living. Husband's petition for restitution of conjugal rights was dismissed, it being held that she had just cause for leaving.

168. *Blunt* v. *B.* (1943) A.C. 513.

169. *Herod* v. *H.* (1939) P. 11; *Brewer* v. *B.* (1961) 3 All E. R. 957.

his wife and the wife later commits adultery of which the husband becomes aware, his desertion comes to an end, because he then has good cause for staying away from her, but this is so only if the wife fails to prove that her adultery has had no effect on her husband's mind and that he would never have come back to her in any event.[170]

4. *REASONABLE CAUSE IN ENGLISH AND HINDU LAW*

If one spouse has just or reasonable cause for leaving the other, the separation is justifiable and there will be no desertion on his part[171] The true test is whether the respondent has left the petitioner without reasonable excuse and with the object of living apart against the will of the petitioner.[172] Such reasonable cause may be either a matrimonial offence, e.g., adultery[173] or cruelty,[174] or some other conduct which is 'grave and weighty'.[175] The position is practically the same at Hindu law. The explanation to S. 10 of the Hindu Marriage Act, 1955 provides that the desertion must be without reasonable cause. Reasonable or just cause may be.[176]:—

1. a cause which would amount to a matrimonial offence, i.e., whatever would be a ground for judicial separation, divorce, restitution of conjugal rights or avoiding the marriage; or

2. a cause which would amount to constructive desertion, i.e., conduct amounting to expulsion; or

3. any other ground which though not in itself sufficient to constitute a matrimonial offence,[177] would be sufficiently

The wife had decided not to live with her husband at his place of service; the husband in fact had started living with another woman; it was held that this did not terminate her desertion as she had already formed a fixed intention to desert.

170. *Richards* v. *R.* (1952) p. 307 (C.A.).

171. *Frowd* v. *F.* (1904) p. 177, 179.

172. *Cowley* v. *C.* (1897) The Times, 3 Feb.

173. *Roe* v. *R.* (1956) 3 All E.R. 478.

174. *Pike* v. *P.* (1954) p. 81, 87 (C.A.).

175. *Edward* v. *E.* (1950) p. 8; *Yeatman* v. *Y.* (1868) L. R. 1 P. & D. 489, 494.

176. S. V. Gupte, *Hindu Law of Marriage*, Bombay, 1961, p. 147. the grounds which constitute a matrimonial offence are given in Ss. 9, 10, 12, 13 of the Hindu Marriage Act, 1955.

177. Anna Saheb v. Tarabai, A.I.R. 1970 Madh. Pr. 36 at p. 37.

grave and weighty to justify desertion, and a reasonable cause which would be a defence to a petition for restitution of conjugal rights.

"Reasonable cause" was defined by Lord Penzance[178] as conduct which must be 'grave and weighty'. Gorell Barnes,[179] J., modified it to conduct so 'grave and weighty' as to make it "practically impossible for the spouses to live properly together." The standard of what amounts to grave and weighty matters was raised by Barnard,[180] J., to conduct so grave and weighty as to render married life impossible. The distinction can be seen in *Clark* v. *C.*[181], where the wife was a voluntary patient in a mental hospital. As she was receiving mental treatment away from her husband, it was practically impossible for her to live with her husband but not quite impossible, for after treatment and recovery she could come back.

What amounts to a grave and weighty matter must of course depend largely on the facts of each individual case, but the courts require a high standard and are reluctant to relieve the spouses of their marital duties merely because of incompatibility of temperament. The situation has to be viewed against the background of conjugal duties, bearing always in mind that each spouse takes the other for better, for worse.[182] Similarly at Hindu law, a husband, having accepted his wife as a gift from God before the nuptial fire, has to make allowance (as we have seen before) for her irritating idiosyncrasies.[183]

The maxim that mere wear and tear of married life does not amount to a just cause for leaving has a stricter application to a Hindu wife, who, having regard to the social conditions and customs in India, is expected, in putting up with the difficulties of married life, to show a more tolerant attitude to her husband and his family than her English sister, who enjoys a higher standard of living, more personal freedom and has a different intellectual and cultural background. The

178. Lord Penzance in *Yeatman* v. *Y.* (1868) L. R. 1 P. & D,. 489-494.

179. Gorell Barnes, J., in *Oldroyd* v. *O.* (1896) p. 175, 184.

180. Barnard, J., in *Dyson* v. *D.* (1954) p. 198, 206.

181. *Clark* v. *C.* (1956) 1 All E.R. 823.

182. *Buchler* v. *B.* (1947) p. 25, 29, 47 (C.A.).

183. *Narayan* v. *Prabhadevi*, A.I.R. 1964 Madh. Pr. 28.

difference can be seen with reference to "mother-in-law cases."

In *Narayan* v. *Prabhadevi*[184] (to which we have already referred at p. 90) a wife was living with her husband and his family (which is the normal mode of Hindu life). The mother-in-law used to interfere in even petty household matters, as telling the wife not to bathe in cold water, not to touch certain things on certain days and not to give presents to people like the maid-servant. The wife resented all this and picked petty quarrels with the husband and his mother; eventually she left him and went to live with her parents, when she was sick. The husband not only made no attempt to bring her back but turned her out, when she came to his house on her own accord after recovering from her illness. After two years he petitioned for judicial separation. It was held that the wife was not in desertion; on the contrary the husband was in constructive desertion in not taking her back. Though her husband resented it, her conduct in being disrespectful to her mother-in-law was not so 'grave and weighty' as to give him just cause for expelling her from the matrimonial home.

This can be compared with the English decision of *Millichamp* v. *M.*[185] where the husband brought his wife to his mother's home. There were frequent quarrels between the wife and the mother, who said that she did not want the wife and told her to clear out; the mother never gave the wife any peace. The wife wanted to live with her husband but not with his mother, whereas the husband said his mother's house was the only one which he could provide. Eventually the wife left and successfully sued for a maintenance order on the ground of wilful neglect to maintain. The husband appealed on the ground that the wife had deserted him and refused to return to him. It was held that the wife was not in desertion; she had just cause to live separate and apart. It was the husband's duty to provide a home for his wife and he had failed in that duty by putting his mother first.

Both the decisions are right in principle and the same test of 'just cause' was applied in both of them, yet the conclusion is different. The facts are similar in so far as the

184. *Narayan* v. *Prabhadevi*, supra.
185. *Millichamp* v. *M.* (1931) 146 L.T. 96.

daughters-in-law were unable to get along with their respective mothers-in-law but in *Narayan* v. *Prabhadevi* (supra) the wife was expected to accept the ill-treatment from her mother-in-law as the ordinary "wear and tear" of married life, while in *Millichamp* v. *M.* the husband's failure to protect the wife from such treatment from his mother was regarded as just cause for the wife to live separate from him.

However, the mutual duty of the spouses to cohabit is not lightly to be abandoned. Thus the neurotic condition of the husband by itself does not entitle the wife to refuse to live with him.[186] Similarly a husband is not justified in leaving his wife because of her irrational behaviour proceeding from mental ill-health.[187]

But a spouse would have just cause for leaving the other for the preservation or protection of his or her health, e.g., in *Clark* v. *C.*[188] a wife was held justified in living separate and apart from her husband because she was receiving treatment in a mental hospital. Likewise in *Espie* v. *E.*[189] a wife, who was in the last stages of consumption, was unable to join her husband as she was being treated in a sanatorium; it was held that she was not in desertion. Where a husband refused to live with his wife on the ground that she was a drunkard, dangerous to herself, to him and to the children, it was held that the marriage relationship is a grave one and refusal of cohabitation is not lightly to be regarded but the right of the wife is subject to the correlative right of the husband and children. Accordingly the husband was justified in refusing to live with her.[190]

Likewise at Hindu law in the recent case of *Meena* v. *Lachman*[191], a husband accused his wife of unchastity. This was held to be a sufficiently grave and weighty matter to entitle the wife to live separate and apart. Similarly, where a wife left her husband because he accused her of immorality and wrote

186. *Leng* v. *L.* (1946) 2 All E.R. 590.
187. *B.* v. *B.* (1962) V.L.R. 378.
188. *Clark* v. *C.* (1956) 1 All E.R. 823.
189. *Espie* v. *E.* (1914) V.L.R. 654.
190. *Fisk* v. *F.* (1920) 122 L.T. 803.
191. *Meena* v. *Lachman*, A.I.R. 1960 Bom. 418; reversed in A.I.R. 1964, S. C. 40.

obscene letters and the wife apprehended that there was danger to her health and happiness, if she returned to him, it was held that she had just cause for leaving him.[192]

Leaving a spouse to protect the health and happiness of the children was recognised as just cause in *G.* v. *G.*[193] A married couple had three daughters. The husband began to show signs of mental instability; he frightened the children by his conduct and caused a serious emotional disturbance in one of them, Susan. The wife, largely for the sake of children, refused to allow him to live with her and children. The wife did not, however, say that she would never live with the husband again. It was held that the wife was not in desertion, as she had just cause for living separate and apart from her husband for the sake of preserving the children's health. The learned President, Sir Jocelyn Simon, held that serious danger to the health of the children, particularly Susan, must be regarded as a grave and weighty matter.

The case is important because it laid down the principle that the duty that husband and wife owe to each other to live together and to keep their family together must be measured against their duty to their children, so that, if it were necessary for a wife to live separately from her husband for the preservation of a child's health, there would be good cause for separation. In other words the interest of the children and the protection of their health can override the duty of cohabitation that spouses owe to each other. In this case the husband's behaviour constituted a threat to the child's health and welfare. As has been said earlier, a spouse is entitled to live separate and apart from the other for the protection of his own health, but in *G.* v. *G.* the court went beyond this, extending the principle to the health of the children of the marriage and balancing their interest against the duties of the spouses to each other.

As sexual intercourse is one of the objects of marriage, a deliberate, unreasonable, unjustified and wilful refusal of sexual intercourse amounts to such a grave and weighty matter as to

192. *Bai Jamna* v. *Dayalji* (1920) 22 Bom. L.R. 214.

193. *G.* v. *G.* (1964) 1 All E.R. 129.

afford a just cause for living separate and apart.[194] This is not so where the refusal is justifiable, e.g., where the wife refuses sexual intercourse because after child-birth she has formed an invincible repugnance to the sexual act.[195] Conversely where a spouse persists in making sexual demands, which are known to be regarded by the other spouse as inordinate or revolting is lack of consideration, which may amount to conduct so grave and weighty as to justify the other spouse in withdrawing from cohabitation.[196]

However, the mere refusal of sexual intercourse, without regard to other circumstances, such as when the spouses are living under the same roof or there is an implied separation amounting to desertion, does not of itself amount to desertion,[197] but it will nevertheless be a good cause for leaving[198]. This is not so where the parties are living separate and apart and the husband refuses to resume cohabitation except on the condition that there should be no sexual intercourse, there being no medical grounds for such refusal. In such a case he is guilty of desertion.[199]

The situation becomes complicated where both the spouses have good reason to separate or both are unreasonable in their demands. In *Walter* v. *W.*[200] the husband and wife were both working in different parts of London. The husband moved to be nearer his place of work and the wife remained in the former matrimonial home. Neither consented to the separation and each had reasonable grounds. Neither party proved that the separation was brought about by the fault of the other so neither was in desertion.

This was criticised by Denning, L. J., in *Hosegood* v. *H.*[201] where the husband wanted the wife to come and live with him in the places to which he was posted from time to time, whereas the wife insisted on living with her mother and daughter. The

194. *Ousey* v. *O.* (1875) L.R. 3 P. & D. 223; *Lawrence* v. *L.* (1950) p. 84.

195. *Beevor* v. *B.* (1945) 2 All E.R. 200.

196. *Holborn* v. *H.* (1947) 1 All E.R. 32.

197. *Weatherlay* v. *W.* (1947) 1 All E.R. 563 (H.L.).

198. *Synge* v. *S.* (1900) p. 180 affirmed (1901) p. 317 (C.A.).

199. *Hutchinson* v. *H.* (1963) 1 All E.R. 1.

200. *Walter* v. *W.* (1949) 65 T.L.R. 680.

Court of Appeal held that the husband was entitled to divorce on the ground of desertion. Denning, L. J., said, "In the choice of the matrimonial home, neither spouse has a casting vote; where both parties are guilty of unreasonable conduct, the court is not bound to choose between the two, but may pronounce each guilty of desertion. In *Walter* v. *W.* (supra) it was held that where each is obstinate, neither is guilty of desertion, whereas the truth is that both may be."

The correctness of this view has been doubted in *Simpson* v. *S.*[202] and expressly disapproved in *Lang* v. *L.*,[203] where the Commissioner found that the parties were in mutual desertion. Somerville, L.J., said that he did not think that it was possible to hold that each party had deserted the other at the same time. Jenkins, L.J., found it hard to understand the concept of mutual desertion, while Hodson, L.J., said that he was unable to appreciate the concept of mutual desertion, though it might be possible to arrive at such a conclusion when the parties have drifted apart in circumstances which amounted to separation by consent.

The difficulty about the concept of mutual desertion is that it is not distinguishable from circumstances which amount to divorce by consensual separation.[204] It has been held in a recent case that it is impossible in law for a husband and wife to have deserted each other but a finding of mutual desertion could only be made, if at all, on very special facts. Mutual desertion could only arise where the act of each spouse was outside the knowledge of the other, so that their conduct would not give rise to an inference of consent.[205]

Doubts as to the validity of the concept of mutual desertion arise from the decision in *Bernett* v. *B.*[206], where the husband left the matrimonial home with the *animus deserendi.* The wife shortly after he left evinced a strong intention not to have him

201. Denning, L. J., in *Hosegood* v. *H.* (1955) 66 T.L.R. 735, 740 (C.A.); Denning, L.J., in *Beigan* v. *B.* (1956) p. 313, 320 (C.A.).

202. Lord Merriman, P., in *Simpson* v. S. (1951) p. 320, 330.

203. *Lang* v. L. (1953) The Times, 7 July (C.A.).

204. *Spence* v. *S.* (1939) 1 All E.R. 52, 58.

205. *Wevill* v. *W.* (1962) 106 Sol. Jour. 155.

206. *Barnett* v. *B.* (1955) p. 21; *Fishbarn* v. *F.* (1955) p. 29. (A similar case).

back by changing the locks on the doors. The husband at no time made any approach to his wife with a view to resuming matrimonial life. The wife was as much at fault in locking her husband out as he was in deserting her. It was held that the husband's desertion had been terminated, for a wife should not be able to claim that she was being wronged by the continuing absence of a husband whom she had decisively declared that she would not have back. She had firmly rejected him and made it practically impossible for reconciliation to take place.

A just cause ceases to be so where the deserted spouse refuses a bonafide offer of resumption of cohabitation made by the other spouse.[207] An unjustifiable refusal not merely terminates the desertion, but also reverses the process, i.e. puts the boot on the other leg and turns the deserted spouse into the deserter.[208] This is not so where the deserted spouse has just cause for refusing the offer, e.g., where a wife knows that incestuous adultery by the husband will continue.[209]

It has been seen that neither spouse has a casting vote as to the choice of the matrimonial home. This is not so at Hindu law, which is inclined to follow the old fashioned English view, according to which the husband, being the bread-winner and head of the household, was entitled to choose the place for the matrimonial home and the wife had to follow him. It was her duty to reside wherever he went. This view has been drastically attacked in England, particularly by Lord Denning in *Dunn* v. *D.*[210] and *Hosegood* v. *H.*[211], where he said that the wife had an equal voice in this matter.

Where the wife refused to resign her job, which compelled her to live away from her husband, she was held to have withdrawn herself without reasonable cause from the society of her husband. Under the Hindu law a wife's duty to her husband is to submit herself obediently to his authority and to remain

207. *Pratt* v. *P.* (1939) A.C. 417 (H.L.).

208. *Thomas* v. *T.* (1924) P. 194, 201; *Bipinchandra* v. *Prabhavati*, A.I.R. 1957 S.C. 176.

209. *W.* v. *W.* (1962) p. 49.

210. *Dunn* v. *D.* (1949) p. 98, 103 (C.A.).

211. *Hosegood* v. *H.* (1955) 66 T.L.R. 735, 740 (C.A.).

under his roof and protection.[212] In *Shakuntala* v. *Baburao*,[213] the wife was living in Indore on the bounty of her aunt, from whom she was hoping to get an annuity, while the husband had to live in Bombay at his place of employment. The wife refused to join him there. It was held that the wife was living away from him without just cause. The husband was not in desertion, because he had gone to Bombay not with the *animus deserendi* but to earn his livelihood. In *Rajaya* v. *Venkata*[214] the wife left her husband and went to live at her parents' house where she wanted the husband to establish the matrimonial home, which he was unwilling to do. On the husband's petition for divorce on the ground of desertion, it was held that her refusal to return to her husband's house was without just cause and amounted to desertion. On marriage the wife passes into the dominion of the husband and, so far as Hindu law is concerned, it is obligatory that she should reside in the house of the husband. The duty imposed upon a Hindu wife to reside with her husband, wherever he may choose to live is a rule of Hindu law and not merely a moral precept. It is not open to a Hindu wife to insist upon her husband's separating himself from his parents or giving up his employment and living in the house or place of her parents.

The test is whether one spouse is acting reasonably in living away from the other. In *Powell* v. *P.*,[215] a young wife was living with her mother in Greece and wanted her husband to go and live with her at her family's place. She was living away from her husband against his will on the pretext that her health could not withstand the rigour of English climate. It was held that she was not justified in refusing to live with her husband at his place of business in England. A similar conclusion was reached in *Thornton* v. *T.*[216], where the wife

212. *Tirath* v. *Kirpal*, A.I.R. 1964 Punj. 28; *Gaya* v. *Bhagwati*, A.I.R. 1966 Madh. Pr. 212.

213. *Shakuntala* v. *Baburao*, A.I.R. 1963 Madh. Pr. 10.

214. *Rajaya* v. *Venkata* (1955) An. W.R. 215. (A case under the Madras Hindu Bigamy Prevention and Divorce Act. 1949); see also *Krishnabai* v. *Punamchand*, A.I.R. 1967 Madh. Pr. 200.

215. *Powell* v. *P.* (1957) The Times , 22 Feb. (C.A.).

216. *Thornton* v. *T.* (1939) 41 Bom. L.R. 1234 (a case under the Indian and Colonial Divorce Jurisdiction Act, 1926).

refused for no adequate reason to live in the country in which her husband was employed.

In India, the wife has a reasonable cause to withdraw from cohabitation, if the husband has been outcaste or has changed his religion.[217] A leprous husband cannot enforce his right of cohabitation upon an unwilling wife and the wife of a Hindu, who is suffering from virulent leprosy, is entitled to live apart from him and claim separate maintenance.[218] If the husband openly keeps a mistress in the house, the wife is justified in living separate from him.[219] If he has another wife living, so that the wife would be entitled to separate residence and maintenance under S. 18 (2) (d) of the Hindu Adoption and Maintenance Act, 1956, she has just cause to refuse to live with her husband[220]. Similarly, where a husband married again before the commencement of the Hindu Marriage Act, 1955 and the second wife is alive, the first wife is justified in refusing to live with him[221].

Where a girl aged 7 years who was married to a man of 54 years of age, refused to live with the husband on attaining puberty and the marriage was never consummated, it was held that in the circumstances her refusal to consummate the marriage was justified as the marriage was an ill-assorted one.[222]

5. *WILFUL NEGLECT*

The explanation to S. 10 of the Hindu Marriage Act, 1955 states that desertion includes the wilful neglect of the petitioner by the other party to the marriage. This, however, does not enlarge the legal definition of desertion by including 'wilful neglect' not amounting to desertion. To amount to wilful neglect there must be deliberate and intentional failure to per-

217. *Paigi* v. *Sheonarain* (1866) 8 All. 78.

218. *Sheenappayya* v. *Rajamma*, A.I.R. 1922 Mad. 399.

219. *Kuppuswami* v. *Alagammal*, A.I.R. 1961 Mad. 391; *Chilha* v. *Chedi*, A.I.R. 1929 Oudh. 121; *Stree* v. *S.*, A.I.R. 1935 Mad. 541 (Special Bench).

220. *Bhagwanti* v. *Sadhu*, A.I.R. 1961 Punj. 181; Mallappa v. Neelamma, A.I.R. 1970 Mys. 59.

221. *Babulal* v. *Shantibai* 1962 M.P.L.J. Notes 90, reported in the Yearly Digest of Indian & Select English Cases, May, 1962, p. 831; *Pullaiah* v. *Rushingamma*, A.I.R. 1963 Andh. Pr. 323; contrast Rohini v. Narendra, A.IR. 1970 All 102.

222. *Gurmukh* v. *Harbans*, A.I.R. 1928 Lah. 902.

form the obligations of married life indicative of a total repudiation of the obligations of marriage. Mere neglect of consorting, indifference or want of proper solicitude for the other spouse is not wilful neglect.[223]

The word 'wilful' has been employed in contradistinction to 'accidental' or ''inadvertent'. It means that the person is consciously acting in a reprehensible manner or is consciously failing in the discharge of his or her marital obligations. It implies abstention from an obvious duty.[224] Wilful neglect can be proved by instances of failure by the husband to provide reasonable maintenance for his wife. Such failure must be wrongful. His act will not be wrong, if the wife herself is guilty of some matrimonial offence, e.g., a husband is not liable to maintain a wife, who is guilty of desertion.[225] Wilful neglect means more than that the husband has not provided reasonable maintenance. It denotes some wrongful default . A reasonable belief in the wife's adultery affords a defence to a charge of wilful neglect.[226] The duty to cohabit and the duty to maintain are coextensive and where circumstances have excused the husband from his duty to cohabit, he cannot be guilty of wilful neglect to maintain.[227]

In establishing that a husband has wilfully neglected to maintain her, a wife has as heavy a burden as if she were seeking to establish desertion without cause and a wife, who has acted unreasonably in leaving her husband, may find it difficult to prove that he is in breach of his obligation to maintain her.[228] Wilful neglect may be inferred where one spouse has deliberately renounced his marital obligations of cohabitation against the wish of the other. Where the wife withdrew to a separate room, had nothing to do with her husband, performed no wifely duties for the husband, cooked no meals for him and avoided meeting him so that the husband was obliged to do his own

223. *Meena* v. *Lachman*, A.I.R. 1960 Bom. 418; see also A.I.R. 1964, S.C. 40 at p. 59.

224. *Manglabai* v. *Deorao*, A.I.R. 1962 Madh. Pr. 193; see also *Khageshwar* v. *Lochan*, 1963 M.P.L.J. (notes) 2, reported in the Yearly Digest of Indian and Select English Cases, April, 1963, p. 763.

225. *Lilley* v. *L.* (1960) p. 158 (C.A.).

226. *Whittakar* v. *W.*, (1939) 3 All E.R. 833, 838.

227. Per Pearce J. in *Chilton* v. *C.* (1952) p. 196.

228. *McGowan* v. *M.* (1948) 2 All E.R. 1032, 1035.

cooking, washing, mending and ironing; they were held to be leading separate lives; such wilful neglect amounted to desertion;[229] such a situation is expressly covered by explanation to S. 10 of the Hindu Marriage Act, 1955.

6. *THE PERIOD OF DESERTION*

In England the petitioner must prove that the respondent has been continuously in desertion throughout the whole course of three years immediately preceding the date of presentation of the petition.[230] Presentation means the date of filing of the petition[231] Two separate periods of desertion cannot be added together to make three years for the purpose of presenting a petition.[232]

To this rule there is an exception that the existence of a non-cohabitation clause in maintenance order precludes any desertion while the clause remains in the order; where the period before the maintenance order was made is less than three years, it may be aggregated with any period elapsing after the non-cohabitation clause has been deleted to provide a period of three years.[233] The same rule applies where the parties are separated under a decree of judicial separation, provided the decree or order has been continuously in force and the parties have not resumed cohabitation since it was granted.

Another exception was created by S. I (2) of the (English) Matrimonial Causes Act, 1965, whereby, in calculating the period for which the respondent has deserted the petitioner without cause and in considering whether such desertion has been continuous, no account is taken of any one period not exceeding three months, during which the parties resumed cohabitation with a view to reconciliation; and for the purpose of a petition for divorce, the court may treat a period of desertion as having continued during time when the deserting party was incapable of entertaining the necessary intention, if the evidence before the court is such that, had that

229. *Walker* v. *W.* (1952) 2 All E.R. 138 (C.A.); see also N.R. Raghavachariar, *Hindu Law*, Madras, 1960, pp. 906-907.

230. *Pratt* v. *P.* (1939) A.C. 417 (H.L.).

231. *Alston* v. *A.* (1946) p. 203.

232. *Jordan* v. *J.* (1939) p. 239, 248-249.

233. *Green* v. *G.* (1946) p. 112.

party not been so incapable, the court would have inferred that that intention continued at that time.

At Hindu law the period of desertion is two years. As at English law it must be continuous till the presentation of the petition. Where a spouse had a right to petition for divorce on the ground of desertion under some previous statute (e.g., under the Bombay Hindu Divorce Act, 1947) until its repeal by the Hindu Marriage Act, 1955, it still remained a vested right which was capable of being enforced after the repeal of that Act.[234] In *Ishwar* v. *Pomilla,*[235] where, after a decree for restitution of conjugal rights had been passed, the husband proceeded with a petition for annulment of marriage. After its dismissal and after the expiry of two years from the date of the passing of the decree for restitution of conjugal rights, he petitioned for divorce on the ground of non-compliance of the decree by the wife. It was held that, it being impossible for the wife to make any effort to comply with the decree for restitution of conjugal rights as long as the husband was proceeding with the petition for nullity of marriage, the husband ought to have waited for two years after the dismissal of his nullity petition, before he could claim a divorce. From this it seems that the period of desertion is interrupted while a nullity petition is pending.

It may be concluded that at Hindu law the definition of desertion is similar to that at English law, because it has been constructed on English case law, but when it is applied to Hindu society the practical result is not always the same, e.g., in a Hindu joint family the acts and faults of the relations of a spouse are capable of being construed as those of the spouse himself at least if he does not dissociate himself from them. The conduct which amounts to a grave and weighty matter at English law may not necessarily be so at Hindu law, when the situation is viewed against the background of Hindu social customs. Under the Hindu Marriage Act, 1955, desertion is not a ground for divorce but only for a decree of judicial separation, if it has lasted for a continuous period of two years. If, however, the parties fail to resume cohabitation for a period

234. *Hirabai* v. *Ramchandra,* A.I.R. 1958 Bom. 26.
235. *Ishwar* v. *Pomilla,* A.I.R. 1962 Punj. 432.

of two years after the passing of a decree for judicial separation, either party can petition for divorce. Thus the whole procedure takes four years before a final release from marriage can be obtained. This is expensive, lengthy and slow. On the contrary English law provides a quick and efficient remedy by giving a direct right of divorce on the ground of desertion for a continuous period of three years. Provision for judicial separation also exists at English law.

Chapter VI

CRUELTY

1. *CRUELTY AS A MATRIMONIAL FAULT*

At English law a petition for divorce or judicial separation may be presented by the husband or the wife on the ground that the respondent has, since the celebration of the marriage, treated the petitioner with cruelty.[1] The same remedies are provided in the (Indian) Special Marriage Act, 1954[2] and the (Kenya) Hindu Marriage and Divorce Ordinance, 1960.[3] The Hindu Marriage Act, 1955 allows either party to a marriage to present a petition for a decree of judicial separation on the ground that the other party has treated the petitioner with such cruelty as to cause a reasonable apprehension in the mind of the petitioner that it will be harmful or injurious for the petitioner to live with the respondent.[4] The words qualifying the word "cruelty" indicate that it is to be interpreted in substantially the same way as in English courts of law. But its application to Hindu society does not always yield the same result, having regard to social, cultural, educational, religious and ethical differences. Cruelty is not, as in England, a ground for divorce at Hindu law but only for a decree of judicial separation. If, however, the parties fail to resume cohabitation for a period of two years or upwards after the passing of such a decree, either of them can petition for divorce, on that ground.[5] Hindu law in Uttar Pradesh[6] is different in that the husband or

1. Ss. 1(1)(c) and 14 of the (English) Matrimonial Causes Act, 1950, re-enacted in Ss. 1 (1) (a) (iii) and 12 of the (English) Matrimonial Causes Act, 1965.

2. Ss. 27(d) and 23 of the (Indian) Special Marriage Act, 1954.

3. Ss. 10(1)(c) and 12(c) of the (Kenya) Hindu Marriage and Divorce Ordinance, 1960.

4. S. 10(1)(b) of the Hindu Marriage Act, 1955.

5. S. 13((1)(viii) of the Hindu Marriage Act, 1955 as amended by the Hindu Marriage Amendment Act, 1964.

6. S. 2(a) of the (*Uttar Pradesh Sanshodhan*) *Hindu Marriage Act*, 1962.

the wife can petition for divorce on the ground that the respondent has persistently or repeatedly treated the petitioner with such cruelty as to cause a reasonable apprehension in the mind of the petitioner that it will be harmful or injurious for the petitioner to live with the respondent.

The language of S. 10(1)(b) of the Hindu Marriage Act, 1955 is partly borrowed from *Russell* v. *R.*[7] The words "such cruelty as to cause a reasonable apprehension in the mind of the petitioner" recognise the test of 'likelihood of injury to health', which was approved by the majority of the Law Lords. The words of the Section differ from those used by Lopes, L.J., who said, "There must be danger to life, limb or health bodily or mental or a reasonable apprehension of it, to constitute cruelty."[8]

Taking the words of S. 10(1) (b) in their ordinary meaning, it appears that cruelty, as there contemplated, must be such as to cause a reasonable apprehension that it will be harmful or injurious for the petitioner to live with the other party. Not only past cruelty but also a reasonable apprehension of its repetition in the future has to be proved. Lord Merriman commented on *Meacher* v. *M.*[9], in the following words, "When the legal conception of cruelty is described as being conduct of such a character as to cause danger to life, limb or health bodily or mental or a reasonable apprehension of it, it is vital to bear in mind that it comprises two distinct elements: first the ill-treatment complained of, and secondly, the resultant danger or the apprehension thereof. Thus it is inaccurate, and liable to lead to confusion, if the word 'cruelty' is used as descriptive only of the conduct complained of, apart from its effect on the victim."[10]

This implies that past ill-treatment amounting to cruelty in the popular sense does not suffice, unless there is need to protect the victim from the danger of such ill-treatment or its

7. *Russell* v. *R.* (1897) A. C. 395, H.L.

8. *Russell* v. *R.* (1895) p. 315, 322 (C.A.); affirmed in (1897) A.C. 395, H.L.

9. *Meacher* v. *M.* (1946) p. 216 (C.A.).

10. Lord Merriman, P., in *Jamieson* v. *J.* (1952) A.C. 525.

repetition in the future. In *Lissack* v. *L.*[11] it was held that, in petitions based on cruelty, the action of the court in interfering in the marriage is intended, not to punish the guilty party for what he did in the past, but to protect the innocent party from harm in the future and the question for the court to decide is whether the innocent party can, with safety to life and health, live with the guilty one. However, this view is not fully justifiable in the light of the following authorities.

In *Meacher* v. *M.*[12], decided five years earlier, a wife was severely assaulted by her husband on several occasions, because she refused to obey his order not to visit her sister. She had a nervous breakdown, and left her husband. Later she petitioned for divorce on the ground of cruelty. Henn Collins, J., held that she was not entitled to a decree, because the court would only intervene to protect parties from what they expected to happen and not from what had already happened. As she was living separate from her husband, she was not in danger of further injury from him and she could prevent such assa ults and injuries by obeying her husband. The wife appealed, whereupon the Court of Appeal unanimously reversed the decision of Henn Collins, J. Morton, L.J., said, "Here then was actual violence and physical ill-treatment and I can find nothing in the authorities to justify the view that, if a wife has suffered assaults on her person, she is not entitled to a decree, unless she can show that these assaults are likely to continue." Bucknill and Somervell, L.JJ., concurred. Bucknill, L.J., observed, "The learned judge appears to have based his decision on the proposition that a decree nisi for cruelty will not be granted in respect of acts of cruelty already committed, unless there is also a reasonable fear that further acts of cruelty will be committed. This seems to me to impose a condition on the statutory right to a decree for cruelty which is not in the Act of 1937."

Thus past cruelty alone was held sufficient for a petition to succeed on the ground of cruelty. This view was followed

11. *Lissack* v. *L.* (1951) p. 1; see also O. Kahn-Freund, "*Mental Cruelty*" (1953) 16 M.L.R. 68-70.

12. *Meacher* v. *M.* (1946) p. 216 at 218 (C.A.); commented upon in (1947) 10 M.L.R. 198; (1946) 62 L.Q.R. 7.

in *Swan* v. *S.*[13], decided after *Lissack* v. *L.*[14], by the Court of Appeal, where Hodson, L.J., observed, "I can find nothing in the old authorities to justify the proposition that a decree based on cruelty is a remedy given not for a wrong inflicted but solely as a protection for the victim." But the development of the concept can be traced from the time of Lord Penzance, who said, "Though the object of this court's interference is safety for the future, its sentence carries with it some retribution for the past."[15] The ruling in *Lissack* v. *L.* (supra) is a development from the dictum of Lord Penzance comparable with development in other fields of law. The English courts, which for some time regarded *mens rea* as an essential element in cruelty as a matrimonial fault have abandoned this attributive. This abandonment is consistent with the view that relief is granted in matrimonial causes to protect the injured, not to punish the guilty. The approach of the courts to *Meacher* v. *M.*[16] seems to have ignored the fact that if the wife had not lived apart from her husband, she would have had to endure assaults endangering her health. The combination of cruelty in the popular sense with a reasonable apprehension of injury to health is manifest in *Russell* v. *R.*[17] and has been incorporated in S. 10 (1) (b) of the Hindu Marriage Act, 1955.

In *Putal* v. *Gopi*[18] the wife was occasionally beaten. She became estranged from her husband and went to her father's house, whereupon the husband launched a criminal prosecution against the father, alleging that he had enticed away the wife for immoral purposes and to procure her remarriage. The father was acquitted. Then the husband applied for restitution of conjugal rights, in defence to which the wife pleaded cruelty and just cause. It was held that cruelty was established. The institution of a criminal case falsely imputing unchastity

13. *Swan* v. *S.* (1953) p. 258 (C.A.).

14. *Lissack* v. *L.* (1951) p. 1.

15. Sir James Wilde (Lord Penzance) in *Hall* v. H. (1864) 3 Sw. & Tr. 347, 349 = 164 E.R. 1309; see also Sir C.K. Allen, "*Matrimonial Cruelty*" (1957) 73 L.Q.R. 316.

16. *Meacher* v. *M.* (1946) p. 216 (C.A.).

17. *Russell* v. *R.* (1897) A.C. 395, H.L.

18. *Putal* v. *Gopi*, A.I.R. 1963 Pat. 93.

to the wife, having regard to the conditions obtaining in India and the importance attached to female chastity was calculated to cause as great mental distress and apprehension of harm and injury as could be conceived. After such treatment from her husband no wife in India could consider herself safe in his company. There would always be a lurking apprehension that the husband would take revenge upon his wife for her failure to submit to his will.

In this case there was past cruelty as well as the apprehension that it would be repeated if the wife resumed cohabitation with the husband. But it is not necessary that the wife should have suffered injury in the past, if the circumstances are such that injury to health, bodily or mental is apprehended in the future. Continuous ill-treatment, cessation of marital intercourse, studied neglect, indifference on the part of the husband and his imputation of unchastity are all factors which may undermine the health of a wife. In such cases it is not unreasonable to hold that the wife may legitimately apprehend that, if she stays with her husband, there will be a repetition of such conduct as may result in a complete breakdown of her health.[19]

So it may be concluded that both at Hindu law and English law in order to amount to legal cruelty, injury to health must have resulted or be reasonably apprehended to result. But injury to health is insufficient, unless the conduct is sufficiently grave and weighty to warrant the description of being cruel. In certain circumstances even one incident of cruelty would be sufficient. In *Railton* v. *R.*[20] the wife persisted in using a typewriter after the husband, who had been dozing in an arm-chair, had asked her to stop. The husband caught hold of her violently, pushed her into an arm-chair and then handled her so roughly that she sustained very considerable bruising on her limbs. He showed no regret for what he had done. It was held that the charge of cruelty had been proved, for no woman could fail to fear a repetition of similar conduct, in the circumstances.

19. *Pancho* v. *Ram Prasad*, A.I.R. 1956 All. 41; a similar conclusion was reached in *Joseph* v. *J.* A.I.R. 1934 Pat. 475 (a case under the Indian Divorce Act, 1869).

20. *Railton* v. *R.* (1962) 106 Sol. Jour. 454.

The rule that the injury must be grave and weighty[21] applies at Hindu law. In *Tulsibai* v. *Bhima*,[22] relying on *Russell* v. *R.*[23] it was held that the accepted legal meaning of the expression 'cruelty' in England and India is 'conduct of such a character as to have caused danger to life, limb, or health, bodily or mental, or as to give rise to a reasonable apprehension of such danger.' Even a single act of violence may be of such a grievous nature as to satisfy the test of cruelty. On the other hand, isolated acts of assault committed at the spur of the moment and on some real or fancied provocation may not amount to cruel treatment. In *Kusum* v. *Kampta*[24] it was held that the reasonable apprehension in the mind of the wife need not be merely physical injury. Apprehension of psychological injury or harm will also suffice.

2. *CHANGES IN THE CONCEPT OF CRUELTY*

Judges have carefully avoided defining cruelty, for its concept changes with the march of time. What is regarded as cruelty by one generation may not be so regarded by another. This can be illustrated by looking at the historical background of 'cruelty'. Blackstone[25] maintains that according to old English law a husband was entitled to correct his wife by beating. Chaucer[26] gives startling examples of punishments inflicted by husbands on their rebellious wives. It is described that a husband, who came to know that his wife had gone to a place he had forbidden her to visit, rode to the town and made an agreement with a surgeon to heal two broken legs, and then on returning home he took a pestle and broke both his wife's legs. In comparison with this the ancient Hindu law is milder

21. *Noble* v. *N.* (1964) 1 All E.R. 577; *Gollins* v. *G.* (1963) 2 All E.R. 966 H.L.

22. *Tulsibai* v. *Bhima*, I.L.R. 1961 Madh Pr. 292.

23. *Russell* v. *R.* (1897) A.C. 395, H.L.

24. *Kusum* v. *Kampta*, A.I.R. 1965 All. 280.

25. W. Blackstone, *Commentaries on the Laws of England*, vol. I, 4th. Ed., Oxford, pp. 444-445.

26. A. Abram, *English Life and Manners in the later Middle Ages*, London, 1913, p. 126; see also A.S. Altekar, *The Position of Women in Hindu Civilisation*, Benares, 1956, p. 94.

for it only gives a husband the right to beat his wife with a rope or a split bamboo.[27] Wife-beating is not uncommon in modern India but judges are reluctant to approve of such behaviour in modern Hindu society and are willing to find cruelty even without proof by medical certificates.

In *Holmes* v. *H.*,[28] decided over two centuries ago, the husband was of a brutish and cruel temper. He abused his wife, calling her by such names as bitch, and swore at her. On one occasion, he, accompanied by two men, came into the parlour, locked the door and demanded sexual intercourse threatening that, if she did not accede to it, the two men would hold her whilst he did it. When she escaped through the window, the men followed her, got hold of her and started dragging her back by the hair. It was held that this was not sufficient cruelty to entitle her to a divorce ! Such a conclusion would be startling in modern society.

The change in the concept of cruelty can be seen by comparison of the case with *Lauder* v. *L.*,[29] a fairly recent decision. The husband had been subject to fits of sulky depression, sometimes lasting for several days. During such periods he would refuse to speak to his wife, even in the presence of third parties, towards whom his behaviour was normal and even cheerful. It was held by the Court of Appeal that the husband was guilty of cruelty. On the other hand in *Cousen* v. *C.*,[30] decided a century ago, indifference, neglect, aversion to the wife's society, cessation of matrimonial intercourse and the husband's carrying on an adulterous intercourse with a servant under the same roof where he was residing with his wife, were held not to amount to cruelty.

In *Oliver* v. *O.*[31], decided a century and a half ago, it was held that violent words do not break bones and it is better that they should be suffered than that a marriage should be broken up, and the husband and wife exposed to temptations of living

27. Manu VIII, 299, S.B.E., vol. 25, Oxford, 1886.

28. *Holmes* v. H. (1755) 2 Lee 116 = 161 E.R. 283; see also J.M. Biggs, *The Concept of Matrimonial Cruelty*, pp. 19, 23, 60.

29. *Lauder* v. *L.* (1949) P. 277 (C.A.).

30. *Cousen* v. *C.* (1864) 4 Sw. & Tr. 164 = 164 E.R. 1479.

31. *Oliver* v. *O.* (1801) 1 Hag. Cons. 361 = 161 E.R. 581, 583.

alone. This is not so in modern society. In *Usmar* v. *U.*[32] it was held that constant nagging by the wife amounted to cruelty.

Similar changes are to be found in Hindu society. In *Kamla* v. *Amar*,[33] it was held that the concept of cruelty undergoes changes corresponding to the changes in social custom and standards of behaviour. Again in *Shyamsundar* v. *Shantamani*[34] it was held that the concept of cruelty is fast changing and the courts have to take cognisance of the changing attitude of Hindus to marriage. It is permissible to say that in taking a second wife and transferring all the love and affection to the newly married wife would amount to such legal cruelty as would entitle the wife to claim separate residence and maintenance. The elements of cruelty have to be defined with regard to social conditions as they obtain today and not against the rigid background of the tenets of the old texts of Manu or other Hindu lawgivers.[35]

Social changes are evident both in India and England in the growth of equality of the sexes, as evidenced by women's right to vote, a more sociable attitude between the sexes and the Indian courts' disapproval of assaults and the use of physical violence by husbands to their wives.[36] Lord Denning has postulated equality even in regard to the matrimonial home. "In the choice of a matrimonial home neither party has a casting vote. These matters are to be settled by agreement, by give and take, and not by the imposition of the will of one over that of the other."[37]

The expansion of the concept of cruelty by the recognition of mental cruelty has been partly due to the progress in medical science, psychology and psychiatry, resulting in the discovery

32. *Usmar* v. *U.* (1949) p. 1.

33. *Kamla* v. *Amar.*, A.I.R. 1961 J. & K 33.

34. *Shyamsundar* v. *Shantamani*, A. I. R. 1962 Orissa 50.

35. *Gurdev* v. *Sarwan*, A.I.R. 1959 Punj. 162, 165, per A.N. Grover, J.

36. *Smt. Pancho* v. *Ram Prasad*, A.I.R. 1956 All. 41; *Gurcharn* v. *Waryam*, A.I.R. 1960 Punj. 422.

37. *Dunn* v. *D.* (1949) P 98, 103 (C.A.); repeated in *Hosegood* v. *H.* (1950) 66 T.L.R. 735; *Gaya* v. *Bhagwati*, A.I.R. 1966 Madh. Pr. 212 at pp. 213-214; see also J.M. Biggs, *The Concept of Matrimonial Cruelty*, Ch. II, p. 17, and ff.; L. Rosen, "*Cruelty in Matrimonial causes*" (1949) 12 M.L.R. 324 (shows how the concept of cruelty fluctuates); M. Puxon, "*The Changing Face of Cruelty*" (1962) 106 Sol. Jour. 579, 602.

of various mental disorders, which may be recognised by law as 'injury to health'.[38] As in England, danger of mental injury has been recognised as an element of cruelty at Hindu law.[39] A woman will nowadays leave her husband for reasons which her grandmother would have considered utterly trivial. Judges will infer cruelty on the part of the husband from conduct which so recent a President as Sir Francis Jeune would have regarded as merely a manly assertion of marital authority. Judicial separations are granted for grounds which our ancestors would have deemed absurd. In fact the law of marriage and divorce has undergone immense changes.[40]

In *Gale* v. *G.*[41], decided over a century ago, the husband amongst other charges accused his wife of having, previous to their marriage, committed incest with her step-father. It was held that such a false charge was not *per se* sufficient to constitute legal cruelty. Earlier in *Durant* v. *D.*[42] a false charge of misconduct and criminality was held not to amount to cruelty in itself though it could be considered with other factors. The change in outlook can be seen in *Walker* v. *W.*,[43] decided at the end of the nineteenth century, where Barnes, J., said that he could conceive nothing more abominable and degrading than for a husband to make an unfounded charge of infidelity against his wife. As Henn Collins, J., remarked less than thirty years ago, "Formerly public opinion permitted the use of the ducking stool and long after that ceased to be in use the husband could, without censure of his neighbours, exercise a far stricter discipline than would be tolerated today and that even of a physical nature."[44]

Similar changes are taking place in India. In *Heather* v. *Thomas*[45] a husband imputed unchastity to his wife by writing

38. J. M. Biggs, *The Concept of Matrimonial Cruelty*, p. 47.
39. *Kusum* v. *Kampta*, A.I.R. 1965 All. 280.
40. Comment in a note in (1922) 66 Sol. Jour. 735.
41. *Gale* v. *G.* (1852) 2 Rob. Ecc. 421=163 E.R. 1366.
42. *Durant* v. *D.* (1825) 1 Hag. Ecc. 733 at 769= 162 E.R. 734.
43. *Walker* v. *W.* (1898) 77 L.T. 715 at 717.
44. Henn. Collins, J., in *Atkins* v. *A.* (1942) 2 All E.R. 637 at 638.
45. *Heather* v. *Thomas*, A.I.R. 1941 Rang. 221 (a case under the Indian and Colonial Jurisdiction Act, 1926).

letters to her, in which he doubted the paternity of the child. She was very much upset by this but it was held that this did not constitute cruelty. Such a view is untenable today. In *Kupuswami* v. *Alagammal*,[46] it was decided that making unfounded allegations of adultery against a chaste wife would amount to cruelty. In *Soosannamma* v. *Varghese*[47] it was held that the progressive tendency of the law and the requirements of modern civilised life have left mere physical violence in the background. The wife may seek redress if she fears the exercise of tyranny by the husband, by subjecting her to constant insults, abuse and accusation of adulterous conduct, which would make married life unendurable. Conduct of this kind is cruelty of a worse kind than physical voilence.

However, Hindu law differs from English law in certain ways. A Hindu wife[48] who bears the reproaches of her husband and his family without complaint is regarded as a virtuous lady. An uncomplaining and obedient wife brings credit to her parents' family. If she is badly treated or occasionally beaten, she will be reluctant to go to court for matrimonial relief. The fear of publicity, social disapproval and the loss of reputation in the estimation of the neighbours make the Hindu wife think twice before taking the desperate step of invoking the help of the court. A recent illustration of this is *A.* v. *B.*[49] where it was pointed out that when dealing with the question of delay one should not ignore the traditional background of Hindu Society and the instinctive reluctance of women to seek legal redress of their grievances against their husbands. In that case the wife's petition was delayed as she had to consider the interests of her parents and other members of the family. She belonged to an orthodox family, which despised divorce.

46. *Kupuswami* v. *Alagammal*, A.I.R. 1961 Mad. 391; a similar conclusion was reached in *Kamla* v. *Amar*, A.I.R. 1961 J. & K. 33.

47. *Soosannamma* v. *Varghese*, A. I.R. 1957 Ttra. C. 277 (a case under the Indian Divorce Act, 1869).

48. This does not apply to all sections of Hindu society Amongst the rich and educated classes equality of sexes is common and the polite behaviour towards women is approved. Indian women in such classes may be even more cultured than European women.

49. *A.* v. *B.*, A.I.R. 1967 Punj. 152.

She concluded that her legal action would make it very difficult to find matches for the daughters of her brothers and sisters and that they would be ostracised by society. But an English wife, brought up in an atmosphere of independence, where the individual is more important than the social group, may take little or no account of considerations, which inhibit her Indian sister from approaching the court.

Although English case law has a great persuasive authority in the Indian courts, so that it has been held that Hindu law takes a similar view of legal cruelty as English law,[50] the application of English principles to facts arising in Hindu society does not always yield the same result as it would in England. In *Atkins* v. *A.*[51] a husband's health was injured by the constant nagging of the wife. He was granted divorce on the ground of his wife's cruelty. A Hindu husband is unlikely to complain of such behaviour as cruelty, as he is the dominating partner in the marriage. Even if he did, mere nagging might be treated as the wear and tear of married life. Nearly a century ago in the Calcutta case, *Jogendro* v. *Hurri*,[52] Garth, C.J., pointed out that the same circumstances as would be an answer to a suit for restitution of conjugal rights in the case of an English spouse might not be sufficient in the case of a Hindu. The habits and customs of the Hindu community, especially as regards the marriage state, are so different from those of English people that Hindu and English spouses cannot always be fairly judged by the same rule.

3. *DEFINING CRUELTY*

Judges have carefully refrained from attempting a comprehensive definition of cruelty for the purpose of matrimonial causes and experience has shown the wisdom of this course.[53] Shearman, J., said, "I do not think there is such a thing as

50. *Yamuna* v. *Narayan* (1876) 1 Bom. 164; *Binda* v. *Kaunsilia* (1891) 13 All. 126, 158 (the broad advantage of consulting the English law is that by analogy it affords valuable help).

51. *Atkins* v. *A.* (1942) 2 All E.R. 637.

52. *Jogendro* v. *Hurri* (1880) 5 Cal. 500, 505.

53. Lord Tucker in *Jamieson* v. *J.* (1952) A.C. 525, 550.

'legal cruelty' as distinct from actual cruelty; cruelty means 'cruel conduct' whether in legal language or the vernacular."[54] But this "common sense" definition is too crude. Scrutton, L.J., while warning against a tendency to take too lenient a view of what constitutes 'legal cruelty', said, "It is not every conduct that causes injury to health which could be considered cruelty."[55] Similarly Bucknill, J., said that mere conduct which causes injury to health is not enough.[56]

As mentioned above, in *Russell* v. *R.*, Lopes, L.J., said, "There must be danger to life, limb or health, bodily or mental or a reasonable apprehension of it, to constitute legal cruelty."[57] This was confirmed on appeal when Lord Herschell, stating the majority opinion, said "I think it may confidently be asserted that in not a single case was a divorce on the ground of cruelty granted, unless there had been bodily hurt or injury to health or a reasonable apprehension of one or other of these."[58]

The foundation for this definition had already been laid down in previous decisions. In *Mytton* v. *M.*,[59] decided eighty years ago, Butt, J., said, "Although I am not aware that there were any blows, still, if the conduct of the husband be such as to endanger the life, or even the health of the wife, that is cruelty in every sense of the word, whether we talk of legal cruelty or anything else." In this case the alleged cruelty, which commenced during the honeymoon, consisted of harsh and irritating and tyrannical conduct which made the wife's life intolerable and seriously injured her health. There was no actual violence, but the husband had shaken his fist in her face, saying at the same time that, being a lawyer, he knew the law too well to commit violence.

Lord Penzance a century ago used similar words, "The

54. Shearman, J., in *Hadden* v. *H.* (1919) The Times, 5th. Dec.

55. Scrutton, L. J., in *Baker* v. *B.* (1919) The Times, 11th. Dec. (C.A.).

56. Bucknill, J., in *Horton* v. *H.* (1940) p. 187, 193.

57. Lopes, L.J., in *Russell* v. *R.*, (1895) p. 315, 322 (C. A.).

58. *Russell* v. *R.* (1897) A.C. 395, H.L.; see also Dominik Lasok, "*The Grounds of Divorce in Transition*" (1963) 2 Slicitor Quarterly 297 at pp. 311-318.

59. *Mytton* v. *M.* (1886) 11 P.D. 141.

essential features of cruelty are familiar. There must be actual violence of such a character as to endanger personal health or safety or there must be reasonable apprehension of it. The court, as Lord Stowell once said, has never been driven off this ground."[60] The usual principles require that complaints should be supported by proofs of violence and ill-treatment, endangering or at least threatening, the life or person or health of the complainant.[61] It is clear from the above definitions that cruelty means not only actual bodily harm, but also a reasonable apprehension of such a harm, for the court is not to wait till the hurt is actually done.[62] This has been constantly followed by the English courts,[63] and also applied in India. In *Joseph* v. *J.*[64] the wife alleged that after the husband had introduced one Doris Adams into the house, his attitude changed completely. He began to neglect her, deprived her of the household purse, the direction of servants, and began to pay attention to Doris Adams. He told the wife to get out of the house and threatened to kill her, if she did not do so. On another occasion he threatened to push her teeth down her throat. The question was whether there was a reasonable apprehension of bodily harm. Following *Russell* v. *R.*[65] and *Evans* v. *E.*,[66] it was held that the acts and words of the husband amounted to legal cruelty.

The apprehension must be reasonable in the sense that it must not arise merely from an exquisite or diseased sensibility of mind.[67] In *Dular Koer* v. *Dwarka*,[68] Harrington, J., said,

60. Lord Penzance in *Milford* v. *M.* (1866) L.R. 1 P. & D. 295: 299.

61. *Waring* v. *W.* (1813) 2 Hag. Cons. 153=161 E.R. 699.

62. Lord Stowell in *Evans* v. *E.* (1790) 1 Hag. Cons. 39–161 E.R. 466.

63. Lord Stowell repeated the principle in *Oliver* v. *O.* (1801) 1 Hag. Cons. 361 at 364 = 161 E.R. 581; *Kirkman* v. *K.* (1807) 1 Hag. Cons. 409=161 E.R. 598; *Harris* v. *H.* (1813) 2 Hag. Cons. 148 at 149= 161 E.R. 697; Sir James Hannen in *Birch* v. *B.* (1873) 42 L.J. P. & M. 23.

64. *Joseph* v. *J.*, A.I.R. 1934 Pat. 475 (a case under the Indian Divorce Act, 1869).

65. *Russell* v. *R.* (1897) A.C. 395, H.L.

66. *Evans* v. *E.* (1790) 1 Hag. Cons. 39=161 E.R 466.

67. *Stuart* v. *S.*, A.I.R. 1926 Cal. 864.

68. *Dular Koer* v. *Dwarka* (1907) 34 Cal. 971, 974, 980.

"I prefer to base my judgement on a principle which is equally applicable to Europeans and Indians alike, namely that the court is not bound to order a wife to return to her husband when there is reasonable ground for apprehending that her return to that husband will imperil her safety." In that case the husband had brought a low caste mistress to the house to live as a member of the family and the wife was driven out. Mookerjee, J., after considering a number of English authorities[69] came to the conclusion that the conduct of the husband constituted, in the language of Lord Stowell, "a grave weighty and serious matrimonial offence" and that it amounted to cruelty.

In *Mackenzie* v. *M.*,[70] Lord Herschell said that a single act of violence would warrant a decree of separation when there was reason to anticipate that it might be repeated. Cases of this type can be found as far back as 1862, when, in *Reeves* v. *R.*[71] it was stated that, where one gross act of cruelty is of such a nature as to raise a reasonable apprehension of further acts of the same kind, the court will grant relief.

Until *Russell* v. *R.* (supra) personal violence was an essential ingredient of cruelty. In *Holmes* v. *H.*,[72] decided over two hundred years ago, the wife had suffered degrading and humiliating ill-treatment but the only evidence of physical violence was that she had been dragged by the hair and this was held insufficient to amount to cruelty. The recognition of mental injury as an alternative was not established until *Russell* v. *R.* reached the House of Lords in 1897. Though nearly a century earlier we had Lord Stowell saying, "Words of menace, imparting the actual danger of bodily harm, will justify the interposition of the court, as the law ought not to wait till the mischief is actually done."[73] He used a similar

69. *Popkin* v. *P.* (1794) 1 Hag. Ecc. 766 = 162 E.R. 745; *Evans* v. *E.* (1790) 1 Hag. Cons. 35 = 161 E.R. 466; *Swatman* v. *S.* (1865) 4 Sw. & Tr. 135 = 164 E.R. 1467; *Cousen* v. *C.* (1865) 4 Sw. & Tr. 164 = 164 E.R. 1479; *Russell* v. *R.* (1897) A.C. 395.

70. *Mackenzie* v. *M.* (1895) A.C. 384, 392 (H.L.).

71. *Reeves* v. *R.* (1862) 3 Sw. & Tr. 139, 141 = 164 E.R. 1227.

72. *Holmes* v. *H.* (1755) 2 Lee 116 = 161 E.R. 283.

73. Lord Stowell in *Oliver* v. *O.* (1801) 1 Hag. Cons. 361 at p. 364 = 161 E.R. 581.

phraseology in *Kirkman* v. *K.*,[74] where he said that the court should not wait till a tragic event has taken place. Words of menace, if accompanied with probability of bodily violence will be sufficient.

Forty years later we find the courts treating grossly insulting behaviour as a ground for apprehending danger, and therefore amounting to cruelty. In *Saunders* v. *S.*[75] the husband spat in the wife's face and this was held to be a threat of actual violence. Dr. Lushington in the course of his judgement said, "Is it possible to imagine that, when a husband has proved himself so utterly insensible to all those feelings which he ought to entertain towards his wife, so brutal, so unmanly, that he would, when his passion was excited, restrain himself within the bounds of law and that his wife would be safe under his control ? Threats of personal ill-usage have been deemed sufficient to justify a separation. I am of opinion that such an outrage as this is more than equivalent to any threat, for it proves a malignity of feelings, which would require only an opportunity to show itself in acts involving greater personal danger but never surpassing in cowardly baseness."

4. *INABILITY TO PERFORM THE DUTIES OF MARRIED LIFE*

Another change in the concept of cruelty came in 1865 with *Swatman* v. *S.*[76] In this case the husband was in the habit of drinking and committing adultery, usually in his own home. The amount of physical violence, if any, suffered by the wife was negligible. But Lord Penzance, holding cruelty established, said, "This conduct made up a burden which the petitioner's health was unable to bear, and under which she could not be expected to discharge the duties of married life." The reference to the duties of married life is an echo of what Lord Stowell had said three quarters of a century earlier. "The

74. Lord Stowell in *Kirkman* v. *K.* (1807) 1 Hag. Cons. 409 = 161 E.R. 598.

75. *Saunders* v. *S.* (1847) 1 Rob. Ecc. 549, 562 = 163 E.R. 1131.

76. *Swatman* v. *S.* (1865) 4 Sw. & Tr. 135 = 164 E.R. 1467.

causes must be grave and weighty and such as show an absolute impossibility that the duties of married life can be discharged."[77] The effect of the decision in *Swatman* v. *S.* (supra) was that physical violence was no longer an essential ingredient of cruelty; it was essential that the guilty spouse's misconduct was so grave and weighty as to render married life impossible.

The concept of matri monial cruelty in Indiaa has developed on somewhat similar lines. In *Kondal* v. *Ranganayaki*[78] the husband falsely accused his wife of an attempt to murder him. He insulted her on several occasions, called her by the most vile epithets, treated her with loathing and digust and abused her, when she tried to serve meals to him; he told her that, if she came back to him, she would be dragged out and beaten with slippers; he threatened to stab her. It was held that cruelty in the legal sense need not be physical. A course of conduct which, if persisted in, would undermine the health of the wife is sufficient to amount to cruelty. Similarly in *Udayanath* v. *Shivapriya*[79] it was held that proof of physical violence is not necessary to establish cruelty. The court will find cruelty proved, if, after taking into consideration the conduct of the husband and all the circumstances of the case, it finds it impossible for the wife to live with her husband with the prestige and dignity of a wife; if the husband remarries and neglects his first wife, she is justified in living separate from him. The concepts of mental cruelty and desertion are fact changing and the courts have to take notice of the modern attitude of Hindus to marriage. It is quite permissible to come to a conclusion that in certain circumstances taking a second wife and transferring all the love and affection to her may amount to legal cruelty to first wife.[80]

In England the necessity of proving personal violence was finally rejected in *Kelly* v. *K.*,[81] decided in 1870. The

77. Lord Stowell in *Evans* v. *E.* (1790) 1 Hag. Cons. 39=161 E.R. 466.

78. *Kondal* v. *Ranganayaki*, A.I.R. 1924 Mad. 49.

79. *Udayanath* v. *Shivapriya*, A.I.R. 1957 Orissa 199.

80. *Shyamsundar* v. *Shantamani*, A.I.R. 1962 Orissa 50.

81. *Kelly* v. *K.* (1870) L.R. 2 P. & D. 31, 35, 38, 59.

husband suspected his wife of plotting against him. He censored her letters, dissociated himself from her, deposed her from the position of mistress of the house, told the servants to ignore her orders and stopped her from attending Holy Communion. Consequently she became ill, lost her appetite and all sense of taste and smell. As she was suspected of suffering from paralysis, she left home for treatment. On her return she was treated even more harshly. She was forbidden to see and receive her friends and was not allowed to go out unless accompanied by a manservant. In the words of Lord Penzance she was treated like a child or a lunatic. He said that such a conduct of the husband 'sets at nought not only his own obligations, but the very ends of matrimony itself, by rendering impossible the offices of domestic intercourse and the reciprocal duties of married life.' Granting the wife a decree of judicial separation, he held that proof of injury to the wife's health was sufficient to establish cruelty and the husband's defence that his conduct did not amount to cruelty, as he had not used personal violence against his wife, failed. He appealed unsuccessfully to the full court, where the decision of the lower court was affirmed; both Channell B. and Hannen. J. held that personal violence had never been essential to the proof of cruelty.

The decision is a landmark in the history of cruelty, for it established the principle that injury to health is the criterion of cruelty and the means by which it is effected are not relevant. This is clear from the words of Channell B., when he said, "It is obvious that the modes by which one of the married persons may make the life or the health of the other insecure are infinitely various."[82] Earlier Sir John Nicholl had said, "Cruelty can only be described generally and rather by effects produced than by acts alone."[83] *Kelly* v. *K.*[84] cleared the way for the recognition of mental harm as cruelty. This can be seen from the words of Karminski, J., over a century later, "It

82. *Kelly* v. *K.* (1870) L.R. 2 P. & D. 31 at p. 61.

83. *Westmeath* v. *W.* (1827) 2 Hag. Ecc. Supp. 1 at 69=162 E.R. 992.

84. *Kelly* v. *K.* (1870) L.R. 2 P. & D. 31.

is implicit in our law since *Kelly* v. *K.* (supra) that to find cruelty it is not necessary to find physical violence. Cruelty by words, by talk, other than violence, may nonetheless be cruelty and possibly in some cases more dastardly cruelty than that inflicted by blows. Nagging will suffice, if persistent; abuse or harsh language may well be cruelty, provided always that it causes either injury to health or a reasonable apprehension thereof."[85]

It was clearly laid down in *Russell* v. *R.*[86] that injury to health, bodily or mental, is the sole criterion of cruelty. In this case the parties were living apart. Lady Russell petitioned for judicial separation, alleging cruelty. She had falsely charged him with unnatural offences. She failed to prove the charge but continued accusing her husband, falsely, and publicly. Later she petitioned for restitution of conjugal rights. In defence the husband put forward the conduct of the wife, which, he alleged, amounted to cruelty, and cross petitioned for judicial separation. Therefore, the sole question to decide was whether the wife's conduct amounted to cruelty. It was argued on her behalf in the Court of Appeal that her conduct, however blameworthy, did not constitute cruelty, as her husband had not suffered any bodily hurt actual or apprehended. Rudeness of language, a want of civil attention, even occasional sallies of passion and what merely wounds the mental feelings do not amount to legal cruelty.[87] On the other hand counsel for the husband contendded that, in order to establish cruelty 'the causes must be grave and weighty, and such as to show an absolute impossibility that the duties of married life can be discharged.'[88]

This 'impossibility theory' was rejected by the Court of Appeal, in *Russell* v. *R.*,[89] which by a majority (Lindley and Lopes, L. JJ.) held that the wife's conduct did not amount to cruelty, because there was no injury to the husband's health so his petition for judicial separation failed. But the Court of

85. Karminski, J., in *Eastland* v. *E.* (1954) P. 403, 412.
86. *Russell* v. *R.* (1897) A.C. 395, H.L.
87. *Evans* v. *E.* (1790) 1 Hag. Cons. 35 at 38=161 E.R. 466.
88. *Evans* v. *E.*, supra, at p. 37.
89. *Russell* v. *R.* (1895) p. 315 (C.A.).

Appeal held unanimously that it was sufficiently grave and weighty to provide a defence to restitution of conjugal rights. Lopes, L.J., delivered the judgement and defined curelty as, "There must be danger to life, limb or health, bodily or mental, or a reasonable apprehension of it, to constitute cruelty." The case then went to the House of Lords, where the minority of the peers (Lord Halsbury, L.C., Lords Hobhouse, Ashbourne and Morris), following the dissenting opinion of Rigby L.J. in the Court of Appeal, were disposed to define cruelty as conduct rendering it impossible to discharge the duties of married life. They wished to expand the concept of cruelty by getting rid of the necessity to establish danger of injury to health, which prevented Earl Russell obtaining relief from the trouble caused by his wife. The majority of the House (Lords Herschell, Shand, Watson, Macnaghten and Davey) however, adopted the 'injury to health test' and affirmed the Court of Appeal decision. The judgement of the majority was delivered by Lord Herschell, who said, "Upon the review of the authorities prior to the time when the Divorce Act came into operation, I think it may confidently be asserted that in not a single case was a divorce on the ground of cruelty granted, unless there had been bodily hurt or injury to health or a reasonable apprehension of one or the other of these. And it may with equal confidence be asserted that no other test was ever applied when it had to be determined whether a sentence of divorce on the ground of cruelty should be pronounced. I can find no case in which the impossibility that the duties of married life could be discharged was treated as the criterion."[90]

Thus both limbs of *Evans* v. *E.*,[91] namely 'the injury to health' and 'impossibility of married life' tests were fully discussed. The rejection of the latter in favour of 'the injury to health' is fully justifiable on the ground that it is not practicable for the court to determine precisely when married life has become impossible, as married behaviour varies from couple to couple and it is not uncommon for a spouse to put forward all

90. *Russell* v. *R.* (1897) A.C. 395 at 456, H.L.
91. *Evans* v. *E.* (1790) 1 Hag. Cons. 35=161 E.R. 466.

sorts of petty reasons which are alleged to have made married life impossible for him or her. Sir Carleton Allen[92] in his very learned article on the subject points out, on the authority of Lord Stowell in *Evans* v. *E.* (supra), that physical danger makes the discharge of domestic duties, e.g., to children so difficult as to render married life impossible. But if there is such physical danger, there is apprehension of 'injury to health' and a consideration of the impossibility of performing the duties of married life becomes redundant.

Though the 'impossibility of married life' was rejected as a test of cruelty in *Russell* v. *R.* (supra), it may still be relied on as evidence of injury to health. *Kelly* v. *K.*[93] abolished the necessity of proving personal violence to establish cruelty and *Russell* v. *R.* clearly recognised injury to mental health. This provided relief in many cases which had previously gone unremedied because the element of personal violence was lacking, e.g., *Hudson* v. *H.*[94] where the judge Ordinary said, "But one feature stands prominent in most, if not all the decided cases, personal violence, or the threat of it, and danger to health or life as the result of it." Now the criterion of cruelty was injury to health, mental or physical. There was no difficulty, if the injury alleged was personal violence such as cuts and bruises but mental injury might be hard to prove. Not every act which produced such injury could be regarded as cruelty, so that it became the practice to plead that the conduct complained of was so grave and weighty as to 'make married life impossible' and therefore amounted to cruelty. A recent example of this can be found in the words of Sir Jocelyn Simon, P., "The test of cruelty or constructive desertion is still: was the conduct of such a grave and weighty nature as to make cohabitation virtually impossible ?"[95]

The position is similar in India. In *Cowasji* v. *C.*,[96] the

92. Sir C.K. Allen, "*Matrimonial Cruelty*" (1957) 73 L.Q.R. 324; J.M. Biggs, *The Concept of Matrimonial Cruelty*, ch. II, p. 43.

93. *Kelly* v. *K.* (1870) L.R. 2 P. & D. 31.

94. *Hudson* v. *H.* (1863) 3 Sw. & Tr. 314=164 E.R. 1296 at 1297; see also *Holmes* v. *H.* (1755) 2 Lee 116=161 E.R. 283.

95. *Saunders* v. *S.* (1965) 2 W.L.R. 32.

96. *Cowasji* v. *C.*, A.I.R. 1938 Bom. 81 (a case under the Parsi Marriage and Divorce Act, 1936).

Bombay High Court, following English cases,[97] held that the causes of disagreement between husband and wife must be grave and weighty so as to show an absolute impossibility that the duties of married life can be discharged. The word 'impossibility' was construed as 'moral impossibility', which was to be determined in accordance with the customs of the community concerned.

The 'impossibility of married life' rule also serves as a check on the undue expansion of the concept of cruelty, as is evident from the words of Scrutton, L.J., "The law of cruelty in divorce should be closely watched against a tendency to take a too lenient view of what constitutes legal cruelty. The court ought to act on the view of Lord Stowell that it was the duty of the courts to keep the rule extremely strict. The causes must be grave and weighty and such as to show an absolute impossibility that the duties of the married life could be discharged. It was not every conduct which caused injury to health which could be considered cruelty."[98]

The 'impossibility of married life' rule was rejected as a criterion of cruelty in *Russell* v. *R.*[99] because it was feared that its adoption would lead to a boundless expansion of the concept of cruelty and make it impossible to draw the line of demarcation between what constitutes cruelty and what does not. There is a danger that the 'injury to health' test may be extended to incompatibility of temperment, as the judges have recognised. Bucknill, J., said, "Mere conduct which causes injury to health is not enough. A man takes the woman for his wife for better for worse. If he marries a wife whose character develops in such a way as to make it impossible for him to live with her, I do not think he establishes cruelty merely because he finds life with her impossible."[100] This is in consonance with the view expressed in 1863 by Sir J. Wilde who said, "This court has neither the power nor the inclination to

97. *Evans* v. *E.* (1790) 1 Hag. Cons. 35=161 E.R. 466; *Russell* v. *R.* (1897) A.C. 395, H.L.

98. Scrutton, L.J., in *Baker* v. *B.* (1919) The Times, 11th. Dec. (C.A.).

99. *Russell* v. *R.* (1897) A.C. 395, H.L.

100. Bucknill, J., in *Horton* v. *H.* (1940) p. 187, 193.

deal with the mere unhappiness of ill-assorted marriages."[101] The same applies at Hindu law, under which a husband, having married his wife before the nuptial fire, is expected to make allowances for her irritating idiosyncrasies; and a line has to be drawn between what is mere unhappiness or the wear and tear of married life and blameworthy conduct.[102]

The courts have tried to keep the concept of cruelty within bounds by imposing restrictions from time to time, e.g., by holding that injury to health is not sufficient, unless there is an intent to injure, and that the cruel acts should be 'aimed at' the injured party,[103] a topic to which we revert presently. But these limitations were rejected by the House of Lords in *Gollins* v. G.,[104] where it was held that the criterion of cruelty is whether the complaining spouse has suffered injury, and not whether the offending one intended to inflict it. Lord Pearce[105] said, "It is impossible to give a comprehensive definition of cruelty but when reprehensible conduct or departure from the normal standards of conjugal kindness causes injury to health or an apprehension of it, it is, I think, cruelty, if a reasonable person, after taking due account of the temperament, and all the other particular circumstances, would consider that the conduct complained of is such that this spouse should not be called on to endure it."

The undue expansion of cruelty is also checked by the requirement that the conduct complained of must be grave and weighty. "From the days of Lord Stowell down to the present day it has been acknowledged that to support a finding of cruelty the matter must be grave and weighty."[106] At present to prove cruelty it must be shown (1) that the conduct complained of is sufficiently grave and weighty to warrant the description of being cruel and (2) that it has caused injury to

101. *Hudson* v. *H.* (1863) 3 Sw. & Tr. 314, 319 = 164 E.R. 1296.
102. *Narayan* v. *Prabhadevi*, A.I.R. 1964 Madh. Pr. 28 (a case on constructive desertion).
103. *Eastland* v. *E.* (1954) p. 403.
104. *Gollins* v. *G.* (1963) 2 All E.R. 966, H.L.
105. Lord Pearce in *Gollins* v. *G.*, supra, at p. 992.
106. Lord Pearce in *Gollins* v. *G.*, supra, at p. 986.
107. *Noble* v. *N.* (1964) 1 All E.R. 577.

health, or a reasonable apprehension of such injury.[107] The same applies at Hindu law.[108]

5. *MENS REA IN CRUELTY*

The principle that the conduct of the offending spouse should be aimed at the other spouse first appeared in *Westall* v. *W.*[109], where Lord Denning said, "Defects of temperament, like defects of health, must ordinarily be accepted for better or for worse. When there is no intent to injure, they are not to be regarded as cruelty, unless they are not aimed at the other party but are also plainly and distinctly proved, not merely to cause passing distress or emotional upset, but actually to cause injury to health." His Lordship made no attempt to define the meaning of 'aimed at' so the matter was left in obscurity until *Keslefsky* v. *K.*[110] In that case the husband petitioned for divorce on the ground of his wife's cruelty, alleging that she had written to him, whilst he was away in the armed forces during the war, that she wanted her freedom and wanted the only child of the marriage to be adopted. On his return from military service she refused him intercourse; she used to stay up late at night, do no work at all and stay in bed late in the morning; she was utterly lazy and grossly neglected the child, a boy aged 3 years. It was held that this did not amount to cruelty as the conduct of the wife was not aimed at the husband, being due to her temperament and character. Denning, L.J., explained what he had meant by 'aimed at' and observed, "In *Westall* v. *W.*,[111] we all said, if I remember rightly, that an essential element in cruelty is that there must be conduct which is, in some way, aimed at one person by the other. I adhere to all I there said but the question now is what is meant by 'aimed at'. The conduct of one party can properly be said to be aimed at the other when it consists of actions or words actually or physically directed at him. Then it may be cruelty,

108. *Tulsibai* v. *Bhima*, I.L.R. 1961 Madh. Pr. 292. Where reliance was placed on *Russell* v. *R.* (1897) A.C. 395, H.L.

109. *Westall* v. *W.* (1949) 65 T.L.R. 337 (C.A.).

110. *Keslefsky* v. *K.* (1951) p. 38 (C.A.).

111. *Westall* v. *W.* (1949) 65 T.L.R. 337 (C.A.).

even though there is no desire to injure the other or to inflict misery on him. It may consist in a display of temperament, emotion or perversion, whereby the one gives vent to his or her feelings, not intending to injure the other but making the other the object—the butt—at whose expense the emotion is relieved. The sick wife in *Squire* v. *S.*[112] had no desire to injure her husband but she was guilty of cruelty, because she made her husband the butt of her inordinate demands. The moody husband in *Lauder* v. *L.*[113] directed his sulkiness at his wife, although he had no wish to hurt her. So also the nagging wife in *Usmar* v. *U.*[114]"[115] With this he compared cases where the act or conduct is not directed at the other spouse. He continued, "When the conduct does consist of direct action against the other, but only of misconduct indirectly affecting him or her, such as drunkenness, gambling or crime, then it can only properly be said to be aimed at the other when it is done, not only for the gratification of the selfish desires of the one who does it, but also, in some part, with an intention to injure the other and to inflict misery on him or her. Such an intention may readily be inferred from the fact that it is the natural and probable consequence of the conduct, especially when the one knows or it has been brought to his notice what the consequence will be and nevertheless he does it, careless and indifferent whether it distresses the other or not."[116]

The object of insisting that the conduct complained of should be "aimed at" the petitioner was to limit the scope of the concept of cruelty. This is evident from his later statement, "We cannot find that she has treated her husband with cruelty. If the door of cruelty were opened too wide, we should soon find ourselves granting divorce for incompatibility of temperament. This is an easy path to tread, especially in undefended cases. The temptation must be resisted, lest we slip into a state of affairs where the institution of marriage itself is imperilled."[117]

112. *Squire* v. *S.* (1949) p. 51.
113. *Lauder* v. *L.* (1949) p. 277 (C.A.).
114. *Usmar* v. *U.* (1949) p. 1.
115. Lord Denning in *Keslefsky* v. *K.* (1951) p. 38 at 45-46 (C.A.).
116. Lord Denning in *Keslefsky* v. *K.*, supra, at p. 46.
117. Lord Denning in *Keslefsky* v. *K.* supra, at p. 48.

Keslefsky v. *K.*[118] was followed at Hindu law in *Putal* v. *Gopi*,[119] where it was held that the acts which are complained of as cruelty must be aimed at or directed to the other spouse directly or indirectly. It is not necessary that the complaining spouse must be the direct target of attack. A husband or wife may not, prima facie, do anything directly against the other and apparently they may be on good terms. Nonetheless the behaviour may be such as to cause an extreme mental distress and consequent detriment to health, as when the husband cohabits with other women.

Keslefsky v. *K.* (supra) was followed in a later English case of *Eastland* v. *E.*,[120] where the couple had three children. The wife alleged that the husband mismanaged his financial affairs and ran into debt. After the failure of his farm he found employment but told his wife virtually nothing of what he was earning and gave her very little, if any, financial support. He ignored her, neglected her and refused to make her any allowance of money for food or any other purpose. He left her to deal with the creditors, knowing well that this was causing great distress and injury to her health. Consequently she was obliged to ask her parents for money in order to pay the rent of the house.

It was held that, although the wife's health had suffered by the husband's grave defects of character and conduct, his conduct was negative; it was not aimed at the wife, nor directed against her, nor did it in any way impinge upon her, so deplorable though it was, it fell short of cruelty. Karminski, J., following the dictum of Lord Denning in *Keslefsky* v. *K.*[121] said, "Great care has to be taken in cases of this kind not to extend light-heartedly the area of legal cruelty.[122]

Eastland v. *E.*[123] was a hard case. The wife had suffered injury to her health because of the conduct of her husband, and still the court withheld its remedy where it was needed most.

118. *Keslefsky* v *K.* (1951) p. 38.
119. *Putal* v. *Gopi*, A.I.R. 1963 Pat. 93.
120. *Eastland* v. *E.* (1954) p. 403.
121. Lord Denning in *Keslefsky* v. *K.* (1951) p. 38 at 48.
122. Karminski, J., in *Eastland* v. *E.* (1954) p. 403 at 411
123. *Eastland* v. *E.* (1954) p. 403.

Therefore, it is hardly surprising that this decision was disapproved by the House of Lords in *Gollins* v. *G.*,[124] where the facts were similar; it was held that in cases where the two spouses are of normal physical and mental health and the conduct of the respondent is so bad that the other should not be called on to endure it, cruelty is established, and then it does not matter what was the respondent's state of mind; it is immaterial whether the respondent's conduct was aimed at the other spouse or was due to unwarranted indifference, attributable, perhaps, to selfishness or laziness.

Lord Reid said, " 'Aimed at' is a phrase in ordinary use understood by everybody. If you aim at something you intend to hit it and if you hit something unintentionally you have not aimed at it. Intention is a state of mind. You cannot see into other people's minds, but ordinary people have little difficulty in inferring intention from what a man does and says, viewed in light of the circumstances. In real life either you see aiming at something or you are not."[125] This shows that Lord Reid was equating 'aimed at' with 'intent to hit' and both of the phrases referred to the element of intention in cruelty. As intention to injure was clearly ruled out in *Gollins* v. *G.* (supra) the 'aimed at' test was set aside. The effect of *Gollins* v. *G.* was to establish that cruelty consists of the effects produced on the injured party by the conduct of the offending spouse, irrespective of whether the latter intended to injure. So *Eastland* v. *E.*[126] is no longer good law, nor is it necessary that the conduct of the offending spouse should be aimed at the injured spouse. Dr. Biggs[127] expected that the 'aimed at' test would be discarded. In *Gollins* v. *G.* this requirement was set aside and the judges look at the conduct itself and its probable consequences in deciding whether the conduct complained of amounts to cruelty, without searching into the motives or intentions that gave rise to it.

124. *Gollins* v. *G.* (1963) 2 All E.R. 966, H.L.

125. Lord Reid in *Gollins* v. supra, at p. 972.

126. *Eastland* v. *E.* (1954) p. 403.

127. J.M. Biggs, *The Concept of Matrimonial Cruelty*, pp. 84-87, 90, 92; see also L. Rosen, "*Cruelty and Constructive Desertion*" (1954) 17 M.L.R. 343.

But the 'aimed at' test is still followed in India. In the recent case of *Kamala* v. *Rathnavelu*,[128] the wife was ill-treated. She was given a separate room, where she had to cook for herself separately, while the husband had his meals prepared by his mother. He doubted the paternity of his child and the wife was given a clear impression that she was unwanted. It was held that, in determining what constitutes cruelty, the history of the couple had to be taken into account. Failure to provide sufficient comforts and amenities and even not showing affection may not amount to cruelty. Negative conduct such as neglect or want of affection, even extracting heavy work may not amount to cruelty but the intentional continuance of a course of conduct 'aimed at' the wife, even though it is not violent, is cruelty.

A criminal Lawyer would regard cruelty as containing two elements : (i) intention to injure, (ii) causing actual injury. On the question of intention, *Gollins* v. *G.*[129] is an important decision in that the House of Lords confirmed the principle that the presence of an intention to injure is not an essential element in cruelty. The facts of the case were simple. The couple had two daughters. The husband ran into debt, sold his farm and bought a house on mortgage, which he transferred, subject to the mortage, to his wife, who had given him or lent him considerable sums. In order to maintain the family the wife ran this house, the matrimonial home, as a guest house. The husband did nothing or little to help her; he could have obtained paid employment, but did not. He was incorrigibly and inexcusably lazy but the evidence did not show any wish on his part to harm the wife nor was he aggressively unkind to her. Creditors of the husband tried to make the wife pay and she did pay some of his debts. His refusal to try to help her or earn money worried her and injured her health. In the result she, who was a normal, active and capable

128. *Kamala* v. *Rathnavelu*, A.I.R. 1965 Mad. 88.

129. *Gollins* v. *G.* (1963) 2 All E.R. 966, H.L.; the case is commented upon in (1962) 106 Sol. Jour. 886; (1964) 108 Sol. Jour 925; (1965) 67 Bom. L.R., Journal, p. 11; R. Lowe, "*A New Look at Cruelty*" (1963) 113 Law Journal, p. 683; L. Neville Brown, "*Cruelty without Culpability or Divorce without Fault*" (1963) 26 M.L.R. 625 at pp. 628-635.

woman, was reduced to a physical and mental state in which she could no longer maintain herself and her children. The question was whether she had been treated with cruelty by her husband.

Eventually the case went to the House of Lords, where it was held that an intention on the part of one spouse to injure the other is not a necessary element of cruelty as a matrimonial offence, though the presence of such an intention, if it exists, is material and may be crucial. Whether cruelty as a matrimonial offence has been established is a question of fact and degree, which should be determined by taking into account the particular individuals concerned and the particular circumstances of the case, rather than applying any objective standard.

The point that intention is not an essential ingredient of cruelty is not novel. It was recognised in the Ecclesiastical courts, in *Kirkman* v. *K.*,[130] decided a century and a half ago, cruelty resulted from the jealousy of the wife. Sir William Scott pointed out that the effects of cruelty were the same, whether it proceeded from disorderly affection or from malignity. So it was not necessary to show that it proceeded from malignity. He was more emphatic in *Holden* v. *H.*[131] when he said, "It is not necessary to inquire from what motive such treatment proceeds; it may be from turbulent passion or sometimes causes which are not inconsistent with affection. If bitter waters are flowing, it is not necessary to inquire from what source they spring."

In *Dysart* v. *D*,[132] Dr. Lushington pointed out that it was not the duty of the court to inquire into the causes of cruel conduct and he would not go out of his way to try to find them. He continued. "When I find conduct towards a wife likely to prove dangerous to her safety, but not in other cases, I shall consider it within my cognisance, whatever may have been the case thereof, whether having arisen from violence of disposition, from want of moral control or from eccentricity. It is for me to consider the conduct itself and its probable consequences;

130. Sir William Scott (later Lord Stowell) in *Kirkman* v. *K.* (1807) 1 Hag. Cons. 409 at 410 = 161 E.R. 598.

131. Lord Stowell in *Holden* v. *H.* (1810) 1 Hag. Cons. 453 at 458 = 161 E.R. 614.

132. Dr. Lushington in *Dysart* v. *D.* (1844) 1 Rob. Ecc. 106 at 116 = 163 E.R. 980 at 983-984.

the motives and causes cannot hold the hand of the court." Lord Penzance in *Hall* v. *H.*[133] also came to a similar conclusion when he said, "With danger to the wife in view, the court does not hold its hand to inquire into motives and causes. The sources of the husband's conduct are for the most part immaterial." But he made an exception in case of insanity and disease of the mind, which is dealt with below at p. 166.

Sir John Nicholl in *Westmeath* v. *W.*[134] had also suggested that the criterion of cruelty should be the effects produced rather than the acts done. With this volume of decisions it is difficult to see how it was held in *Astle* v. *A.*,[135] decided a quarter of a century ago, that malignity or intention is an essential in gredient of cruelty. In *Astle* v. *A.* (supra) intention was equated with malignity and in *Jamieson* v. *J.*[136] it was equated with unwarrantable indifference as to the consequences to the victim. In *Kellock* v. *K.*[137] the wife committed acts which were dangerous to the health and life of the husband. She was suffering from depressive insanity but it was held that she was guilty of cruelty, as she had acted with a consciously wicked mind. Similarly in *Horton* v. *H.*[138] it was held that the "husband must prove that she has committed wilful and unjustifiable acts inflicting misery and pain upon him and causing him injury to health."

The matter came to ahead in *Squire* v. *S.*[139] where the wife continuously for nights on end prevented the husband from sleeping, demanding that he read to her or converse with her.

133. Wilde, J.O., (Lord Penzance) in *Hall* v. *H.* (1864) 3 Sw. & Tr 347 at 349 = 164 E.R. 1309.

134. Sir John Nicholl in *Westmeath* v. *W.* (1827) 2 Hag. Ecc. Supp. 1 at 69 = 162 E.R. 992.

135. *Astle* v. *A.* (1939) p. 415 (this is discussed fully in relation to insanity as a defence).

136. *Jamieson* v. *J.* (1952) A.C. 525 at 535, H. L.

37. *Kellock* v. *K.* (1939) 3 All E.R. 972 (simply followed *Astle* v. *A.* (1939) p. 415.

138. Bucknill, J., in *Horton* v. *H.* (1940) p. 187 at 193, followed in *Usmar* v. *U.* (1949) p. 1 (C.A.).

139. *Squire* v. *S.* (1949) p. 51 (C.A.); commented upon in (1948) 92 Sol. Jour. 318; K T. Samson, "*Motive as an Element of Cruelty in Divorce*" (1948) 11 M.L.R. 88.

If he showed signs of sleep, she unreasonably demanded that he should perform various menial services for her, whereby the husband was deprived of sleep and suffered in health. Finnemore, J., came to the conclusion that, in order to establish cruelty, the conduct must be deliberate, malignant and intended. As the wife's conduct resulted from illness, she had no intention to be cruel and consequently no cruelty was established. The Court of Appeal reversed the decision, holding that malignant intention was not an essential element of cruelty, Hodson, J., dissenting, and that the evidence clearly established cruelty. The dictum of Shearman, J., in *Hadden* v. *H*,[140] "I do not question the evidence of the husband that he had no intention of being cruel to her, but I hold that his intentional acts amounted to cruelty", was approved.

Thus the rule that malignity or intention is an essential ingredient of cruelty was eliminated. But in order to prove the cruel conduct, resort was had to the presumption that a person is presumed to intend the natural and probable consequences of his acts. But why should an intention be imputed to a person, if the evidence clearly proves that he had no such intention ? This difficulty was clearly pointed out by Professor Goodhart.[141] in his very learned article on the subject, where he states that in *Gollins* v. *G*.[142] the main evidence in favour of the presumption was that the husband's neglect to maintain his wife "amounted to a course of conduct intentionally pursued." There is no doubt that he intended not to work, but that he did so for the purpose of injuring his wife seems improbable. The application of this presumption was rejected by the House of Lords.

Dr. Biggs[143] suggested that the test of cruelty should be whether the respondent foresaw the consequences of his act or conduct, and, where such foresight could not be proved, it might be presumed by resort to the presumption that a person

140. Shearman, J., in *Hadden* v. *H*. (1919) The Times, 5th. Dec.

141. A.L. Goodhart, "*Cruelty, Desertion, and Insanity in Matrimonial Law*" (1963) 79 L.Q.R. 98.

142. *Gollins* v. *G*. (1963) 2 All E.R. 966, H.L.

143. J.M. Biggs, *The Concept of Matrimonial Cruelty*, pp. 94-98.

intends the natural and probable consequences of his acts.[144] He regards the presumption as irrebuttable in the sense that it is invoked only in the last resort where there is no adequate evidence to prove either the existence or the absence of foresight in the respondent. However, this test was rejected by Lord Reid, who said, "To attribute to a man an intention which he did not have is to base oneself on a fiction and that is bound to lead to trouble. However useful fictions may have been in the past in other branches of the law, they seem to be both unnecessary and confusing in the realm of cruelty....If the conduct complained of and its consequences are so bad that the petitioner must have a remedy, then it does not matter what was the state of the respondent's mind. In other cases the state of his mind is material and may be crucial."[145] The test is positive.[146]

Applying this principle, many cases, where there is no express intention to injure the other spouse, become reconciled as cases of cruelty. It brings within the concept a spouse who commits sexual offences against third parties, which are breaches of conjugal obligations. In *Ivens* v. *I.*[147] a husband had committed indecent assaults on the wife's daughter by a previous marriage, a child between 13 and 15 years of age. The girl informed her mother, who protested to her husband, and he promised not to repeat it. He failed to keep his promise and resumed his inde-

144. *Lang* v. *L.* (1955) A.C. 402; see comments in (1962) 106 Sol. Jour., pp. 293-294; A.L. Goodhart, "*Constructive Desertion*" (1955) 71 L. Q.R. 32; J.C. Hall, "*Matrimonial Cruelty and Mens Rea*" (1963) 104 Cambridge Law Journal 104 at p. 106.

145. Lord Reid in *Gollins* v. *G.* (1963) 2 All E.R. 966, 973, 974.

146. 'Positive' will be used to describe the state where the effect of the consequences resulting from the act or conduct of the offending spouse, is so bad and injurious on the health of the injured party, that a reasonable man who has witnessed the scene can come to the conclusion that the victim has been treated with cruelty.

147. *Ivens* v. *I.* (1955) p. 129 (C.A.); similar offences were committeed in the following cases, but there was no evidence that the husband had intended to injure the wife. The conduct of the husband had disastrous effects on the health of the wife as it had in *Gollins* v. *G.*, supra; *Thompson* v. *T.* (1901) 17 T.L.R. 572; *Bosworthick* v. *B.* (1901) 18 T.L.R. 104; *Cooper* v. *C.* (1955) p. 99; *Crawford* v. *C.* (1956) p. 195; *W.* v. *W.* (1962) p. 49.

cent conduct, with the result that his wife's health was affected. It was held that a criminal and indecent assault by a husband on a child was cruelty to the child's mother, although no intention to injure the mother was shown. Both Lord Goddard, C.J., and Vaisey, J., spoke in terms of 'foresight of consequences'. Lord Goddard, C.J., said, "I can imagine nothing which would be more likely to affect the woman's health, as in fact it did, and I can conceive of no conduct more calculated to justify the court in saying that the husband knew perfectly well what the effect of his conduct would be upon his wife and upon the state of her health and yet, careless of or indifferent to what the effect would be, continued to carry on this filthy conduct."[148] Vaisey, J., agreeing said, "The indecent conduct of the husband towards the wife's own daughter was not done in order to hurt the wife but it had that consequence, as the evidence quite clearly shows, and as the husband must have known that it would or might."[149] The same is true in cases where the husband is carrying on an improper association with another woman, which results in injury to the wife's health. His intention may not be to hurt the wife deliberately, but merely to enjoy the other woman.[150] Applying *Gollins* v. *G.*[151] the effect on the wife's health amounts to cruelty and the intention of the husband is irrelevant. In such cases the conduct is so bad that the victim must have a remedy.

In *Eastland* v. *E.*[152] the facts were identical to those in *Gollins* v. *G.* (supra). The husband's failure to provide maintenance for his wife and children; his irresponsibility and shiftlessness, which had brought him into debt, injured the wife's health. As his acts were not intended to injure the wife, it was held that his conduct did not amount to cruelty. But since *Gollins* v. *G.* such a finding is wrong. *Cox* v. *C.*[153] was also

148. Lord Goddard, C.J., in *Ivens* v. *I.* (1955) p. 129 at 132 (C.A.).
149. Vaisey, J., in *Ivens* v. *I.* (1955) p. 129 at 133 (C.A.).
150. *Walker* v. *W.* (1962) p. 42 at 46; *Windeatt* v. *W.* (1962) 1 All E.R. 776 (C.A.). The facts in both the cases were identical, but the intention to injure was inferred from the circumstances in the latter case.
151. *Gollins* v. *G.* (1963) 2 All E.R. 966, H.L.
152. *Eastland* v. *E.* (1954) p. 403.
153. *Cox* v. *C.* (1952) 2 T.L.R. 141 (C.A..)

wrongly decided in the light of *Gollins* v. *G.* In that case the husband was improperly associating with other women with consequential injury to the wife's health. It was held that the wife must show an intention on the part of the husband to inflict misery on her. It was subsequently held in *Walker* v. *W.*,[154] that such an association was cruelty. In *Windeatt* v. *W.*,[155] the inference of intent to injure the wife was drawn in similar circumstances.

In *Gollins* v. *G.*[156] Lord Reid said, "Why should we have to drag in intention at all ? It seems to me a very poor defence to say, 'I know the disastrous effects on my wife of what I have been doing. Probably I could have resisted temptation, if I had really tried, but my conduct is innocent, because I had not the slightest desire or intention to harm my wife. I have acted throughout from pure selfishness." Though the evidence may make it clear that he had no active intention of causing pain or misery to his wife, if his conduct was unjustifiable or inexcusable and, if he knew or the evidence shows that he must have known that the effect of his conduct would be to cause pain and suffering to his wife, who was not unusually sensitive and was mentally normal, why does intention matter?

Lord Evershed,[157] while agreeing that malignity or intention is not an essential ingredient of cruelty, said that the test is whether the acts or conduct of the man or woman charged is cruel and not whether he or she is cruel. Thus the criterion is the effect of the cruel conduct on the victim. The question is whether, in all the circumstances of the case, a reasonable man witnessing the scene can come to the conclusion that the victim has been treated cruelly by the offending spouse. If the answer is in the affirmative then the state of the respondent's mind is immaterial.

This test is recognised in Hindu law but where the joint

154. *Walker* v. *W.* (1962) p. 42 at 46.

155. *Windeatt* v. *W* (1962) 1 All E.R. 776 (C.A.).

156. Lord Reid in *Gollins* v. *G.* (1963) 2 All E.R. 966 at 971.

157. Lord Evershed in *Gollins* v. *G.*, supra, at 976; see also M. Puxon, "*'Cruel' means Cruel*" (1964) 108 Sol. Jour. 786; L. Rosen, "*Legal Cruelty and Cruelty*" (1964) 108 Sol. Jour. 887; comments in (1965) 67 Bom. L.R., Journal, p. 11.

family system is still practised, the acts of the husband's relations are capable of being imputed to the husband, at least when he makes no attempt to protect his wife. In *Anjani* v. *Krushna*[158] the wife alleged that she was hated and neglected; the husband called her ill-bred and illiterate. She was not given food and drink like a member of the family; she was compelled to do menial work in the household, including cleaning the cowshed and utensils. She was also physically tortured, slapped and kicked by the mother-in-law. Her husband joined hands with his parents in harassing her. She was deprived of all the pleasures of married life. It was held that the conduct of the husband amounted to cruelty.

In *Sayal* v. *Sarala*,[159] the marriage was not a happy one. In order to improve the unhappy relationship, the wife on the advice of someone administered a love potion to her husband. As a result of this the husband became ill, developed various bodily disorders and ultimately had a breakdown. She had clearly no intention to hurt her husband and throughout his illness showed great concern for his health. It was held that her act amounted to cruelty. The wife's administration of the love potion emanated from the laudable object of bringing about domestic amity in the house but it had produced more deleterious effects on the husband than he be called upon to endure. The situation was viewed from the victim's suffering and not from the respondent's intention. It was held that the husband was in need of protection from danger of a similar act in the future.

The principle of *Gollins* v. *G.*[160] would be appropriate in such cases. The rule that intention is not an essential ingredient of cruelty does not imply that it is irrelevant. This of course may be decisive in cases where it exists. All the circumstances of the case have to be considered. The matter is well put by Lord Reid, "Much must depend on the knowledge and intention of the respondent, on the nature of his or character, and on the character and physical and mental weaknesses of the

158. *Anjani* v. *Krushna*, A.I.R. 1954 Orissa 117.

159. *Sayal* v. *Sarala*, A.I.R. 1961 Punj. 125.

160. *Gollins* v. *G.* (1963) 2 All E.R. 966, H.L.

spouses, and probably no general statement is equally aplicable in all cases, except the requirement that the party seeking relief must show actual or probable injury to life, limb or health.[161]"

The question was also considered by Lord Normand in the House of Lords in *Jamieson* v. *J.*,[162] "The conduct alleged must be judged up to a point by reference to the victim's capacity for endurance, in so far as that capacity is or ought to be known to the other spouse ... that leaves it open to find, after evidence, that the petitioner was the victim of his or her abnormal hypersensitiveness and not of cruelty inflicted by the respondent." Each case must depend on its own individual facts; if the wife suffers from a heart disease and the husband, being aware of her condition, gives her a sudden shock, he is guilty of cruelty.[163] Similarly when the wife is very sensitive and is upset by her husband's association with another woman, even though the association involves no sexual impropriety, if the husband persists in such conduct, which results in injury to the wife's health, he is guilty of cruelty.[164] But such conduct may not amount to cruelty, if it is provoked by the complaining spouse.[165]

Health and capacity for endurance are important factors; the emotional susceptibilities of women and the normally stronger physique of men have to be considered. In *Jilling* v. *J.*,[166] the wife had persistently nagged her husband over financial matters. Her conduct was unjustifiable but, as the husband was a strong and healthy man, it had not injured his health. Consequently there was no cruelty.

In *Niblett* v. *N.*,[167] a husband falsely, maliciously and wil-

161. Lord Reid in *Gollins* v. *G.* (1963) 2 All E.R. 966 at 969.

162. Lord Normand in *Jamieson* v. *J.* (1952) A.C. 525 at 535, H.L. (accepting the Lord President's view in the court below).

163. *Barrett* v. *B.* (1903) 20 T.L.R. 73.

164. *Windeatt* v. *W.* (1962) 1 All E.R. 776 (C.A.).

165. *Robinson* v. *R.* (1961) 105 Sol. Jour. 950; *King* v. *K.* (1953) A.C. 124.

166. *Jillings* v. *J.* (1958) The Times, 11th. Dec. (C.A.); in *Usmar* v. *U.* (1949) p 1, such nagging amounted to cruelty.

167. *Niblett* v. *N.*, A.I.R. 1935 Oudh. 133 (a case under the Indian Divorce Act, 1869).

fully charged his wife with unchastity. She failed to show that she had suffered mental or physical injury to health as a result of the imputations. Following *Russell* v. *R.*[168], it was held that cruelty was not established. This case was no doubt correctly decided, having regard to the current attitude towards sex in England but it should be followed with caution, if at all in India. In *Kupuswami* v. *Alagammal*[169] the husband's unfounded charges of unchastity against his wife and his keeping a mistress openly in the house, were held to be cruelty. In *Iqbal* v. *Pritam*[170] the wife sought a deree of judicial separation on the ground of cruelty, alleging that her husband indulged in the business of speculation and lost heavily. He did not desist from such a ruinous course in spite of her protests. On the contrary he beat her when she protested. He wanted her unmarried daughter for immoral purposes. He imputed unchastity to her and threatened to kill her, so that proceedings were instituted to have him bound over to keep the peace under S. 107 of the Code of Criminal Procedure. In his defence the husband alleged that the wife was living in adultery. It was held that the petitioner had been treated with such cruelty as to cause a reasonable apprehension in her mind that it would be harmful and injurious to live with him.

In *Kusum* v. *Kampta*[171] the question was whether the wife had been treated with cruelty. She alleged that the husband had, without any foundation, accused her of unchastity, in a communication from his lawyer, and in the pleadings, in circumstances from which malice could be inferred. She deposed that these false allegations caused her much pain and suffering and that the husband was in the habit of making such accusations. When she was ill, she was not given medical attention, so she had to go to her parents in Delhi for treatment. The husband insisted upon sexual intercourse after childbirth, when it was harmful and injurious to her health. On this evidence, it was held that the cruelty is lack of regard and consideration for the other spouse. It includes selfish brutality and disregard for

168. *Russell* v. *R.* (1895) p. 315 (C.A.).
169. *Kupusuami* v. *Alagammal*, A.I.R. 1961 Mad. 391.
170. *Iqbal* v. *Pritam*, A.I.R. 1963 Punj. 242.
171. *Kusum* v. *Kampta*, A.I.R. 1965 All. 280, 285, 286, 283.

the health, needs, desires, and feelings of the other spouse, even in such a matter as sexual relations between the two. Relying on *Holborn* v. *H.*,[172] it was laid down that persistence in inordinate sexual demands or malpractices by either spouse can be cruelty, if it injures the other spouse. Indeed, according to matrimonial experts, this sphere of conjugal life ought to be more sedulously guarded against psychological injuries than any other. Each spouse is entitled to expect the other to show due consideration and respect for the health, requirements, feelings, and sentiments of the other. The learned judge, Beg, J., said, "Courts trying matrimonial cases must maintain an attitude of sympathetic understanding for both sides, if they are to successfully judge psychological situations and subjective factors, which they are necessarily called upon to do in such cases. It is not reasonableness and unreasonableness of the antipathy felt by either spouse for the other which has to be determined by the court with a view to punishing an erring party. It is only the reasonableness or otherwise of the apprehension that the mental or physical health of the complaining spouse will suffer by living together, which has to be adjudicated upon in a suit for judicial separation. There is a good deal to be said for consultations with competent psychiatrists by the parties themselves, before rushing to court or, failing that, for obtaining the opinions of psychiatrists as experts before a court, which entertains doubts upon such a matter, gives its decision. In the absence of opinions of competent psychiatrists who are, unfortunately, very scarce in this country, the court should undertake the task of such an expert itself before pronouncing upon the question. The guiding consideration should be the welfare of the spouse alleging reasonable apprehension of injury." On the authority of D. Tolstoy in "The Law and Practice of Divorce and Matrimonial Causes", 1963, it was held that the test of cruelty is subjective and the mental and physical condition of the spouse must be taken into consideration in determining whether the conduct amounts to cruelty in the particular case. A reasonable apprehension of psychological injury or harm is enough for granting a decree for judicial separation.

172. *Holborn* v *H.* (1947) 1 All E.R. 32 at p. 33.

Medical evidence of injury to health is not essential in India, whatever the position in England. The situation is well defined in *Kaushalya* v. *Wisakhi*,[173] where it was held that, in view of the submissive nature of Hindu women, the mere absence of a medical certificate will not discredit the testimony with respect to maltreatment of the wife at the hands of her husband. I.D. Dua, J., in the course of his judgement stated, "There is public policy clearly discernible in the recent legislative measures, whereby attempts have been made to raise the social status of women in India. New rules of social behaviour and conduct towards women in the Indian Society of today must be recognised and kept in the forefront by the courts, while determining cruelty under the Hindu Marriage Act, 1955." In that case cruelty was obvious from the facts of the case. The wife deposed that her husband used to beat her with sticks and place her hands beneath the charpoy. Once he had attempted to set fire to her clothes, so she had to report to the police about his behaviour. In the circumstances of the case there was no need to produce medical witnesses.

There is no difficulty in finding cruelty where there is evidence of personal violence. In *Gurdev* v. *Sarwan*,[174] the husband got a restitution decree from which the wife appealed, alleging that she was always subjected to cruel treatment ; she was beaten and had suffered a severe injury on her eye. The husband wanted her to submit to his brother and other people. He slapped her before the Panchyat when the latter came to remonstrate with him. She was being kept in illegal confinement by the husband, until her mother applied to a magistrate for a search warrant under S. 100 of the Code of Criminal Procedure. It was held that keeping a wife in illegal confinement is certainly an act of a nature which is cruel and is bound to have harmful and injurious effect on her health.

The social position of the parties is a relevant factor. The

173. *Kaushalya* v. *Wisakhi*, A.I.R. 1961 Punj. 521, 624; C.K. Allen, "*Matrimonial Cruelty*" (1957) L.Q.R. 316 at pp. 320-321 (about the endurance of ill-treated wives and medical evidence in English law); Donald Blair, "*Proof in Matrimonial Proceedings : the Medical Aspect*" (1965) 5 Medicine, Science and the Law 65 at pp. 66-70.

174. *Gurdev* v. *Sarwan*, A.I.R. 1959 Punj. 162.

following passage in *Westmeath* v. *W.*,[175] decided nearly a century and a half ago, illustrates the point clearly. "A blow between the parties in the lower conditions and in the highest stations of life bears a very different aspect. Among the lower classes blows sometimes pass between married couples who, in the main, are very happy and have no desire to part; amidst very coarse habits such incidents occur almost as freely as rude and reproachful words; a word and a blow go together. Still amongst the very lowest classes, there is generally a feeling of something manly in striking a woman, but if a gentleman, a person of education, the discipline of which *emollit mores*[176] and tends to extinguish ferocity; if a nobleman of high rank and ancient family uses personal violence to his wife, his equal in rank, the choice of his affection, the friend of his bosom, the mother of his offspring—such conduct in such a person carries with it something so degrading to the husband, and so insulting and mortifying to the wife, as to render the injury itself far more severe and insupportable."

In *Stourton* v. *S.*,[177] a case decided very recently, the court made a similar approach. This was a tragic one, because the high social position of the parties, their respective ages, their religious beliefs, the long period during which the marriage had subsisted, and the inevitable repercussions on a family of honourable and ancient lineage made it a disagreeable task to grant a decree on the ground of cruelty.

Similarly at Hindu law the situation has to be viewed against the background of the whole marital relationship of the spouses, bearing in mind the educational, cultural, intellectual and social standard of the parties. Even a single act of violence may be of such a nature as to satisfy the test of cruelty. On the other hand isolated acts of assaults committed in agony or resulting from provocation may not amount to cruelty. The court has to take into account the ordinary weaknesses, short-

175. *Westmeath* v. *W.* (1827) 2 Hag. Ecc. Supp. 70, 73 = 162 E.R. 992.

176. 'Smoothens' or 'polishes the manners'.

177. *Stourton* v. *S.* (Lord Mowbray's case) (1961) The Times, 2nd. and 16th. May.

comings and failings as well as the strength of human nature.[178] In *Gurcharn* v. *Waryam*,[179] the husband was held guilty of cruelty on proof by the wife that he had charged her with adultery without any foundation. He had doubted the paternity of his child and had taken no interest in its birth. The wife was maltreated, neglected and beaten. Dua, J., propounded the test of cruelty in the following words, "Whether or not isolated acts of violence amount to cruelty normally depends on the facts and circumstances of each case and the modern tendency of the society is at least to treat with disapproval acts of violence or assault towards women. New rules of social behaviour and conduct must, therefore, be recognised by the courts in determining what would amount to cruelty in the present set-up, and the court would be disinclined to dismiss lightly the so called isolated acts of violence and assault as not amounting to cruelty, if the victim of such assaults resents and takes exception to them."

Like the English law, Hindu law takes account of impact of the personality and conduct of one spouse on the mind of the other. If the general conduct of the husband tends to degrade the wife and subject her to a course of indignity (e.g., the imputing of unchastity) injurious to her health, cruelty will be established.[180] *Kohli* v. *Kohli*[181] decided that there are few things which a woman, especially in the background of Indian traditions, cherishes more than chastity, so where a husband makes an unfounded allegation of adultery against his wife, it must in the very nature of things cause her extreme anguish and amounts to cruelty.

Whether conduct is cruel is to be judged by its effect on the person to whom it is directed so that the personality of the agrieved spouse is relevant.[182] A suggestion that cruelty should be defined as conduct which no reasonable man should be

178. *Tulsibai* v. *Bhima*, I.L.R. 1961 Madh. Pr. 292; *Shyamlal* v. *Saraswati*, A.I.R. 1967 Madh. Pr. 204 at p. 205; see also *Sarah Abraham* v. *Pyali Abraham*, A I.R. 1959 Ker. 75 (a case under the Indian Divorce Act, 1869).

179. *Gurcharn* v. *Waryam*, A.I.R. 1960 Punj. 422, 425.

180. *Kamla* v. *Amar*, A I.R. 1961 *J.* &. K. 33.

181. *Kohli* v. *K.*, A.I.R 1967 Punj. 397 at p. 399.

182. Pearce, J., in *Lauder* v. *L.* (1949) p. 277 at 308 (C.A.).

expected to endure, was rejected by the Royal Commission[183] on the ground that injustice would be done, where conduct did not measure up to the standard set and yet was serious enough to injure the health of a person of delicate physique or susceptible temperament.

Both at Hindu law and English law the criterion of cruelty is whether, after considering all the circumstances of the case and making allowance for the temperament of the spouses, the conduct of the delinquent spouse has been such as to cause reasonable apprehension of injury to health. If the answer is in the affirmative, the intention of the respondent is immaterial.

6. *PROTECTION OF THE AGGRIEVED SPOUSE*

Redress is provided in matrimonial causes to protect the aggrieved spouse. The history of this principle can be traced from the time of Lord Stowell, who, over, a century and a half ago, put the duty of self-preservation before that of marital cohabitation, when he said, "In a state of personal danger no duties can be discharged; for the duty of self-preservation must take place before the duties of marriage, which are secondary both in commencement and in obligation."[184] In *Kirkman* v. *K.*,[185] while emphasising the need to protect the injured party he observed, "The persons of both parties, however, must be protected from violence, and I cannot accede to what has been said in argument, that the court should wait till there has been actual violence of such a nature as may endanger life." He used a similar phraseology in *Holden* v. *H.*[186] when he said, "Everything is in legal construction, *saevitia*, which tends to bodily harm, and in that manner renders cohabitation unsafe;

183. Royal Commission on Marriage and Divorce (1956) Cmd. 9678, para 130; C.K. Allen, "*Matrimonial Cruelty*" (1957) 73 L.Q.R. at p. 321.

184. Sir William Scott (later Lord Stowell) in *Evans* v. *E.* (1790) 1 Hag. Cons. 39 = 161 E.R. 466.

185. Lord Stowell in *Kirkman* v. *K.* (1807) 1 Hag. Cons. 409 = 161 E.R. 598.

186. Lord Stowell in *Holden* v. *H.* (1810) 1 Hag. Cons. 453 at 458 = 161 E.R. 614.

whenever there is a tendency only to bodily mischief it is a peril from which the wife must be protected; because it is unsafe for her to continue in the discharge of her conjugal duties; and to enforce that obligation upon her might endanger her security and perhaps her life."

Similarly in *Otway* v. *O.*[187] a wife obtained a separation *a mensa et thoro* (judicial separation) on the ground of her husband's adultery and cruelty. She alleged that the husband was in the habit of giving way to violent passion, of following her from room to room, abusing her, calling her by the most opprobrious names and accusing her of adultery and incest. She was so terrified by his conduct that she quitted the house twice. She suffered fits from his violent conduct and her health had been materially affected. The husband would not allow her to have medical treatment till he was told that she was in danger. It was held that she needed protection from this cruelty.

In *Prichard* v. *P.*,[188] decided a century ago, the husband petitioned for judicial separation on the ground of his wife's cruelty. The wife was a lady of unrestrained violence. She habitually abused her husband in foul language and from time to time struck him. Finally, when he went to divine service, she thrust herself in front of him on the steps of the chapel and assailed him with abuse and blows, in consequence of which he suffered nervous shock and much mental and bodity suffering. A decree of judicial separation was granted to the husband, not because he needed protection from the wife's assaults and violence, for he was physically stronger than the wife but because the wife herself was in personal danger, as she was likely to provoke the husband, who might use more physical violence in retaliation and self-defence !

In *Curtis* v. *C.*[189] the husband suffered from 'brain fever',

187. *Otway* v. *O.* (1812) 2 Phill. Ecc. 95 = 161 E.R. 1088

188. *Prichard* v. *P.* (1864) 3 Sw. & Tr. 523 = 164 E.R. 1378; see also *White* v. *W.* (1859) 1 Sw. & Tr. 591 = 164 E.R. 874. Where the husband himself was in need of protection from the danger arising out of the intemperate and violent habits of the wife, who was at times confined as insane.

189. *Curtis* v. *C.* (1858) 1 Sw. & Tr. 192 = 164 E.R. 688 at 698; *Cook* v. *C.* (1863) 32 L.J. (P.M. & A.) 81. Where a return to cohabitation was dangerous to the wife.

was subject to fits of ungovernable passion and had treated the wife in a harsh and degrading manner. It was held that the husband's misconduct was dangerous to the wife and rendered cohabitation unsafe, so she was entitled to protection by decree. In *Marsh* v. *M.*[190] the husband was intemperate and had suffered from delirium tremens. He had occasionally inflicted bodily injury on his wife and had by his general conduct towards her materially injured her health. The wife was granted a decree of judicial separation, because the court was satisfied that she could not return to cohabitation without incurring great peril of a renewal of the bodily injuries inflicted upon her. Persisting in drunkenness, knowing that such a course of conduct is injurious to the other spouse may of itself amount to cruelty. Where the husband was a habitual drunkard, who attacked his wife with words and violence which brought her to the verge of a nervous breakdown and she would have suffered further injury had she remained with him, on her petition for divorce, it was held that the husband's conduct amounted to cruelty.[191]

There have been comparable decisions in Hindu law. In *Sayal* v. *Sarala*,[192] the married life of the spouses was unhappy. The wife for the purpose of improving their marital happiness administered a love potion to her husband. As a result the husband became ill with slow fever, giddiness and ultimately a nervous breakdown with vomitings, loss of weight, abdominal burning, backache, heart trouble and various other complications. On the husband's petition for judicial separation on the ground of his wife's cruelty, it was held that the crucial point to determine was whether there was reasonable apprehension in the mind of the husband of a similar act from his spouse in future. The husband's fear for the future was based on the instinct of self-preservation. The wife believing in the potency

190. *Marsh* v. *M.* (1858) 1 Sw. & Tr. 312 = 164 E.R. 744; see also F.W. Whitlock, "*Insanity, Drunkenness and Divorce*" (1964) 4 Medicine, Science and the Law 81 at 87.

191. *Baker* v. *B.* (1955) 3 All E.R. 193; J.M. Biggs, *The Concept of Matrimonial Cruelty*, pp. 127-130.

192. *Sayal* v. *Sarala*, A.I.R. 1961 Punj. 125 (cited above at p. 151) (the case is also a reflection on the social life of the people).

of the love potion had put the life of her husband in danger so he was held entitled to seek the protection of the court for the future. The husband was granted the decree, it being held that the court was not to wait for the recurrence of the peril to afford remedy to the petitioner. In another case the wife was beaten and turned out of the house. Once the husband lost his temper and slapped her face with the result that her nose began to bleed. She was held justified in apprehending that it would be harmful and injurious for her to live with her husband.[193]

In *Tulsibai* v. *Bhima*,[194] the wife petitioned for judicial separation on the ground of cruelty, alleging, when she cooked rice for him, the husband, on the pretence that it was not properly cooked, pierced her legs with a hot 'konchu' (an edged instrument used for cooking). When the injujuries started bleeding, chillies were put on the injured parts, so that it took 6 months for her to recover in her father's house. On an assurance of good behaviour being given by the brother of the husband, she returned to reside with the husband but she was again beaten and kicked so that one of her fingers was fractured. It was held that having faced these ordeals, she was likely to meet the same or graver type of trouble in the future. She was in need of protection from the recurrence of cruelty.

In *Kondal* v. *Ranganayaki*[195] the husband petitioned for restitution of conjugal rights in defence to which the wife pleaded cruelty. Devadoss, J., having in view the safety of the injured spouse said, "Before passing a decree in favour of the husband, the court should be satisfied that, by giving its aid to him, it does not thereby endanger the life, limb, liberty or the health of the wife. If there is danger to any of these, the court would be amply justified in refusing to grant a decree for restitution."

193. *Mt. Padama* v. *Parma*, A.I.R. 1959 Pr. 37.

194. *Tulsibai* v. *Bhima*, I.L.R. 1961 Madh. Pr. 292; see also *Tulsa* v. *Pannalal*, A.I.R. 1963 Madh. Pr. 5. A case on cruelty, where the wife was beaten for getting up late in the morning. She was neglected and not given proper food and clothing.

195. *Kondal* v. *Ranganayaki* (1923) 46 Mad. 791, 807=A.I.R. 1924 Mad. 49.

Similarly in *Putal* v. *Gopi*[196] it was held that where defence to a petition for restitution of conjugal rights is based on cruelty, the court interferes not to punish the husband for what he has done but to protect the wife for the future, so the important question is whether the wife can with safety to life and health live with the husband.

In *Mango* v. *Prem*[197] the husband petitioned for restitution of conjugal rights to which the wife pleaded, cruelty as just cause for living separate from her husband, alleging maltreatment and legal cruelty by the husband and his father, the latter having the intention to enjoy her personally. She also alleged that her husband wanted her to submit to others. It was held that the wife was fully justified in living apart from the husband, as it was not safe for her to live in the house of her husband, where her father-in-law was suspected of intending to outrage her modesty. Likewise in *Ram* v. *Dev*[198] on the husband's petition alleging desertion, the wife pleaded cruelty as just cause, alleging that the husband's father had made improper overtures to her. He had asked her to massage him and to remove her veil. She complained to her husband, who resented it and beat her. It was held that she had just cause for living separate on account of the conduct and treatment of the husband and his father.

It is clear from these cases that the object of granting matrimonial relief is to protect the injured spouse. In the earlier English cases if the suffering party was not in any danger of life or health no remedy was granted, e.g., in *Dysart* v. *D.*,[199] decided over a century ago, a wife pleaded cruelty in defence to her husband's petition for restitution of conjugal rights. She failed on the ground that the evidence did not warrant "that a return to cohabitation would expose to danger or reasonable risk thereof, the personal safety of the lady."

Relief will be granted not only to protect a spouse from

196. *Putal* v. *Gopi*, A.I.R. 1963 Pat. 93.
197. *Mango* v. *Prem*. A.I.R. 1962 All. 447.
198. *Ram* v. *Dev*, A.I.R. 1950 E. Punj. 317.
199. Per Dr. Lushington in *Dysart* v. *D.* (1844) 1 Rob. Ecc. 106= 163 E.R. 980 at 993.

physical injury but also from danger to mental health. In *Atkins* v. *A.*,[200] the court intervened when the nagging and bickering was of such a kind and so constant as to endanger the health of the spouse on whom it was inflicted. In *Kamla* v. *Amar*[201] cruelty was found when the husband made false allegations against the wife's chastity, involving her in a criminal case, which affected her reputation and her health. The protection of the health and safety of the spouse is the guiding principle. Physical violence is not the sole ingredient of cruelty. It may be physical or mental. Anguish of mind may be more severe than bodily pain and a husband disposed to evil may cause more misery to a sensitive and affectionate wife by a course of conduct addressed only to the mind than, if, in fits of anger, he were to inflict occasional blows upon her person.[202] In *Pancho* v. *Ram*[203] the wife alleged that she was ill-treated and turned out of the house and the husband had remarried. It was held by Roy, J., that continuous ill-treatment, cessation of marital intercourse, studied neglect, indifference on the part of the husband and an assertion on the part of the husband that the wife is unchaste are all factors which may undermine the health of a wife. In such cases it would not be unreasonable to hold that the wife may legitimately apprehend that, if she goes back to her husband, there will be a repetition of such conduct, which may result in a complete breakdown of her health. When a husband habitually insults his wife and behaves towards her with neglect and unkindness, so as to impair her health, he must be held to be guilty of cruelty.

The earlier English cases cited above emphasise the need of protection for the injured party. Though protection is still the object which a court seeks to achieve by granting redress, in *Swan* v. *S.*[204] Hodson, L. J., said, "I can find nothing in the old authorities to justify the proposition that a decree based on cruelty is a remedy given not for a wrong inflicted but solely

200. *Atkins* v. *A.* (1942) 2 All E.R. 637.

201. *Kamla* v. *Amar*, A.I.R. 1961 J. & K. 33; see also *Umri Bai* v. *Chittar*, A.I.R. 1966 Madh. Pr. 205.

202. *Sarah Abraham* v. *Pyali Abraham*, A.I.R. 1959 Ker. 75.

203. *Pancho* v. *Ram*, A.I.R. 1956 All. 41, 43.

204. Hodson, L.J., in *Swan* v. *S.* (1953) p. 258 at 267 (C.A.).

as a protection for the victim." Disaproving *Lissack* v. *L.*[205] he continued, "To treat cruelty in the light only of need for protection would be to take it out of the realm of matrimonial oal offences altogather, which is not, to my mind, consistent with the language of the legislature nor with the decisions of the ecclesiastical courts which have laid the foundations of the law on the topic."

The object of matrimonial relief is twofold; on this view it relates to both the spouses. The injured spouse is protected from further cruelty and the offending is punished by loss of right to consortium. A century ago Sir James Wilde, later Lord Penzance, in *Hall* v. *H.*[206] said, "Though the object of this court's interference is safety for the future, its sentence carries with it some retribution for the past. "Twenty years ago in *Meacher* v. *M.*[207], though the wife was not likely to suffer cruelty in the future, it was held by the Court of Appeal that cruelty in the past was sufficient to entitle her to a decree of divorce. But *Meacher* v. *M.* (supra) was criticised in *Jamieson* v. *J.*[208] by Lord Merriman in the House of Lords in the following words, "When the legal conception of cruelty is described as being conduct of such a character as to cause danger to life, limb, or health bodily or mental or a reasonable apprehension thereof, it is vital to bear in mind that it comprises two distinct elements; first the ill-treatment complained of, and secondly the resultant danger or apprehension thereof. Thus it is inaccurate and liable to lead to confusion, if the word 'cruelty' is used as descriptive only of the conduct complained of, apart from its effects on the victim."

In the recent case of *Williams* v. *W.*,[209] Willmer, L.J., said, "It must now be accepted, I think, that cruelty as understood in this context contains both a subjective and objective element. The contrary view, namely, that relief is granted, not for a

205. *Lissack* v. *L.* (1951) p. 1.

206. Sir James Wilde (Lord Penzance) in *Hall* v. *H.* (1864) 3 Sw. & Tr. 347. 349 = 164 E.R. 1309-1310.

207. *Meacher* v. *M.* (1946) 2 All E.R. 307 (C.A.)

208. Lord Merriman in *Jamieson* v. *J.* (1952) A.C. 525, 545, H.L.; see also C.K. Allen "*Matrimonial Cruelty*" (1957) 73 L.Q.R., pp. 325-327.

209. *Williams* v. *W.* (1962) 3 All E.R. at 447 (C.A.).

wrong inflicted, but solely as a protection for the victim, so that only the impact on the innocent spouse of the conduct complained of has to be considered, is no longer open to us since the decision of Pearce, J., in *Lissack* v. *L.*[210] was overruled by this court in *Swan* v. *S.*[211]

On appeal to the House of Lords the decision was reversed. *Lissack* v. *L.* (supra) was approved and *Swan* v. *S.* (supra) not followed. It was held that the test was an objective one, i.e., the question whether actions are cruel must be judged wholly objectively, that is to say, whether the act complained of would be regarded by any reasonable man if done by one ordinary person to another as being cruel to the spouse affected.[212] The test is not whether a spouse is cruel, but whether his conduct as affecting the victim is cruel from a reasonable man's point of view. The principle that the court's duty is to protect the injured spouse as applied in *Lissack* v. *L.* (supra) is maintained. From the victim's point of view the pain is the same whether suffering is caused by accident or by the act of the madman.[213]

In *P.* v. *P.*[214] a wife petitioned for divorce on the ground of her husband's cruelty, alleging that her husband refrained from sexual intercourse with her, in spite of her requests, so that her health suffered. Her evidence showed that he was not interested in women at all and had no desire for sexual life. There was no evidence that he was cruel to her in any other respect. The wife's health had suffered largely from the unnatural life she lived over the years. It was held that cruelty was not established as the husband had no control over the absence of his sexual desire. *Gollins* v. *G.*[215] was distinguished on the ground that it proceeded on the basis of inexcusable conduct of the husband, because he could control his conduct to the extent of working and providing maintenance for his

210. *Lissack* v. *L.* (1951) p. 1.
211. *Swan* v. *S.* (1953) p. 258 (C A.).
212. Per Lord Evershed in *Williams* v. *W.* (1963) 2 All E.R. 994. H.L.
213. Lord Hodson in *Williams* v. *W.* (1963) 2 All E.R. 994, 1010. H.L.
214. *P.* v. *P.* (1964) 3 All E.R. 919.
215. *Gollins* v. *G.* (1963) 2 All E.R. 966, H.L.

wife but he did not do so with cruel consequences on his wife. But if *Williams* v. *W.*,[216] where cruelty had resulted from the insanity of the husband, over which he had no control, was rightly decided, *P.* v. *P.* (supra) seems to be wrong. In the latter although the husband had not intended to be cruel, his abstinence from sexual intercourse had cruel effects on the health of the wife.

In a case of cruelty the petitioner must prove that his health has suffered injury from the conduct of the offending party. Thus in a recent case of *P.* v. *P.*[217] (1965), a husband petitioned for divorce on the ground of cruelty, alleging that his wife refused to permit sexual intercourse or to have a child. The husband's health had been materially prejudiced in consequence and the situation was such as the husband should not be called upon to endure. It had been brought about by the wife's deep-rooted fear of cenception, not through any intention to injure the husband or selfishness or indifference on her part. Applying a dictum of Lord Reid[218] to the effect, that no one would now maintain that cruelty cannot be proved against a person whose acts are sufficiently grave and really imperil the other spouse so as the latter is in need of protection, it was held that the fact that the wife's conduct was not her fault, being due to neurosis, even if she was unaware of it, could not prevent a finding of cruelty in law. The need for protection lay at the root of the problem. Thus the principle that the object of the court is to protect the injured spouse is as important today as it was in the earlier cases and the punishment of the guilty spouse by loss of consortium is incidental. The fact, that the break-up of a marriage is regarded less seriously today than it was a hundred years ago, has not added any qualification to it.[219]

7. *INSANITY AS A DEFENCE TO CRUELTY*

The principle that the court acts to protect the injured spouse is of particular importance when the petitioner complains

216. *Williams* v. *W.* (1963) 2 All E.R. 994, H.L.

217. *P.* v. *P.* (1965) 1 W.L.R. 963.

218. Lord Reid in *Williams* v. *W.* (1963) 2 All E.R. 994, 1004, H.L. (1964) AC. 698, 722.

219. Lord Evershed in *Williams* v. *W.* (1963) 2 All E.R. 994 at 1009.

of ill-treatment by an insane partner. In *Hayward* v. *H.*,[220] decided over a century ago, the husband turned his wife out of his house, because she was deranged and dangerous due to her insanity, She petitioned for restitution of conjugal rights and the husband raised the defence of her insanity. Cresswell, J.O., gave the following decision, "I find no authority for holding that that is an answer to a claim for restitution of conjugal rights. A husband is not entitled to turn a lunatic wife out of doors. He may be rather bound to place her in proper custody, but he is not entitled to turn her out of his house. He is less than ever justified in putting her away, if she has the misfortune to be insane.'"

The wife's insanity was accepted as a defence to cruelty and the need to protect the husband was ignored. A few years later in *Hall* v. *H.*,[221] though it was held that the motives of the cruel conduct of the husband are immaterial so far as the protection of the victim is concerned, an exception was recognised in case of insanity. Wilde, J.O., said, "I have no doubt that cruelty does not cease to be a cause of suit if it proceeded from 'violent and disorderly affections' as said in one case, or from 'violence of disposition, want of moral control or eccentricity' as said in another, or from a 'liability to become excited in a controversy' in the language of another; but madness, dementia, positive disease of the mind, this is quite another matter. An insane man is likely enough to be dangerous to his wife's ersonald safety, but the remedy lies in the restraint of the husband, not the release of the wife." This recognised a distinction between insanity and such defects as violence of disposition, want of moral control and eccentricity which are no defence to cruelty, because protection can be afforded by the confinement of the lunatic.

This was followed in *Hanbury* v. *H.*,[222] where a distinction was drawn between permanent insanity and recurrent fits of

20. Cresswell, J.O., in *Hayward* v. *H.* (1858) 1 Sw. & Tr. 81 = 164 E.R. 639.

221. Lord Penzance (Sir James Wilde) in *Hall* v. H. (1864) 3 Sw. Tr. 347 at 349 = 164 E.R. 1309.

222. *Hambury* v. *H.* (1892) p. 222; on appeal (1892) 8 T.L.R. 559.

insanity. The same distinction appears in *Astle* v. *A.*,[223] where Henn Collins, J., said, "If the insanity were such as to require permanent restraint, then and then only, would a decree be refused", the lunacy laws being assumed to afford a sufficient protection. In *Astle* v. *A.* (supra) the husband had been guilty of violent attacks on the wife. He was certified insane. On his discharge and when not under certification, he came home and threatened his wife with violence telling her that he had decided to kill her and commit suicide. She was terribly alarmed and sought police protection. Ultimately she petitioned on the ground of cruelty, to which the husband raised the defence of insanity. It was held that insanity was a defence only if it came within the M'Naghten-rules, i.e., at the time of the committing of the act, the party at fault must be labouring under such a defect of reason, from disease of the mind, as not to know the nature and quality of the act he was doing or, if he did know it, that he did not know he was doing what was wrong. Applying the M'Naghten rules, it was found that the husband was insane during the earlier violent attacks but sane at the time of the threatened violence to his wife and the family, so the wife got a decree of divorce. Henn Collins,[224] J., applied M'Naghten rules simply because in his opinion 'the' test applied in all other courts', but these rules were only applied in criminal courts to charges of homicide. They are not applicable in cases of contract or tort.

The M'Naghten rules apply to criminal law, the object of which is quite different from matrimonial law. In criminal law the standard of proof is based on the balance of probabilities and the accused is given the benefit of the doubt. The range of mental disorders is so variable that it is difficult to apply the rules to all sorts of mental defectives. Therefore, they do not cover insanity accurately and scientifically.[225]

223. *Astle* v. *A.* (1939) P. 415; this was followed in *Robins* v. *R.* (1960) 3 All E.R. 66. Where M'Naghten rules were applied.

224. The decision of Henn Collins, J., in *Astle* v. *A.* (1939)p. 415 was vigorously criticised in '*Insanity as a Defence to Cruelty*' (1940) 189 Law Times 342 (Journal and Record); '*Cruelty and Insanity*' (1947) 204 Law Times 281 (Journal and Record).

225. See also F.W. Whitlock "*Insanity, Drunkenness and Divorce*" (1964) 4 Medicine, Science and the the Law 81; H. Tarlo, "*Intention and Insanity in Divorce Law*" (1963) 37 Aust. L.J. 3 at pp. 16-19.

The M'Naghten[226] rules are substantially reproduced in section 84 of the Indian Penal Code, which is as follows, "Nothing is an offence which is done by a person who, at the time of doing it, by reason of unsoundness of mind, is incapable of knowing the nature of the act, or that he is doing what is either wrong or contrary to law." and apply to any criminal charge. As in England so in India[227] the M'Naghten rules have been criticised on the ground that they were devised at a time when there was not enough scientific knowledge of mental disorders to make it possible to devise a satisfactory test of criminal responsibility. Modern psychiatrists recognise the importance of emotional, as opposed to rational, influences in determining behaviour. This knowledge puts a medical witness in a difficult position when he is obliged to apply the M'Naghten rules to a question of responsibility for conduct. He feels frustrated when he fails to convince the court that, although the accused person concerned is not insane by the M'Naghten rules, he is not mentally normal in medical opinion, and thinks the law should be amended so as to take modern psychiatric opinion into account. There are mental conditions and psychopathic disorders falling short of insanity which deserve consideration for exemption from criminal responsibility. The words 'reason', 'quality', 'nature', 'know', and 'wrong' in the M'Naghten rules cannot be clearly defined by a medical specialist. Thus to define 'sanity' and 'insanity' is a difficult task.

In *White* v. *W.*[228] the wife had been very violent to her husband. She had physically attacked him; had falsely accused him of adultery, and eventually she was certified and confined. The husband petitioned for divorce on the ground of cruelty. The Court of Appeal held that the mere fact that the respondent was insane, at the time she committed the acts of cruelty is no defence. Bucknill and Asquith, L.JJ., agreed that it cannot be affirmed that no type or degree of insanity

226. M'Naghten rules (1843) 10 Cl. & F. 200=8 E.R 718.

227. H.S. Mehta in *Contributions to Synthetic Jurisprudence*, edited by M.J. Sethna, Bombay, 1962, pp. 216-220, and also pp. [illegible]2-260.

228. *White* v. *W.* (1950) p. 39 (C.A.).

can excuse acts which in a sane person, would amount to cruelty. But for the defence of insanity to succeed, the insanity must at all events, not fall short of such insanity as is covered by the M'Naghten rules in a criminal defence. Thus *Astle* v. *A.*[229] was approved on that point. Applying the M'Naghten rules the wife was held to be sane. Denning, L.J., came to the same conclusion but for different reasons. He found the wife insane by the M'Naghten rules and proceeded on the basis whether insanity was a defence to cruelty. He expressed the view that the primary purpose of the matrimonial law was to give relief to the injured spouse from a situation which had become intolerable, and not to punish the offender. The fact that the respondent suffered from mental disease made this relief more and not less necessary.[230] He was averse to introducing the tests of criminal into civil law.

Lord Denning's view was followed in *Lissack* v. *L.*,[231] where a wife alleged that her husband had killed the only child of the marriage and had attempted to commit suicide. These events greatly shocked her. To her charge of cruelty, the husband raised the defence of insanity, which was rejected on the ground that such a defence to a petition based on cruelty was not in accord with the true view of the law relating to cruelty. Pearce, J., maintained that matrimonial relief is intended not to punish the guilty spouse but to protect the injured one from the danger and said, "To withdraw from the ambit of cruelty, conduct which is intolerable, but is due to insanity, is to make the court powerless to help in cases where help may be most needed." It was held that insanity was not a defence, and even if it were, the husband was not insane by M'Naghten rules.

The decision is in consonance with the earlier case law emphasising the court's duty to protect the injured party but it was overruled by the Court of Appeal in *Swan* v. *S.*,[232] where

229. *Astle* v. *A.* (1939) p. 415.

230. Lord Denning in *White* v. *W.* (1950) p. 39, 57 (C.A.).

231. *Lissack* v. *L.* (1951) p. 1. 7; commented on in "*Insanity as a Defence to Cruelty*" (1951) 14 M.L.R. 86.

232. *Swan* v. *S.* (1953) p. 258, 267 (C.A.).

the husband had been a voluntary patient in a mental hospital. The wife sought a divorce, alleging cruelty, to which the husband raised the defence of insanity. It was held that one spouse cannot be said to have been treated with cruelty by the other, when the other was at the time suffering from such a defect of reason, from disease of the mind as not to know the nature and quality of the acts complained of.

The first limb of the M'Naghten rules was applied in *Swan* v. *S.* (supra) but the Court of Appeal was divided as to the application of the second limb but, as Hodson, L. J., said, "The two branches of the rule have hitherto always been treated together and I am not satisfied that in civil, as opposed to criminal matters, they can properly be treated in isolation from one another."[233] The Court was, however, unanimous in holding that insanity was a defence.

The question of insanity came up again in *Palmer* v. *P.*[234], where the insame husband had imputed unchastity to his wife and had violently assaulted her on a number of occasions. It was held that he knew what he was doing and knew it was wrong and both limbs of the M'Naghten rules applied. Lord Goddard, C.J., could "see no good reason for saying that when one is dealing with insanity and the inflcting of personal injury or assaults upon another, there should be any difference between the rule applied by the Divorce Division and in the criminal courts."

The principle, that insanity is a defence, laid down by the Court of Appeal, was qualified by the House of Lords in *Williams* v. *W.*,[235] which held that insanity is not necessarily

233. Hodson, L.J., in *Swan* v. *S.*, supra, at p. 268; see comments in (1954) 17 M.L.R. 76; (1953) 69 L.Q.R. 439; (1953) 216 Law Times 587 (Journal and Record).

234. *Palmer* v. *P.* (1955) p. 4, 7, 9 (C.A.); commented on in (1955) 71 L.Q.R. 11; both *Swan* v. *S.* (supra) and *Palmer* v. *P.* were followed in *Elphinstone* v. *E.* (1962) 2 All E.R. 766; commented on in (1962) 106 Sol. Jour. 377-378.

235. *Williams* v. *W.* (1963) 2 All E.R. 994, H.L.; see also R. Lowe, "*A New Look at Cruelty*" (1963) 113 The Law Journal 731, and also at pp. 473-474; A. Samuels, "*Cruelty and Mental Illness*" (1963) 2 Solicitor Quarterly 97; S.P. Khetarpal, "*Cruelty and Insanity in Divorce Law*" (1964) Malayan Law Journal at p. LXXX; M. Puxon, "*The Changing Face of Cruelty*" (1962)

a defence. In that case the husband had injured the health of his wife by deliberately accusing her of adulterous association but he thought that such accusations were justified because he believed that they were true, having been induced to think so by imaginary voices, which informed him of them as fact. The wife petitioned for divorce on the ground of cruelty. On appeal from the Court of Appeal on the point that the second limb of the M'Naghton rules applied, the House of Lords held that the fact, that the husband did not know that his acts were wrong, did not of itself constitute the defence to cruelty. Reversing the decision of the Court of Appeal it was held that insanity, within the scope of the M'Naghten rules, that is to say when, owing to disease of the mind, the spouse at fault was unaware of the nature and quality of his or her acts, or if aware of that, did not know the acts to be wrong, is not necessarily a defence to a suit for divorce on the ground of cruelty but insanity is a factor to be taken into account in applying the test, (which Lord Evershed said was an objective one) whether in all the circumstances of the case the respondent's conduct is of such gravity that he has by his acts treated the petitioner with cruelty. If the conduct were such that it would not amount to cruelty in the absence of an actual intention to hurt, an insane spouse, who could not form such an intention, would not be guilty of cruelty. Where, however, the conduct would be held to be cruelty, regardless of motive or intention to be cruel, insanity should not bar relief.[236]

The decision is a remarkable one. By the approval of *Lissack* v. *L.*[237] the theory of protection was revived. In the opinion of Asquith, L.J., in *White* v. *W.*[238] to the effect, that the sole object of granting matrimonial relief in cases of cruelty is the protection of the victim, who is just as much injured or im-

106 Sol. Jour. 600; A.L. Goodhart, "*Cruelty, Desertion and Insanity in Matrimonial Law*" (1963) 79 L.Q.R. 98 at pp. 116-125; L. Neville Brown, "*Cruelty without Culpability or Divorce without Fault*" (1963) 26 M.L.R. 625 at pp. 635-646.

236. Lord Pearce in *Williams* v. *W.* (1963) 2 All E.R. at p. 1029.

237. *Lissack* v. *L.* (1951) p. 1.

238. Asquith, L.J., in *White* v. *W.* (1950) p. 39, 51 (C.A.).

perillied by the acts of the mad spouse as by those of one who is sane, found support in the words of Lord Hodson who said, "From the victim's point of view the pain is the same, whether suffering is caused by accident or by the act of the madman."[392] Punishment is clearly not the object of matrimonial law, although some punishment automatically ensues as a by-product of the decree, for the guilty party loses the right of consortium in judicial separation and severence of the marriagebond by divorce.

The duty of the court to protect a spouse from injury is as clear as it was one hundred years ago,[240] In the words of Lord Reid, "No one would now maintain that cruelty cannot be proved against a person, if his acts are sufficiently grave and really imperil the other spouse. It is often untrue that such a man is able to exert his reason so as to control his acts in the normal way or even that he is capable of forming a rational decision about them. Yet these are often the cases where the other spouse is most in need of protection..The test of culpability has broken down..In my judgement a decree should be pronounced against a person, not because his conduct was aimed at his wife, nor because a reasonable man realised the position, nor because he must be deemed to have foreseen or intended the harm he did, but simply because the facts are such that, after making all allowances for his disabilities and for the temperaments of both parties, it must be held that the character and gravity of his acts was such as to amount to cruelty."[241]

This of course was logically sound, because, once it had been established in *Gollins* v. *G.*,[242] that intention is not a necessary ingredient of cruelty, it followed automatically that insanity cannot be a defence. This, however, does not mean that intention is irrelevant. The state of mind is a question of fact. It is open to a court to find cruelty against an insane spouse, whether or not such insanity falls within the M'Naghten rules. The test is an objective one, namely, whether, in all the cir-

239. Lord Hodson in *Williams* v. *W.* supra, at p. 1019.
240. Lord Evershed in *Williams* v. *W.* (1963) 2 All E.R. at p. 1009.
241. Lord Reid in *Williams* v. *W.*, supra, at p. 1004.
242. *Gollins* v. *G.*, (1963) 2 All E.R. 966, H.L.

cumstances of the case, it should fairly be said that the spouse charged has treated the other with cruelty.[243]

The conduct complained of has to be judged in relation to the parties, taking account of their individual characters and temperaments; the assessment of this conduct has to be made from the reasonable man's point of view, i.e., the question is whether a reasonable man who had witnessed the scene would come to the conclusion that the victim had been treated with cruelty.

It should be noted that *Williams* v. *W.*[244] was concerned with cruelty. The position of insanity as a defence to a charge of adultery[245] or desertion[246] remains unchanged, as the considerations applicable to these cases are different from those applicable to cruelty.[247] Both at Hindu and English law the complaining spouse must show that the conduct complained of is sufficiently grave and weighty to amount to cruelty, and that he has suffered injury to health, or has a reasonable apprehension of such an injury. Intent to injure, if it exists, is relevant to prove the gravity of the offence, but is not an essential ingredient of cruelty.

The question of insanity came up in the recent case of *Bhagwat* v. *B.*,[248] where the husband got into financial difficulties and lost his job. This shocked him so much that the balance of his mind was disturbed and he was admitted to a mental hospital. After his discharge he used to quarrel with his wife and beat the children of the marriage without any reason. He would sit for hours doing nothing and he refused to let his wife

243. Lord Evershed in *Williams* v. *W.* (1963) 2 All E.R. at p. 1009.

244. *Williams* v. *W.* (1963) 2 All E.R. 994, H.L.

245. *S.* v. *S.* (1962) p. 133 (insanity is a defence to a charge of adultery).

246. *Perry* v. *P.* (1964) 1 W.L.R. 91. Where a wife left her husband's home and never returned, because she suffered from delusions that the husband intended to murder her, that he had broken her shoulder, and that he carried on adulterous associations with various women. She was suffering from paranoid psychosis so she had not the mental capacity to form the intention to desert. She had established plea of insanity and this was a valid defence to a charge of desertion.

247. R. Lowe, "*A New Look at Cruelty*" (1963) 113 Law Journal at pp. 732-733.

248. *Bhagwat* v. *B.*, A.I.R. 1967 Bom. 80.

take any employment to support the family. When a marriage took place in the home of his wife's parents, he wished to give a present to the bridegroom but he could not afford it because of his financial difficulties. This completely upset him, with the result that his mind became deranged. He was again admitted to the mental hospital as a voluntary patient. After some months he was discharged but he continued to be erratic, eccentric and moody. Later he started teaching students, one of whom was Suresh, a brother of his wife. One day he was explaining a problem but, being unabe to find a solution, he started shouting. Suresh brought him home. The same night he tried to strangle Suresh by squeezing his neck. On the following morning he pounced on his own child and tried to strangle it. The same day he was sent to the mental hospital.

The wife continued to live in the matrimonial home until she learned that the husband was to be discharged, when she went to her parents' home. The husband asked her to return, but she refused and petitioned for a decree of judicial separation, alleging that the husband had wilfully deserted her over the statutory period and that he had treated her with such cruelty as to cause reasonable apprehension in her mind that it was harmful for her to live with him. The trial court held that desertion was not proved and that, since the husband's alleged cruelty took place while he was insane, she was not entitled to relief under S. 10(1)(b) of the Hindu Marriage Act, Act, 1955. She appealed and succeeded, it being held by the appellate court, that taking an overall view of the conduct of the husband and the peculiar circumstances under which he was placed, his behaviour amounted to legal cruelty. The husband filed a second appeal to the High Court.

Relying on the English decisions,[249] he pleaded the M'Naghten rules, but in vain, It was held by Naik, J., that the conduct of the husband was such as to amount to cruelty within the meaning of the statute, regardless of his motive or intention and that insanity was not a defence to a plea of cruelty.[250]

249. *Swan* v. *S.* (1953) p. 258, C.A.; *Palmer* v. *P.* (1955) p. 4, C.A

250. Reliance was placed on the celebrated cases of the House of Lords in *Williams* v. *W.* (1963) 2 All E.R. 994 and *Gollins* v. *G.* (1963) 2 All E.R. 966.

The apprehensions entertained by the wife were well founded, as there was no certainty when the husband would relapse into a state of schizophrenia, in which case any thing might happen. Therefore the wife was entitled to a decree of judicial separation.

Chapter VII

INSANITY

1. *INSANITY AS A GROUND FOR RELIEF IN MATRIMONIAL CAUSES*

At English law either spouse can petition for divorce[1] or judicial separation[2] on the ground that the respondent is incurably of unsound mind and has been continuously under care and treatment for at least five years immediately preceding the presentation of the petition. Under S. 1 (3) of the (English) Matrimonial Causes Act, 1965, for the purposes of this section, a person of unsound mind shall be deemed to be under care and treatment while,

(a) he is liable to be detained in a hospital, mental nursing home or place of safety under the Mental Health Act, 1959 or in a hospital or place of safety under the Mental Health (Scotland) Act, 1960;

(b) he is detained in pursuance of an order for his detention or treatment as a person of unsound mind or a person suffering from mental illness made under any law for the time being in force in Northern Ireland, the Isle of Man or any of the Channel Islands (including any such law relating to criminal lunatics) or is receiving treatment as a voluntary patient under any law so in force;

(c) he is receiving treatment for mental illness as a resident in—

(i) a hospital or other institution provided, approved, licensed, registered or exempted from registration by any Minister or other authority in the United Kingdom, the Isle of Man or the Channel Islands; or

(ii) a hospital or other institution in any other country, being a hospital or institution in which his treatment is com-

1. S. 1 (1) (d) of the (English) Matrimonial Causes Act, 1950, re-enacted in S. 1 (1) (a) (iv) of the (English) Matrimonial Causes Act, 1965.

2. S. 14 (1) of the (English) Matrimonial Causes Act, 1950, re-enacted in S. 12 (1) (a) of the (English) Matrimonial Causes Act, 1965.

parable with the treatment provided in any such hospital or institution as is mentioned in (i) above; and in determining whether any period of care and treatment has been continuous, any interruption of the period for twentyeight days or less shall be disregarded.

S. 13 (i) (iii) of the Hindu Marriage Act, 1955 allows divorce on the ground of incurable unsoundness of mind for a continuous period of not less than three years immediately preceding the presentation of the petition. This section has to be distinguished from S. 10 (e)[3], under which either spouse may petition for a decree of judicial separation on the ground of the other's unsoundness of mind for a continuous period of not less than two years. Here the word 'incurable' has been omitted. On the construction of the sentence it is evident that mere unsoundness of mind (whether curable or incurable) for a continuous period of two years entitles the petitioner to judicial separation. However, if the spouses after such separation fail to resume cohabitation for a period of two years, either spouse can petition for divorce.[4] Thus the importance of the provision of S. 13 (1) (iii) that the unsoundness has to be incurable is in practice much reduced.[5] The expression 'incurably unsound mind' cannot be so widely interpreted as to cover feeble-minded persons or persons of dull intellect who understand the nature and consequences of their acts, and are therefore, able to control themselves and manage their affairs.[5a]

Under S. 10 (1) (d) of the (Kenya) Hindu Marriage and Divorce Ordinance, 1960, a petition for divorce may be presented by either spouse on the ground that the respondent is incurably of unsound mind and has been continuously under care and treatment for a period of at least five years immediately preceding the presentation of the petition. Under S. 10 (2),[6] for the purpose of this section a person of unsound mind shall be deemed to be under care and treatment while he is detained, whether in the colony or elsewhere, in an institution duly

3. Hindu Marriage Act, 1955; *Mehta* v. *Vasumati*, A.I.R. 1969 Guj. 48.

4. S. 13 (1) (viii) of the Hindu Marriage Act, 1955 as amended by the Hindu Marriage Act, 1964.

5. S. V. Gupte, *Hindu Law of Marriage*, Bombay, 1961, p. 196.

5a. *Mehta* v. *Vasumati*, A.I.R. 1969 Guj. 48.

6. The (Kenya) Hindu Marriage and Divorce Ordinance, 1960.

recognised by the government as an institution for the care and treatment of insane persons, lunatics or mental defectives or is detained as a criminal lunatic under any law for the time being in force in the colony. A certificate under the hand of the minister that any place is a duly recognised institution for the purpose of this section shall be received in all courts as conclusive evidence of that fact.

The English and Kenya statutes provide relief on the ground of insanity only when it is sufficiently grave to require care and treatment, which is not the test prescribed in the Hindu Marriage Act, 1955. This is probably due to the fact that facilities for treatment of mental disease in India are inadequate. H. S. Mehta[7] points out that people who suffer from mental disorders, though not dangerous to themselves or others, psychopaths, imbeciles and idiots, who suffer from retarded mental development or feeblemindedness are detained in mental hospitals, where they have no opportunity for proper mental treatment and rehabilitation and are reduced to a worse psychotic condition than when they entered.

The law presumes sanity, so the burden of proving that the respondent is of incurably unsound mind is on the petitioner.[8] But if the respondent has been judicially declared insane, it shifts to the respondent. In *Snook* v. *Watts*[9] aftera bill to foreclose, the mortgagor was found lunatic by inquisition, at a date over-reaching the mortgage deed. At the hearing an issue was directed as to his sanity at the date of the mortgage. It was held that the finding of the jury upon a commission of lunacy, that a party is a lunatic, throws the burden of proof on those who contend the contrary. This was followed in *Seshamma* v. *Padamanabha*,[10] where the question related to the properties and adoption of a lunatic. It was held that the effect of an adjudication under the (Indian) Lunacy Act (No. XXXV) of 1858, that a person is a lunatic is to raise a pre-

7. H. S. Mehta in *Contributions to Synthetic Jurisprudence*, edited by M. J. Sethna, Bombay, 1962, pp. 212-214.

8. *Swettenham* v. *S.* (1938) p. 218; *Mahomed* v. *Abdul*, A.I.R. 1923 Pat. 187 (the person who relies on the unsoundness of mind must prove it).

9. *Snook* v. *Watts* (1848) 11 Beav. 105=50 E.R. 757.

10. *Seshamma* v. *Padamanabha* (1917) 40 Mad. 660; D.H. Chaudhari, *The Hindu Marriage Act*, 1955, Calcutta, 1957, p. 228.

sumption, that he continued to be of unsound mind until the contrary is shown. Similarly in *Mohanlal* v. *Vinayak*[11] in which the validity of a deed was in dispute it was laid down that though the onus of proving insanity is in the first place on the person who alleges it, the normal presumption being of sanity, once it has been established that the person is usually of unsound mind the burden of proof is on the party who alleges that the document was executed during a lucid interval.

2. *THE TEST OF UNSOUNDNESS OF MIND*

There must be medical evidence to the effect that the respondent is incurably of unsound mind. "Incurable" is tantamount to "irrecoverable". In *Swettenham* v. *S.*[12] the respondent was suffering from insanity of a confusional type and had a history of intermittent outbreaks of mania, dementia and hysteria; her conversation was rambling, erratic and at times quite incoherent, inconsistent and irrational; it was held that she was irrecoverably of unsound mind. In *Greer* v. *G.*[13] the medical superintendent of the mental hospital, in which the wife had been a certified patient suffering from schizophrenia, expressed the opinion that it was most unlikely that she would make a full social recovery. A consultant psychiatrist stated that she was an improved, 'burnt out' schizophrenic, still showing residue of illness, for which there was no medical cure; her condition unlikely to be substantially improved by further rehabilitation and retraining and she would remain of unsound mind. It was held that the wife was incurably of unsound mind. It was also pointed out that in view of the advancement in recent years in the treatment of mental disorders, changes which were reflected in the law effected by the Mental Health Act, 1959, the relatively slight evidence of incurability, which would have sufficed twenty years ago to establish the ground for relief, could no longer be safely relied upon.

English decisions on the point of medical examination of the alleged lunatic can have no application in cases arising under the Hindu Marriage Act, 1955, because under the Matri-

11. *Mohanlal* v. *Vinayak*, A.I.R. 1941 Nag. 251.
12. *Swettenham* v. *S.* (1938) p. 218.
13. *Greer* v. *G.* (1961) 105 Sol. Jour. 1011.

monial Causes Rules in England specific provision has been made for examination by medical inspectors. There is no such provision in India. In *Bipinchandra* v. *Madhurben*[14] a wife petitioned for divorce under S. 13 (1) (iii) of the Hindu Marriage Act, 1955, alleging that her husband had been insane for the last eleven years and his insanity was increasing day by day. His insanity was manifested by his breaking window-panes, his attempt to break doors and quarrels. She stated that his sense of discrimination between good and evil, right and wrong became less and less as time went on and had ultimately vanished. In 1949, when she had gone to her father's place, she was informed that her husband had run away and was not to be found. When he was found, his name and address had to be tattooed on his hand, so that, if he again ran away, he could be restored to his house. She also alleged that he was given electric shocks by a psychiatrist at Bombay.

In order to prove unsoundness of mind as required by law, she applied to the trial court for an order for compulsory medical examination of the husband. The learned trial judge said that it was necessary to find out whether the husband was of unsound mind and, if so, what was the nature of the insanity. As this could only be done by medical examination, he held that the court had inherent jurisdiction, even in the absence of a specific provision in the Code of Civil Procedure, to direct medical examination. He accordingly ordered that the husband be subjected to the medical examination to determine the unsoundness of his mind and whether this unsoundness was incurable or not.

The friends and relations of the husband did not desire him to be medically examined, so an application was filed to set aside the order for medical examination and it was contended on behalf of the husband that the learned judge had no jurisdication to pass an order to compel medical examination. It was argued that there was no provision either in the Hindu Marriage Act, 1955 or under the Code of Civil Procedure (which is made applicable to petitions filed under the Hindu Marriage Act, 1955 by S. 21 thereof), under which it would be open to the court to compel a party to be medically examin-

14. *Bipinchandra* v. *Madhurben*, A.I.R. 1963 Guj. 250.

ed. It was held that compulsion to undergo medical examination is an interference with the personal liberty of a citizen, which could only be interfered with by a penal enactment or law. There is no provision under the Hindu Marriage Act, 1955 or the rules framed thereunder or in the Code of Civil Procedure or the Indian Evidence Act or any other law, which would show any power in the court to compel any party to undergo medical examination. Medical examination for ascertaining the presence or the extent of insanity, even if it be mere questioning, is as much interference with personal liberty as a real physical interference such as the drawing of blood or the personal examination of the body.

In *Birendra* v. *Hemlata*,[15] a case in which the question whether a party was infected with syphilis arose, it was observed that the courts exercise wide discretion in ordering physical examination and always do so subject to such conditions as will afford protection from violence to natural delicacy and sensibility but it was not specifically laid down that a party under a court's order could have the other party compulsorily medically examined. In that case the party concerned did not object to a proper medical examination, so the question of compulsory examination did not arise. It is not open to a court to invoke section 151 of the Code of Civil Procedure for ordering a medical examination of a party without his consent.[16]

The fact that a party from ulterior motives adopts an obdurate and obstructive attitude does not render the courts helpless to counteract it. Where a party refuses to submit to a medical examination, in a case where the whole case depends on the state of his mind or body, it will be open to the court to draw an adverse inference or presumption against him. Such a party is on a par with the one who wrongfully withholds evidence in his possession. The adverse inference that may be drawn by any court is from the circumstances in each case and having regard to the refusal to let in the best evidence before the court.

Although medical evidence is the best way of proving

15. *Birendra* v. *Hemlata*, A.I.R. 1921 Cal. 459 (a case under the Indian Divorce Act, 1869).

16. *Ranganathan* v. *Chinna Lakashmi*, A.I.R. 1955 Mad. 546.

unsoundness of mind the court has the discretion to over-ride it. In *W.* v. *W.*[17] medical evidence was given to the effect that the husband was suffering from incurable paranoia and that he had delusions of suspicion and mistaken identity. It was held that the opinions of medical experts were in no sense conclusive, though they had to be given great weight. The court has to be satisfied that the unsoundness is in kind and degree within S. 1 (1) (d) of the (English) Matrimonial Causes Act, 1950. His Lordship agreed with the judgement of Phillimore, J., in *Whysall* v. *W.*[18] in holding that the proper test to be applied is that of a reasonable man in looking after his own affairs and the husband's capacity to lead a normal married life must be related to a wife who would receive him as a husband, the term 'incurably' being construed broadly.

In *Whysall* v. *W.* (supra) the husband was suffering from paranoid schizophrenia and was detained under care and treatment in a mental hospital. There was no sign of any lasting improvement in his condition but he had recently shown much improvement as a result of treatment with drugs. Medical evidence was given to the effect that, although there was no prospect, according to present medical knowledge, of full clinical recovery, there was possibility of some social recovery. It was even possible that the husband might be able to be discharged from hospital in about six months. But in case of his discharge, he would still have to continue taking drugs to maintain his recovery. His was a chronic case and there was no hope of more than a partial recovery, such as would enable him to live a life where he had the benefit of sympathetic supervision and care. His wife having petitioned for divorce on the ground of his incurable unsoundness of mind, it was held that there was no prospect of the husband's returning to a really normal life, where he could manage himself and his affairs. The test is whether by reason of his mental condition he is, according to the standard of a reasonable man, capable of managing himself and his affairs, and if not, whether he

17. *W.* v. *W.* (1962) 106 Sol. Jour. 450.

18. *Whysall* v. *W.* (1960) p. 52 at 66, 68; applied in *Robinson* v. *R.* (1964) 3 W.L.R. 935; see also Donald Blair, "*Proof in Matrimonial Proceedings: the Medical Aspect*" (1965) 5 Medicine, Science and the Law 65 at pp. 70-73.

can hope to be restored to a state in which he will be able to do so. The husband was found to be of incurably unsound mind, although there was some prospect of his partial recovery, which could be maintained by drugs and supervision by relations or friends. The intention of Parliament was to enable one spouse to obtain a dissolution of marriage when the mental incapability of the other, despite five years' treatment, was such as to make it impossible for them to live a normal married life together and when there was no prospect of any improvement in mental health which would make it possible for them to do so in the future. The state of mind envisaged was accordingly a degree of unsoundness or incapacity of mind properly called insanity.

But in *Chapman* v. *C.*[19] the wife's petition for divorce on the ground of her husband's incurable unsoundness of mind failed. In that case the husband was continuously under care and treatment first as a certified patient and later as a voluntary one. Later he left the hospital, the doctors being of the opinion that he was well enough to be discharged, if he continued to take a drug. It was held that the treatment ceased at this point, although he continued to take drugs on discharge. He was no longer subject of a reception order; was able substantially to control his condition by drugs; was able to work and earn wages. He was living normally at a Church Army hostel without any special supervision or care. The wife had failed to establish that the husband was incapable of managing himself and his affairs, including his ability to secure employment and his duties in society and as a husband.

The word 'incurable' has to be interpreted in the light of common sense and with regard to the popular understanding of the term. A person who has recovered from a severe mental or physical disease cannot always expect to enjoy a mind or body as robust or healthy as before. Nevertheless such a person is regarded as cured when he is discharged from hospital and has resumed a normal life. The mere fact that he was to take drugs to maintain his cure does not class him as incurable. But once it has been found that the respondent is of

19. *Chapman* v. *c.* (1961) 3 All E.R. 1105.

unsound mind, the degree of unsoundness is immaterial,[20] nor is it necessary that the respondent should be certified. In *Lock* v. *L.*,[21] the wife was suffering from dementia. The medical evidence showed that in the light of present day medical knowledge, she was incurably of unsound mind and no further improvement was possible but she was not certified. This was held to be sufficient for the purpose of incurable unsoundness of mind under the (English) Matrimonial Causes Act, 1950.

It was laid down in *Harrod* v. *H.*[22] that unsoundness of mind may be occasioned either by perversion of intellect, manifesting itself in delusions, antipathies or the like; it may arise from defects of the mind, which are of two kinds. The mind may be originally so deficient as to be incapable of directing the person in any matter which requires thought or judgement, which is ordinarily called idiocy or the defect may arise from the weakening of the mind, originally strong, by disease or some accident of a physical nature, by which memory is lost and the faculties are paralysed, although there is no perversion of the mind, nor any species of that insanity which is ordinarily called mania.

In the matter of *Cowasji*[23], an old man had been for some months past entirely incapable of managing himself and his affairs. Medical evidence showed that his mental infirmity was not unsoundness of mind but weakness of mind or imbecility resulting from old age. A medical expert witness deposed that, as a medical term, unsoundness of mind answers to what is popularly styled lunacy, and is applied only to the state of mind resulting from disease, not to congenital imbecility or senile decay of the mental powers; it might be put down to amentia not dementia. The court held that the term 'unsound mind' comprehends imbecility, whether congenital or arising from old age, as well as lunacy or mental alienation resulting from disease. This test was relied on in *Lalita* v. *Nathuji*[24]

20. *Randall* v. *R.* (1939) p. 131; *Swettenham* v. *S.* (1938) p. 218 (the degree of insanity is immaterial).

21. *Lock* v. *L.* (1958) 3 All E.R. 472.

22. *Harrod* v. *H.* (1854-55) Kay & Johnson's Rep. 1 at 8.

23. In the matter of *Cowasji* (1882) 7 Bom. 15; *Empress* v. *Husen* (1881) 5 Bom. 262.

24. *Lalita* v. *Nathuji*, A.I.R. 1939 All. 333.

where it was explained that the term 'unsoundness' denoted an incapacity to manage affairs. The court further accepted the dictum of Lord Eldon in *Ridgeway* v. *Darwin*[25] to the effect that the test was not whether the person in question was absolutely insane but whether the court thought itself authorised to issue a commission, provided it be made out that the person is unable to act with proper or providential management.

In *George* v. *Edwin*[26] Mr. Justice Jackson observed, "It would appear that unsoundness of mind taken by itself is not sufficient to bring a person within the term 'lunatic', unless it would incapacitate him from managing his own affairs: nor on the other hand, will a person who is incapable of managing his affairs be a lunatic, unless that incapacity is produced by unsoundness of mind." Relying on these observations, it was held in *Mazaharuddin* v. *Sarajuddinkhan*[27] that a lunatic must be incapable of managing his own affairs, and must also be of unsound mind. Though the appellant was, by reason of weak intellect, incapable of managing his own affairs, yet he could not be declared to be a person of unsound mind in the present case.

There is a distinction between mere weakness of intellect and lunacy. A court cannot find a person 'of unsound mind' because some or all of his relations have declared that he is a lunatic.[28] A person who is not sufficiently intelligent to manage his own affairs is not necessarily of unsound mind. The question of 'unsoundness of mind' must depend mainly on the evidence of medical experts. Thus where the medical evidence showed that the appellant's mental condition was normal and his intelligence was of an average illiterate person though he was of very weak intellect, it was held that it was quite impossible on this evidence to hold that the appellant was of unsound mind; it might well be that he was feeble-minded and incapable of managing his affairs.[29]

In *Randall* v. *R*[30]., an English case, the husband was suffering from a defect of the mind which was manifested by an absence

25. *Ridgeway* v. *Darwin* (1802) 8 Ves. 65.
26. *George* v. *Edwin* (1875) 24 W.R. 124. A case under the (Indian) Lunacy Act (No. XXXV) of 1858
27. *Mazaharuddin* v. *Sarajuddinkhan* (1906) 4 Cal. L.J. 115.
28. *Teka* v. *Gopal, A.I.R.* 1930 Lah. 289.
29. *Mahipati* v. *Mt. Changuna*, A.I.R. 1934 Nag. 27.
30. *Randall* v. *R*. (1939) p. 131.

of will-power. He was perfectly sensible in all intellectual matters, and could discuss subjects sensibly; he had no delusions of any sort. What was alleged was that his volition was so defective as to amount to unsoundness of mind justifying his detention. It was held that he was of unsound mind, and the degree of unsoundness was immaterial. It should be noticed that the wife succeeded mainly on the ground that he was in need of care and treatment.

It was held in *Rameshwar* v. *Nageshwar*[31] that it is not enough to find that the person concerned is of undeveloped mind or incapable of managing a large estate but it must be shown that he is subject to delusions. This is not correct; the test of unsoundness of mind is not that the person in question must be subject to delusions. Unsoundness of mind may be of various types, and only in some kinds are delusions of importance. In *Sonabati* v. *Narayanchanden*[32] the lunatic was a young man, whose mother had died when he was about two years old. He had been an invalid all his life and suffered from daily epileptic fits, so that his mental condition had been seriously weakened. It was held that a person might conceivably have all kinds of delusions but, if his conduct remains normal, there is no power under the (Indian) Lunacy Act, 1912, to deal with him, because the law of lunacy deals with conduct and the proper test for insanity is not the beliefs that the person concerned may entertain but the conduct exhibited by him.

This test was approved by Mushtaq Ahmad, J., in *Joshi* v. *Rukmini*,[33] where it was held that unsoundness of mind implies some unusual feature of the mind which tends to make it different from the normal and has in effect impaired the man's capacity to look after his affairs in the same manner as a person without such mental irregularity. There must be some derangement of the mind, whatever its degree and it must not be confused with or taken as analogous to mere mental weakness or lack of intelligence. A man may find it difficult to answer questions of a particular class but if he intelligently answers

31. *Rameshwar* v. *Nageshwar* (1905) 2 All. L.J. 154.

32. *Sonabati* v. *Narayanchanden*, A.I.R. 1935 Pat. 423; P. V. Deolalkar, *The Hindu Marriage Act*. 1955, *Nasik City*, 1959, p. 37.

33. *Joshi* v. *Rukmini*, A.I.R. 1949 All. 449, 453.

questions concerning himself, his family and property, he cannot be classed with men of unsound mind, unable to manage their affairs. If a man's inability to understand and answer questions is restricted to those relating to arithemetical calculations, he cannot be regarded as mentally unsound, although he might have a weak or undeveloped mind. In *Upendra* v. *Narendra*[34] it was pointed out that a person whose mental condition had been affected by a paralytic stroke, so that this and old age had seriously affected his memory and he was unable to recognise his relations but was able to answer questions with regard to his estate and questions with regard to his family with intelligence, could not be said to be of unsound mind and incapable of managing his affairs.

The term 'unsoundness of mind' is to be taken in its ordinary connotation, which means madness. The terms unsound mind and insanity as used under the (English) Matrimonial Causes Act, 1950 mean the same thing[35]. According to J. P. Modi[36] an idiot is one who is of unsound mind from the birth without lucid intervals. A lunatic is one who is of unsound mind only at certain periods. "Unsound mind" covers a wide range of mental conditions including insanity, lunacy, madness, mental derangement, mental disorder and mental aberration. All these terms are used for disordered state of the mind in which the individual loses the power of regulating his actions and conduct according to the rules of society in which he is moving.

In the United States statutes dealing with unsoundness of mind and its consequences use a variety of terms such as insanity, permanent insanity, incurable insanity, incurably insane, permanently and incurably insane, hopelessly and incurably insane, incurable chronic mania or dementia, paranoia, paresis and dementia praecox. Some states require that the person must have been adjudged insane, while the others require continuous confinement in an 'insane asylum.'[37]

34. *Upendra* v. *Narendra*, A.I.R. 1926 Cal. 155.

35. Halsbury's *Laws of England*, 3rd. Ed., Vol. 12, p. 233.

36. J. P. Modi, *Medical Jurisprudence and Toxicology*, 10th Ed., 1949 p. 849, cited in D.H. Chaudhari, *The Hindu Marriage Act*, 1955, Calcutta, 1957, p. 206, see also pp. 172, 227-228.

37. W. E. McCurdy, "*Insanity as a Ground for Divorce*" in *Selected Essays*

The dictionary[38] defines an idiot as "a person so deficient in mental or intellectual faculty as to be incapable of ordinary acts of reasoning or rational conduct. Applied to one permanently so afflicted, as distinguished from one who is temporarily insane, or 'out of his senses' and who either has lucid intervals, or may be expected to recover his reason." An idiot or fool is a person who from his birth, by a perpetual or incurable infirmity, is of unsound mind.[39] An idiot is congenitally incapable of distinguishing right from wrong and is of unsound mind from his birth without lucid intervals.[40]

The word 'idiocy' conveys the meaning of congenital defect in mental faculty. It denotes an extreme form of mental unsoundness. 'Lunacy' and 'idiocy' are stronger terms than 'unsound mind'.[41] The question of unsound mind and its curability has to be determined in the light of medical evidence. Persons differ from one another in degree of intelligence. The word 'idiot' must be read in its ordinary significance as meaning a person so deficient in mental or intellectual faculty as to be incapable of ordinary acts of reasoning or rational conduct. His mental faculties and intelligence have not developed at all.[42]

The words 'unsound mind' in common parlance denote the state of mind of a person who has lost his reason. Insanity can be hereditary or caused by disease, grief, accident or decay of mental faculty due to old age. It may be manifested by various ways, e.g., by the irrational thinking and abnormal behaviour of the person concerned.

3. *THE STATUTORY PERIOD*

It must be proved that the respondent is incurably of unsound mind and has been continuosly under care and treat-

on Family Law, published by the Association of American Law Schools, 1950, pp. 325-334.

38. *A New English Dictionary, edited by J.A.H. Murray*, vol. 5, Oxford, 1901, pp. 21-22.

39. Earl Jowitt, *The Dictionary of English Law*, p. 934.

40. J.D.M. Derrett, *Introduction to Modern Hindu Law*, p. 153; see also P. V. Deolalkar, *The Hindu Marriage Act*, 1955, Nasik City. 1959, p. 37.

41. Shiva Gopal, *The Hindu Code*, Allahabad, 1964, pp. 356-357, 343-345.

42. *Titali* v. *Alfred*, A.I.R. 1934, All. 273.

ment for at least five years immediately preceding the presentation of the petition.[43] The same rule applies to Hindus in Kenya under S. 10 (1) (d) of the Hindu Marriage and Divorce Ordinance, 1960. The law under the Hindu Marriage Act, 1955 is different in that the period is three years in case of divorce and two years in case of judicial separation. The provision for care and treatment is also absent from the Indian scene. The unsoundness of the mind must be continuous and two separate periods cannot be added together to make the required period. Continuity of care and treatment is not broken merely because a mental patient is transferred from one hospital to another, as short breaks are bound to occur during transference of the patient from one country to the other[44] nor is the continuity of time broken by the temporary absence of the patient from the mental institution. Thus in *Swymer* v. *S.*[45] the husband was of unsound mind. He was sent for treatment for a fractured leg to another hospital and remained there from January to May, returning to the mental hospital when the leg had healed. His name remained on the books of the mental hospital during his absence and regular reports were made to the superintendent of the mental hospital. It was held that the five years period of continuous care and treatment had not been interrupted by the absence of the voluntary patient.

However, the continuity of time is broken if the respondent ceases to be a mental patient. In *Measure* v. *M.*[46] the wife was a voluntary patient in a mental hospital. Later she was admitted to a sanatorium for treatment of tuberculosis. She ceased to be a patient of the mental hospital and was no longer on the books of that hospital. She remained in the sanatorium for 11 weeks; when her mental condition deteriorated she was re-admitted to the same mental hospital, where she remained till and during the hearing of the petition. It was held that the husband had failed to establish that the wife had

43. S. 1 (1.) (d) of the (English) Matrimonial Causes Act, 1950, re-enacted in S. 1 (1.) (a) (iv) of the (English) Matrimonial Causes Act, 1965.

44. *Frank* v. *F.* (1951) p. 430 (C.A.).

45. *Swymer* v. *S.* (1955) p. 11 (C.A.).

46. *Measure* v. *M.* (1960) 2 All E.R. 233.

been incurably of unsound mind or had been continuously under care and treatment for five years, because at the date of the wife's admission to the sanatorium, it was an open question whether she was incurably of unsound mind and because during the period of 11 weeks while she was at the sanatorium, she was not receiving mental treatment.

It is not necessary that every part of the treatment should be administered in a hospital. In *Dunn* v. *D.*[47] the wife had, throughout the relevant period of five years, been in a mental hospital, first as a voluntary patient and later as an informal patient. On two occasions she had been absent for periods of more than 28 days, living with her step-mother, with the approval of the hospital authorities, who had entrusted to the step-mother the duty of administering medicines. The court decided that the wife was during her temporary absences receiving treatment as a resident in hospital, the absences during which she lived with the step-mother being part of the care and treatment and therefore not an interruption of it.

In *Shipman* v. *S.*[48] a mentally unsound wife was first detained under a reception order. Later she was discharged. After two years she was again certified. Thereafter she was released from the mental hospital for various periods, which she spent with a sister. Her absences from the mental hospital purported to be sanctioned by orders which were expressed to be by way of provisional discharge. The husband's petition for divorce failed on the ground that there was no such thing as a 'provisional discharge'. Once the order for discharge has been made, the procedure for certification, reception and detention must, if it becomes necessary, begin afresh.

This decision is open to criticism and was expressly disapproved by the Court of Appeal in *Safford* v. *S.*,[49] where the husband was incurably of unsound mind since his admission to the hospital. The superintendent of the mental hospital stated that, since the husband's admission into the hospital, the reception order had been continuously in force. In exercise of his powers he had from time to time permitted the husband to visit his father and allowed him to go home on two

47. *Dunn* v. *D.* (1962) p. 192; followed in *Head* v. *H.* (1963) p. 357.
48. *Shipman* v. *S.* (1939) p. 147.
49. *Safford* v. *S.* (1944) p. 61 (C.A.).

occasions. During those periods of leave 'on trial' the reception order continued in force and the husband was under the control of his father, who promised to keep him under observation and to report from time to time. It was held that continuity of period was not broken by these absences. In *Shipman* v. *S.*[50] a distinction was drawn between a case where there is a liability to be detained if and when a reception order is called out of abeyance and a case of actual detention under an order which is being enforced. The opinion that during absence on probation a reception order is in abeyance is not correct; the reception order is in force throughout. Power to release a mental patient on probation is part of the treatment which a person authorised to receive him has statutory power to give. Detention is to be regarded as a status rather than the physical fact of being kept under lock and key.[51] In *Shipman* v. *S.* (supra) this was ignored.

A petitioner is not entitled to a decree if his conduct has conduced to the insanity of the respondent. In *Greenstreet* v. *G.*[52] husband's petition for divorce on the ground of his wife's unsoundness of mind was contested on the ground that the wife's alleged insanity was caused by the petitioner's cruelty. He had for a period of two years assaulted the respondent, caused bruises on her arms, locked her out of her bedroom and made her sleep in the kitchen, thrown dirty water over her and falsely accused her of attempting to poison him. There was a separation agreement and the parties never resumed cohabitation. Eventually she was admitted to a mental hospital suffering from schizophrenia. The judge described the petitioner's treatment of his wife as 'a calculated series of cruelties affecting her mental condition to such an extent that, though he did not succeed in deranging her mind, he brought her into a condition of mind...the consequence of which was that, when she suffered a serious motor accident, the shock of that accident, aggravated by her predisposing condition of strain, produced the insanity'. The petitioner was not entitled to a decree because his conduct had contributed to the malady of his wife.

50. *Shipman* v. *S.* (1939) p. 147.
51. *Safford* v. *S.* (1944) p. 61 at p. 66.
52. *Greenstreet* v. *G.* (1948) Weekly Notes 172.

The situation is similar in Hindu law. S. 23 (1) (a) of the Hindu Marriage Act, 1955 provides specifically that the court has to be satisfied that the petitioner is not taking advantage of his own wrong or disability. As conduct conducing is a discretionary bar, the judge can overrule it; in *Dodd* v. *D.*[53] a husband was granted divorce on the ground of his wife's incurable insanity notwithstanding that his own adultery had conduced to the wife's mental condition.

Under S. 23 (1) (e) of the Hindu Marriage Act, 1955, the court has to be satisfied that there is no other legal ground why relief should not be granted. This raises the question whether a petition can be brought on behalf of an insane spouse on the ground of the other spouse's insanity. In *Baker* v. *B.*[54] it was held that the committee of a person of unsound mind can petition for dissolution of his marriage on the ground of his wife's adultery. There is no distinction between lunatic petitioners and lunatic respondents. A lunatic respondent is liable to be sued and the fact that insanity may preclude an effectual defence being set up must be regarded as a misfortune resulting from the respondent's condition, and does not affect the petitioner's right to sue any more than the death or insanity of a material witness for the defendant. The learned President stated that 'great wrong might arise from holding that no proceedings for divorce can be maintained against the adulterous wife of a lunatic. She might be left in possession of property settled on her by her husband, which she and her paramour might enjoy to the exclusion of the lunatic. She might exercise power of appointment in favour of the paramour or the children of her and his adultery, a spurious offspring might be foisted upon her husband and his family, by which the devolution of estates or titles might be diverted in favour of illegitimate objects. These evils would only be avoided by a dissolution of the marriage.' In that case a decree of divorce was sought on the ground of the lunatic's wife's adultery. There is no reason why the same should not apply by analogy to a case where the ground relied on is insanity.

53. *Dodd* v. *D.* (1954) The Times, 26th. Oct.

54. *Baker* v. *B.* (1880) 5 P.D. 142 at pp. 145-146, 151; affirmed on appeal in (1881) 6 P.D. 12.

It may be concluded that both at Hindu and English law the respondent must be proved to be of incurably unsound mind. Such unsoundness must be continuous for the required period of time. The words 'under care and treatment'[55] do not appear in the Hindu Marriage Act, 1955. Therefore, unlike English law and Hindu law in Kenya[56] it is not necessary that the respondent should be receiving mental treatment in an approved institution. The fact that he had been continously of unsound mind for the requisite time will suffice, and medical evidence is given great weight for this purpose. For a decree of divorce under S. 13 (1) (iii) of the Hindu Marriage Act, 1955, a temporary or curable unsoundness of mind or where there have been lucid intervals is not enough. But where a decree of judicial separation is sued for under S. 10 (1) (e) it is not necessary to prove 'incurability'. The test of unsoundness of mind is whether the person concerned is incapable of managing himself and his affairs, bearing in mind that 'affairs' include the problems of society and of married life and this has to be judged by the standard of the reasonable man, but without reference to the cause of such incapacity.[57]

55. For comments and recommendations on the words 'care and treatment' see the Report of the Royal Commission, 1956, Cmd. 9678, paras 172-209.

56. S. 10 (1) (d) of the (Kenya) Hindu Marriage and Divorce Ordinance, 1960.

57. *Robinson* v. *R.* (1964) 3 W.L.R. 935 at 943.

Chapter VIII

DISSOLUTION OF MARRIAGE BY PRESUMPTION OF DEATH

1. *PRESUMPTION OF DEATH AS A GROUND FOR DISSOLUTION*

In England any married person who alleges that reasonable grounds exist for supposing that the other party to the marriage is dead may present a petition to the court to have it presumed that the other party is dead, and to have the marriage dissolved; the court, if satisfied that such reasonable grounds exist, may make a decree of presumption of death and dissolution of marriage. In any such proceedings the fact that, for a period of seven years or upwards, the other party to the marriage has been continuously absent from the petitioner and the petitioner has no reason to believe that the other party has been living within that time, shall be evidence that he or she is dead, until the contrary is proved.[1] The words 'may make a decree' invest the courts with discretionary power to refuse a decree if the circumstances are such that injustice would result[2] or adjourn the case until further inquiries have been made.[3]

This can be compared with the Hindu Marriage Act, 1955,[4] according to which any marriage solemnised, whether before or after the commencement of the Act, may, on a petition presented by either the husband or the wife, be dissolved by a decree of divorce on the ground that the other party has not been heard of as being alive for a period of seven years or more by those persons who would naturally have heard of it, had that party been alive. The origin of this rule in India,

1. S. 16 (1), (2) of the (English) Matrimonial Causes Act, 1950, re-enacted in S. 14 (1) of the (English) Matrimonial Causes Act, 1965.

2. *Thompson* v. *T.* (1956) p. 414; D. Tolstoy, *The Law and Practice of Divorce*, London, 1963, p. 70.

3. *N.* v. *N.*; *L.* v. *L.*; *C.* v. *C.* (1957) p. 385.

4. S. 13 (1) (vii) of the Hindu Marriage Act, 1955.

is S. 108 of the Indian Evidence Act, 1872, which provides that when the question is whether a man is alive or dead, and it is proved that he has not been heard of for seven years by those who would naturally have heard of him if he had been alive, the burden of proving that he is alive is shifted to the person who affirms it.

Before the enactment of the Evidence Act, 1872, according to A. Steele[5] who relies on Hindu *sastric* law, the rules were that if nothing is heard of an absentee during twentyfour years, in case he should be under fifty years of age, or twelve years, in case he should be above that age, his relations may consider him dead, perform his funeral rites in effigy, offer the periodical oblations and inherit his property.

2. *PRESUMPTION OF CONTINUANCE OF LIFE*

Once a person is proved to be alive and in normal health, he is presumed to continue so for a reasonable time, unless the contrary is proved. It was held in *Tani* v. *Rikhi*[6] that the presumption is in favour of the continuance of life and the onus of proving the death of a person lies on the party who asserts it. In the very old case of *Wilson* v. *Hodges*[7] where the question related to debt on recognisance of bail, the point to decide was, on whom did the onus lay to prove the death of one Michell. It was held there being presumption of continuance of life, it was for the party who asserts the death of a person to discharge the burden of proof. A similar conclusion was reached in *Lambe* v. *Orton*.[8] The court held that it is a preliminary presumption of evidence that a party living at a

5. A. Steele, *The Law and Custom of Hindoo Castes*, London, 1868, pp. 62-63; Sir Thomas Strange, *Hindu Law*, Vol. I, London, 1830, p. 188 (if no intelligence be received during twelve years of an absentee, the law requires his son to perform obsequies for him presuming his death); see also West & Buhler, *A Digest of the Hindu Law*, London, 1919, p. 626; *Mussumat Anundee* v. *Khedoo* (1872) 14 M.I.A. 412, 413 (a member of a joint Hindu family, of weak mind, went on a pilgrimage and was not heard of for twelve years, his death was presumed).

6. *Tani* v. *Rikhi* (1920) 56 I.C. 742 (Lah. H.C.); the same view was followed by the Bom. and Hyd. High Courts in *Jeshankar* v. *Bai Divali* (1920) 57 I.C. 525; *Balwant* v. *Kerba*, A.I.R. 1953 Hyd. 187.

7. *Wilson* v. *Hodges* (1802) 2 East 312=102 E.R. 388.

8. *Lambe* v. *Orton* (1859) 8 Wk. Rep. 111; see also "*Presumption of death*" (1890) 34 Sol. Jour. at p. 247.

given time is alive at a subsequent time within a reasonable limit. The onus is on him who asserts death.

But if a person is very old and in bad health, the presumption would be that he will not live much longer and in any case the presumption of continuance of life grows weaker with lapse of time so eventually both English law and Hindu law apply the rule that a person who has not been heard of as being alive for seven years is presumed to be dead.[9] But the mere lapse of time without more is not sufficient to raise the presumption. The plaintiff must prove that the missing person has not been heard of by those who would have heard of him if he had returned. In *Doe d. France* v. *Andrews*,[10] which was an ejectment action from land leased for three lives, two of the beneficiaries were dead and nothing whatever was known about the third; no witness was called who had known him; except the mention of him in the lease, there was no proof that he had ever existed. No evidence of search for him was given. It was held that, to raise the presumption of his death, there should have been evidence that he had not been heard of by those persons who would naturally have heard of him had he been alive or that search had been ineffectually made to find such a person.

In *Re Watkins*[11] the question was when a wife's first husband died, she, her two sons, the father and a sister of the husband were the nearest relations; none of them had heard of the missing husband from 1922 to 1948. It was held that she was entitled to assume that he was dead.

In *the goods of Mathews*,[12] a testator aged 73 years disappeared from his home and was not heard of subsequently. Searches had been made by members of his family, advertisements had been published in newspapers, the register of deaths

9. *Doe* v. *Jesson* (1805) 102 E.R. 1217 at 1219; in the goods of *Ganesh Das*, A.I.R. 1926 Cal. 1056. (The presumption of the continuance of life ceases at the expiration of seven years if nothing is heard of the absentee, relying on *Tani* v. *Rikhi* (1920) 56 I.C. 742.)

10. *Doe d. France* v. *Andrews* (1850) 117 E.R. 644, 760; the principle of this case was applied in *Prudential Assurance Co.* v. *Edmonds* (1877) 2 A.C. 487 at 508.

11. In *Re Watkins* (1953) 2 All E.R. 1113.

12. In the goods of *Mathews* (1898) p. D. 17.

had been searched and the police communicated with, all without result. The court on proof of these inquiries, which were ample, allowed the death of the testator to be presumed three years after his disappearance. In the goods of *Robertson*,[13] where a person had not been heard of for twentyfive years, the court ordered advertisements requesting information concerning him to be published in newspapers. But such service was dispensed with in *N.* v. *N.*; *L.* v. *L.*; *C.* v. *C.*,[14] where the persons whose deaths were in question had last been seen or heard of during the war, in territories which were or had come within the U.S. S.R. and exhaustive efforts to trace the respondents, short of attempts which might have involved risk to others, had failed.

In *Bullock* v. *B.*[15] the husband deserted his wife, who obtained an order in the magistrate's court for the payment of maintenance. In 1930 the husband being in arrears, a committal order was made. A warrant was issued directing the police to arrest the husband but was not executed by them as he could not be found. The wife made no further inquiries about him and never heard of him again. In 1944, describing herself as the widow of her husband, she remarried. In 1959 the second husband contended that his marriage was bigamous and void *ab initio*, because the wife had made no inquiries about her first husband's death before her remarriage. The court held that the inference that the first husband died before remarriage was rightly drawn. The fact that the police were unable to execute the warrant against the first husband amounted to sufficient inquiries.

Similar inquiries are expected to be made under S. 108 of the Indian Evidence Act, 1872. In *Kahan Chand* v. *Jawandi*[16] the dispute centered on properties of the deceased. It was contended that the plaintiff was not entitled to sue as her mother, who had a prior right, was alive. The plaintiff produced the woman's mother, brother, step-brother and uncle all of whom declared that they had not heard of her within the past seven years. On this evidence the presumption of death was drawn. On the other hand in *Badal* v. *Saraswati*,[17] one Ram Baksh,

13. In the goods of *Robertson* (1896) p. 8.
14. *N.* v. *N.*; *L.* v. *L.*; *C.* v. *C.* (1957) p. 385.
15. *Bullock* v. *B.* (1960) 2 All E.R. 307.
16. *Kahan Chand* v. *Jawandi*, A.I.R. 1923 Lah. 174.
17. *Badal* v. *Saraswati*, A.I.R. 1927 All. 687.

who would have been entitled to the estate in dispute as nearer reversioner, left the village with his wife, thirty years ago or more. At that time they had no children. There was no evidence that they had not since been heard of by persons who would be likely to hear of them and no evidence that inquiries were made as to what happened to them after they left the village. It was held that in such a case, where a reversioner is suing persons who are merely trespassers, no strong proof is required of the death of a nearer reversioner. But it is submitted that there was no evidence to lead to the presumption that Ram Baksh was dead. The plaintiff could very well have caused some inquiries to be made but as no evidence of such inquiries was adduced, the presumption of death should not have been drawn.

The presumption of death of a spouse will not be drawn from absence of communication from the other spouse, if the failure to communicate can otherwise be accounted for. It was held *Kamtabai* v. *Umabai*[18] that a wife, who had left her husband and was in the keeping of another as his concubine, was not such a person as would naturally hear of her husband, had he been alive, so the presumption of death could not be drawn. A similar conclusion was reached by the English court in *Chard* v. *C.*,[19] where the wife was last heard of in 1917. As a normally healthy woman who would, in 1933, have attained the age of fortyfour years but she had reasons for not wishing to be heard of by her husband and his family and it was not possible to trace anyone who would naturally have heard of her. In such circumstances the presumption of death of the wife was not drawn.

In *Willyams* v. *Scottish Widows Fund Life Assurance Society*[20] the plaintiff had insured the life-interest of one Hall with an

18. *Kamtabai* v. *Umabai*, A.I.R. 1929 Nag. 127.

19 *Chard* v. *C.* (1956) p. 259; see also *Bowden* v. *Henderson* (1854) 65 E.R. 436. (The presumption of death does not arise where the probability of intelligence is rebutted by circumstances).

20. *Willyams v. Scottish Widows Fund Life Assurance Society* (1888) 52 J. P. 471; see also *Wills* v. *Palmer* (1904) 53 Wk. Rep. 169 (where the presumption of death was drawn, although the person whose death was presumed was a bankrupt and absconding solicitor and it was in his interest to keep his identity concealed); 12 Halsbury's *Laws of England*, 3rd. Ed., pp. 287-288.

insurance company to secure advances made to Hall. The plaintiffs claimed that, as Hall had not been seen or heard of for a period of over seven years, his death should be presumed and the plaintiffs declared entitled to the amount of life policy. It was held that the mere disappearance of Hall was not sufficient ground to infer death. No inquiries had been made; indeed Mrs. Hall would be the last to see or hear of her husband, who had treated her badly. In *Bennett* v. *B.*[21] the parties married in 1950. The wife had been previously married in Jamaica but in 1945 her former husband had wounded one of the children of the marriage and disappeared, since then, despite limited inquiries made by both the wife and the police, he had never been seen or heard of. In 1960 the second husband petitioned for nullity on the ground that, at the time when the marriage was celebrated, the wife was already married. It was held by Holroyd, L.J., that the first husband was forty years of age when he left the wife and there was no suggestion that his health was poor. He had reasons for evading both his wife and his matrimonial obligations and the police, so that the presumption of death could not be drawn.

The presumption of death should not be drawn if the person whose death is to be presumed has reason to keep his identity concealed, and the plaintiff is a person who is unlikely to hear of him, if he were alive, unless there is clear evidence establishing the death of the person in question.

The phrase in S. 16 (2) of the (English) Matrimonial Causes Act, 1950 'that the petitioner has no reason to believe' is to be interpreted as meaning 'if nothing has happened within the period of seven years to give the petitioner reason to believe that the other party was then living.' 'Reason to believe' relates to the standard of the reasonable man and not that of the particular petitioner. The petitioner is required to make inquiries and produce that the near relatives or persons, who would naturally hear of the missing spouse, have not heard of him or her.[22] Where there is no evidence one way or the other as to the respondent being alive or dead within the seven years and the matter is of pure speculation, the court is entitled

21. *Bennett* v. *B.* (1961) 105 Sol. Jour. 885.

22 *Thompson* v. *T.* (1956) p. 414; see also "*Presumption of death*" (1956) 58 Bom. L. R. 105 (Jour.).

to hold that there is, in fact, no reason to believe that the missing spouse has been living within that time.[23]

Presumptions come into operation only when the facts on which they may be based have been proved by evidence. It was held in *Mac-darmaid* v. *Attor.-Gen.*[24] that each case must be determined on its own facts. Where, therefore, it was proved that the petitioner's father had been married to a person who was last seen, at the age of twentyseven years, in normal health and circumstances, some three years before the petitioner's birth and of whom nothing had since been heard, it was held that the proper inference to draw on the probabilities of the case was that the father's first wife was still alive when the petitioner was born. The petitioner was, therefore, not the legitimate child of the subsequent marriage of her parents. She could not rely on the presumption of death, since the first wife had been seen within seven years of the birth of the petitioner. The case is supposed by *R.* v. *Harborne Inhabitants.*[25] where Lord Denman said, "I must take this opportunity of saying, that nothing can be more absurd than the notion that there is to be any rigid presumption of law on such question of fact, without reference to accompanying circumstances, such, for instance, as the age or health of the party. There can be no strict presumption of law."

R. v. *Harborne Inhabitants* (supra) was applied in *Chard* v. *C.*,[26] where the validity of the second marriage of a husband was in dispute; it was held that it was for him to prove facts from which a cessation of his earlier marriage could be inferred, and that there was no presumption of law either as to the continuance of life or as to death having supervened; the question had to be determined on evidence on its own facts. Due weight should be given to different circumstances, e.g., whether the missing person was a friendless orphan, or a gregarious man

23. *Parkinson* v. *P.* (1939) p. 346.

24. Mac-darmaid v. Attor.-Gen. (1950) p. 218; see also in re *Aldersey* (1905) 2 Ch. D. 181 at 186 (there is no presumption in favour of continuance of life; it is entirely a matter of evidence).

25. *R.* v. *Harborne Inhabitants* (1835) 2 Ad. & El. 540 = 111 E.R. 209.

26. *Chard* v. *C.* (1956) p. 259, 273, 270; see also *Rango* v. *Mudiyeppa* (1899) 23 Bom. 296 (there is no presumption that a person who was alive in 1877, was alive in 1878; this has to be established by evidence).

in public life, whether in good or in bad health and whether following a quiet or dangerous occupation.

The position in India under the Indian Divorce Act, 1869 is not dissimilar. S. 7 of that Act states that courts shall in all suits and proceedings thereunder act and give relief on principles and rules which, in their opinion, are as nearly as may be conformable to the principles and rules on which the court for divorce and matrimonial causes in England for the time being acts and gives relief. In *Greenwood* v. *G.*[27] a husband had been previously married, but had not heard of his wife for over seven years; presuming her to be dead, he married again. Later on the second wife petitioned for nullity of the marriage on the ground that the husband's first wife was still alive. It was held that she must prove positively that her husband's first wife was alive at the date of the second marriage, which she failed to do.

In *Tirathpati* v. *Ranjit*[28] the man, whose properties were the subject of dispute, had not been heard of for forty years. Evidence was given to the effect that he had died of cholera. One witness deposed that he had accompanied the deceased to Burma, where he saw him die of cholera. This was held to be sufficient to support the presumption of death. Where the right of a party claiming to succeed to the property of another is based on the allegation that the latter has not been heard of for more than seven years, the question to be decided is one of evidence, and not a part of the substantive law.[29]

In *Lalchand* v. *Mahanth*[30] it was not considered necessary to determine on whom the onus of proving the date of death lay, because there was clear evidence, adduced by the plaintiff himself, that his predecessor, whose death it was sought to presume, died in 1892. The question whether or not presumption of death is to be drawn is a matter of fact, which has to be established by evidence, having regard to all the circumstances of the case.

27. *Greenwood* v. *G.*, A.I.R. 1946 Mad. 65.
28. *Tirathpati* v. *Ranjit*, A.I.R. 1931 Oudh. 40.
29. *Dhondo* v. *Ganesh* (1887) 11 Bom. 433.
30. *Lalchand* v. *Mahanth* (1926) 5 Pat. 312.

It was held in *R.* v. *The Inhabitants of Twyning*[31] that the law always presumes against the commission of crime, so where a woman, twelve months after her husband was last heard of, remarried and had children by the second husband, the second marriage was held to be valid, because the law not only presumes the continuation of life but also that crime is not committed. There was a conflict of presumptions but the death of the first husband was presumed, on the ground that the law would not presume that the woman had committed bigamy.

But, as was explained in *Lapsley* v. *Grierson*,[32] there is no absolute presumption of law as to the continuance of life, nor any absolute presumption against a party doing an act because the doing of it would make him guilty of an offence against the law. In every case the circumstances and evidence must be considered. On a prosecution for bigamy, it is incumbent on the prosecutor to prove that the former spouse of the accused was alive at the date of the second marriage. The existence of the other spouse of first marriage at a time preceding it may or may not afford a reasonable inference that he or she was alive at the date of the second marriage. If it were proved that the missing person was in good health on the day preceding the second marriage, the inference would be strong, almost irresistible, that he was alive on the latter day. On the other hand this would not be so if it were proved that he was then in a dying condition, and nothing further was proved. The question is entirely for the jury and the law makes no presumption either way.[33]

3. *PRESUMPTION AS TO THE DATE OF DEATH*

Nepean v. *Doe d. Knight*[34] laid down that, when a party has been absent for seven years without having been heard of, the presumption is that he is dead, but there is no legal presumption as to the time of his death. If it is important to anyone to establish the precise time of such person's death, he must

31. *R.* v. *Inhabitants of Twyning* (1819) 106 E.R. 407, 408.
32. *Lapsley* v. *Grierson* (1848) 1 H.L.C. 498=9 E.R. 853.
33. *R.* v. *Lumley* (1869) 20 L. T. 454, 456.
34. *Nepean* v. *Doe d. Knight* (1837) 2 M. & W. 894 = 150 E. R. 1021, 1028.

do so by evidence. This was followed in *Lambe* v. *Orton*,[35] where it was held that there is no presumption that the missing person died either in the first half or the second half of the seven years. The onus of showing that a party was dead at a given time lies on the one who asserts it.

In *Re Phene's Trust*[36] it was sought to make title to a share in a residuary estate by establishing that Nicholas Phene Hill was alive on Jan. 5, 1861. He was a sergeant of marines in good health when he disappeared while on leave from his ship and had not since been heard of for more than seven years. It was not proved affirmatively that he survived seven months from the time his leave was up. Sir G. M. Giffard enunciated the law as follows, "The true proposition is that those who found a right upon a person having survived a particular period must establish that fact affirmatively by evidence; the evidence will necessarily differ in different cases, but sufficient evidence there must be or the asserting person will fail."

An Indian court in *Ponnaloori* v. *Chilakapathi*,[37] held that it is for the party who wants the court to presume that a person was dead at a particular time, to establish that fact affirmatively by evidence. The same test was applied in *Bal Naicken* v. *Achama Naicken*,[38] where, on the authority of *Re Phene's Trusts*[39] and *Nepean* v. *Doe d. Knight*[40] and Halsbury's *Laws of England*, it was held that, while there is a presumption that a person who has not been heard of for seven years is presumed to be dead, there is no presumption as to the particular date on which he died.

Rango v. *Mudiyeppa*[41] decided that there is no presumption as to the date of death. Anyone, who has to establish the precise date on which a person died, must do so by evidence and can neither rely upon the presumption of death nor on the

35. *Lamba* v. *Orton* (1859) 8 Wk. Rep. 111; see also *Willyams* v. *Scottish Widows Fund Life Assurance Society* (1888) 52 J. P. 471 (there is no presumption as to the actual time of death).

36. *Re Phene's Trusts* (1870) 5 Ch. Ap. 139.

37. *Ponnaloori* v. *Chilakapathi* (1917) 42 I.C. 241 (Mad. H. Ct.).

38. *Bal Naicken* v. *Achama Naicken*, A.I.R. 1921 Mad. 285.

39. *Re Phene's Trusts* (1870) 5 Ch. Ap. 139.

40. *Nepean* v. *Doe d. Knight* (1837) 2 M. & W. 894=150 E.R. 1021, 1028.

41. *Rango* v. *Mudiyeppa* (1899) 23 Bom. 296.

continuance of life. This was approved in *Lal chand* v. *Mahanth*,[42] where, applying *Re Phene's Trusts* (supra), it was held that, when the court has to determine the date of the death of a person, who has not been heard of for seven years, there is no presumption that he died at the end of the first seven years or at any particular date. In this respect there is no difference between the law of India, as declared in the Indian Evidence Act, 1872 and the law of England.

Following *Lal chand* v. *Mahanth* (supra) and *Nepean* v. *Doe d. Knight* (supra), it was held in *Punjab* v. *Natha*[43] that, where a person has not been heard of for seven years, there is no presumption as to the date of his death, but it is presumed under S. 108 of the Indian Evidence Act, 1872 that he was dead at the institution of the suit. The same view was taken in *Hari* v. *Moro*,[44] which decided that where a presumption of death is permissible, the person concerned is regarded as dead at the time when the suit is filed, but no presumption arises as to the particular date of his death, which has to be proved in the same way as any other relevant fact in the case.

The wording of S. 13 (1) (vii) of the Hindu Marriage Act, 1955 has been criticised by P. V. Deolalkar[45] on the ground that death in fact dissolves the marriage, leaving no occasion for divorce; when death is presumed, there should be a decree of presumption of death and consequent dissolution of marriage. When a decree for divorce is granted, after presuming the other party to be dead, the court would appear to exercise jurisdiction over a dead person. This anomaly could have been avoided, if the language of the English statute had been reproduced in the section. However the practical result is the same under S. 13 (1) (vii) of the Hindu Marriage Act, 1955 and S. 16 (1) (2) of the (English) Matrimonial

42. *Lalchand* v. *Mahanth* (1926) 5 Pat. 312 at P. 322 (P.C.).

43. *Punjab* v. *Natha,* A.I.R. 1931 Lah. 582 F.B.; see also *Muhammad* v. *Abdul* (1921) 64 I.C. 468 (Lah.). The death of a person is presumed at the time the question of such death is first raised.

44. *Hari* v. *Moro* (1887) 11 Bom. 89; see also *Jeshankar* v. *Bai Divali* (1920) 57 I.C. 525 (Bom. H. Ct.). The earliest date at which the death can be presumed can only be the date when the suit is filed.

45. P. V. *Deolalkar, The Hindu Marriage Act*, 1955, Gavakari Press, 1959, p. 114.

Causes Act, 1950, the difference being that the word 'dissolution' is used by the latter instead of 'divorce'.

Under S. 10 of the (English) Matrimonial Causes Act, 1950[46] the court can invoke the help of the Queen's Proctor to argue any question in relation to the matter which the court thinks to be necessary or expedient to have fully argued or any person may give the Queen's Proctor information of any matter material to the decision of the case. There is no such safeguard in the Hindu Marriage Act, 1955.[47]

In conclusion it may be said that there are no absolute presumptions of law as to the continuance of life or death but when a person has not been heard of for seven years by those who would naturally have heard of him, had he been alive, and inquiries have been made as to his whereabouts, he is presumed to be dead. However, there is no presumption as to the date of his death. Anyone asserting any particular time must prove it by evidence. At English law a petitioner must prove that reasonable grounds exist for him to believe that the other party is dead. The practical result is the same under both systems. The question of presumption of death depends on proof of facts; if this is done, anyone asserting that the person whose death is presumed is alive must prove it by evidence.

46. Re-enacted in S. 6 of the (English) Matrimonial Causes Act, 1965.

47. S. V. Gupte, *Hindu Law of Marriage*, Bombay, 1961, p. 198.

Chapter IX

GROUNDS OF DIVORCE AVAILABLE ONLY TO THE WIFE

1. *SEXUAL CRIMES*

Rape, sodomy and bestiality first appeared as a ground for divorce available to a wife only under the (English) Matrimonial Causes Act, 1857[1]. This provision was included in S. 10 of the Indian Divorce Act, 1869, S. 27 (j) of the Special Marriage Act, 1954, S. 13 (2) (ii) of the Hindu Marriage Act, 1955, S. 5 (2) of the (Uganda) Divorce Ordinance (15 of 1904)[2] and S. 10 (1) (f) of the (Kenya) Hindu Marriage and Divorce Ordinance, 1960. Rape, sodomy and bestiality are each a ground for divorce in itself. They do not have to be coupled with adultery of the husband.[3] They are also crimes both at English law and Hindu law. None of the above statutes defines these offences, so the same definitions are resorted to for matrimonial purposes as exist at criminal law.

It is interesting to note that these offences were crimes even at Hindu *sastric* law. Rape was heavily punished. In certain cases the penalty was death.[4] Unnatural intercourse with a man or a woman was punished by a fine of 40 panas;[5] bestiality, i.e., intercourse with animals was punishable with 100, and in case the animal was a cow the fine was 500.[6]

1. S. 27 of the (English) Matrimonial Causes Act, 1857, re-enacted in S. 1 (1) of the Matrimonial Causes Act, 1950 and again in s. 1 (1) (b) of the (English) Matrimonial Causes Act, 1965.

2. Laws of Uganda, Cap. 112, applicable by S. 9 (2) of the (Uganda) Hindu Marriage and Divorce Ordinance, 1961.

3. It was wrongly suggested by Hodson , L.J., in *Bampton* v. *B.* (1959) 2 All E.R. 769, B-C, that sodomy had to be coupled with the husband's adultery; see also Alan Milner, "*Sodomy as a ground for divorce*" (1960) 23 M.L.R. 43.

4. Yaj. 2, 288, *Yajnavalkya Smriti*, an English translation by J. R. Gharpure, vol. II, Bombay, 1939: Ganganatha Jha, *Hindu Law in its Sources*, Allahabad, 1930, pp. 493-496.

5. Yaj. 2, 293; Ganganatha Jha, *Hindu Law in its Sources*, p. 502.

6. Yaj. 2, 289; Ganganatha Jha, *op. cit.*, p. 503; Vishnu V. 44, 42, S.B.E., Vol. 7, Oxford, 1880.

(i) *Rape*

Under S. 375 of the Indian Penal Code 1860 rape is committed (except in certain circumstances) when a man has sexual intercourse with a woman under circumstances falling under any of the following descriptions :—

(a) against her will;

(b) without her consent;

(c) with her consent where it was obtained by putting her in fear of death or of hurt;

(d) with her consent where the man knew that he was not her husband, and that her consent was given because she believed that he was another man to whom she was or believed herself to be lawfully married;

(e) with or without her consent where she was under 16 years of age.

This definition of 'rape' is virtually the same as at English law, and has been built on English case law. At English Common law as declared by the judicial decisions the crime of rape consists in having unlawful carnal knowledge of a woman without her consent.[7] "Unlawful carnal knowledge" consists in a man having sexual intercourse with a woman to whom he is not entitled at law.[8] Penetration must be proved but rupture of the hymen is not essential.[9]

It is essential for the offence of rape that the accused should not be legally entitled to have sexual intercourse with the woman concerned. Thus a husband cannot be guilty of rape on his own wife, unless the duty to cohabit has been terminated by law. In *R.* v. *Clarke*[10] the wife was living apart from her husband under a separation order at the time of the alleged offence. It was held that as a general proposition of law a husband cannot be guilty of rape on his wife, but where justices had made an order containing a non-cohabitation clause, the consent to marital-intercourse impliedly given by

7. *Russel on Crime*, 12th. Ed., London, 1964, vol. I, ch. 40, p. 706; Harris, S.F. *Criminal Law*, London, 1954, p. 271.

8. R. v. *Allen* (1839) 9 C. & P. 31 at p. 34; *R.* v. *Russen*, 1 East P.C 439; R. v. *Hughes* (1841) 9 C. & P. 752 = 173 E.R. 1038.

9. *Mt. Jantan* v. *Emp*. A.I.R. 1934 Lah. 797.

10. *R.* v. *Clarke* (1949) 2 All E.R. 448; *R.* v. *Miller* (1954) All E R. 529 (where there was no separation order or judicial separation, the husband was held not guilty of rape on his wife).

the wife at the time of the marriage was revoked, therefore, the husband was not entitled to have intercourse with her without her consent, with the result that he could be guilty of a rape.

The absence of consent on the part of the woman is an essential ingredient of the offence of rape. 'Against her will' or 'by force' are generally considered as synonymous with 'without her consent'.[11] Although some sort of violence is normally accompanied by this offence, it is not necessary to prove violence in every case. In *R.* v. *Day*,[12] on an indictment for attempting to carnally know and abuse a girl of 10 years of age, it appeared that no violence had been used by the accused and no actual resistance was made by the girl. It was held that, although consent on the part of the girl would put an end to the charge, the mere submission would not, and the difference between the two was enormous. In the case of a child it has to be considered whether submission on her part was voluntary or was the result of fear. Consent has to be distinguished from submission; every consent involves a submission, but it by no means follows, that a mere submission involves consent.

A woman's apparent consent can be vitiated by the following circumstances, i.e., by force or fear of bodily hurt, by fraud or by personation of her husband or when she is asleep or so unconscious due to imbecility as not to know the nature of the act. In *R.* v. *Hallett*[13] the evidence of the prosecutrix showed that, on the night of the alleged offence, eight persons followed her to the door of her lodgings. They held her with her back against the door, all of them committing the offence one after the other. Non-resistance on the part of the prosecutrix proceeded merely from her being overpowered by actual force, or from her not being able from want of strength to resist any longer and from the number of persons attacking her she considered resistance dangerous and

11. "*Forcible and Statutory Rape: the operation and objectives of the consent standard*" (1952) 62 Yale Law Journal P. 55.

12. *R.* v. *Day* (1841) 9 C. & P. 722 = 173 E.R. 1026-1027; *R.* v. *Dimes* (1912) 76 J.P. 47 (C.C.A.) (there must be something in the nature of permission and not merely submission to the act of the accused) at p. 48.

13. *R.* v. *Hallett*, 9 C. & P. 748 = 173 E.R. 1036.

useless. Thus consent of the woman was vitiated by force and fear of bodily hurt.

In *R.* v. *Williams*[14] consent of the girl was obtained by fraud. The accused was employed to give lessons in singing and voice production to a girl of 16 years of age. He had sexual intercourse with her under the pretence that her breathing was not quite right, and that he had to perform an operation to enable her to produce her voice properly. The girl submitted to what was done under the belief, wilfully and fraudulently adduced by the accused, that she was being medically and surgically treated and not with any intention that he should have sexual intercourse with her. The accused was convicted of rape. Similarly in *R.* v. *Flattery*[15] a quack doctor had sexual intercourse with a girl of 19 years on the pretence that he was performing a surgical operation on her. It was held that the accused was guilty of rape.

In *R.* v. *Young*[16] while a married woman was asleep in bed with her husband, the accused got into the bed and proceeded to have connection with her, she being then asleep. On waking up she at first thought that he was her husband, but on hearing him speak, she flung the accused off and called out to her husband, while the accused ran away. The jury found that the prosecutrix did not consent before, after or at the time of the accused's having intercourse with her. It was against her will. The accused was convicted of rape. In *R.* v. *Camplin*[17] the consent of the woman was vitiated, because of her drunken state of mind. The accused had caused the insensibility of the woman by giving her liquor for the purpose of exciting her. When she became heavily drunk, he had sexual intercourse with her. It was held to be an act of rape and the fact that the woman did not resist was no defence. A similar conclusion was reached by the Indian court in *Mst. Bhonri* v. *State*[18] where it was held that sexual intercourse under the influence of drink cannot be said to be with consent under Ss. 375-376 of

14. *R.* v. *Williams* (1923) 1 K.B. 340.

15. *R.* v. *Flattery* (1877) 2 Q.B. 410; *R.* v. *Jones* (1861) 4 L.T. 154. (These cases have already been dealt with in the chapter on adultery).

16. *R.* v. *Young* (1878) 14 Cox's C.C. 114 (C.C.A.).

17. *R.* v. *Camplin* (1845) 1 Den. 89 = 169 E.R. 163.

18. *Mst. Bhonri* v. *State*, A.I.R. 1955 Raj. 473 (N.U.C.).

the Indian Penal Code, 1860, because the girl was incapacitated from putting up resistance due to drink. Under S. 375, the question of consent would be relevant only where the victim is over 16 years of age. Where the girl is only about 12 years of age her consent, assuming such a consent was given, would be no consent in the eye of law.[19]

This is analogous to English law. Thus in *R.* v. *Harling*[20] it was laid down that where the charge is one of rape it is necessary in every case that the prosecution should prove that the victim did not consent and the crime was committed against her will. But where the rape is committed on a girl under the age of 16 years, she is incapable of giving consent at law, therefore, the defence is not open to the accused. In *R.* v. *Fletcher*[21] it was held that upon an indictment for rape there must be some evidence that the act was done without the consent of the woman, even where she is an idiot but this is not good law in view of the following authorities.

In *R.* v. *Barratt*[22] the prosecutrix was 14½ years old. She was blind and so unsound of mind that she was hardly capable of understanding anything, although she could go up and down the stairs by herself and could feed herself a little. If she was placed in a chair by anyone she would remain there till night and, if told to lie down, she would do so. It was further proved that her father, on returning home one day, looked through the window of the sitting-room and saw the accused committing the offence. The jury found the prisoner guilty of an attempt to rape on this evidence.

This case has been discussed mainly on the question of consent where the victim is an idiot or of defective mind. It should be noted that a mere attempt to rape will not give a ground for divorce to the wife. For the purpose of the matrimonial law (both English and Hindu) it must be proved that the husband has been guilty of rape but it is not necessary to prove that he has been criminally convicted. The matrimonial offence has to be proved *de novo* with the same strictness and certainty of proof as is required in a criminal case. The matter

19. *Madho* v. *State*, A.I.R. 1955 Him. Pr. 1805 (N.U.C.).
20. R. v. *Harling* (1938) 1 All E.R. 307 (C.C.A.).
21. *R.* v. *Fletcher* (1866) L.R. 1 C.C.R. 39.
22. R. v. *Barratt* (1873) L.R. 2 C.C.R. 81.

is well defined by *Virgo* v. *V.*[23] There a wife petitioned for divorce on the ground of her husband's incestuous adultery. It appeared that a jury in a criminal court had acquitted the respondent of the more serious charge but convicted him of an attempt to carnally know the child. The court, notwithstanding the certificate of conviction, allowed evidence to be given to prove that incestuous adultery had, in fact, taken place, and, finding this as a fact, dissolved the marriage. Similarly in *Bosworthick* v. *B.*[24] it was held that a wife may obtain a divorce from her husband for rape, although he has been prosecuted and convicted for indecent assault only. A respondent committing rape would normally be guilty of adultery also.[25]

In *R.* v. *Ryan*[26] the prosecutrix was an idiot and when asked questions in the witness-box was unable to understand right from wrong. It was held that where a girl is in a state of utter unconsciousness, whether occasioned by the act of the prisoner or otherwise, a person having connection with her during that time is guilty of a rape. Similarly in *R.* v. *Fletcher*[27] the girl was proved to be of 13 years old. She was of weak intellect and therefore incapable of distinguishing right from wrong. When the accused had sexual intercourse with her, she offered no resistance. It was held that the girl was incapable of giving consent from defect of understanding and the accused was rightly convicted of rape. In the Indian case of *Lalu Kamumal* v. *State*[28] the victim of rape was a woman in advanced stage of pregnancy. It was held that the fact that there was no resistance from her would not make her a consent-

23. *Virgo* v. *V.* (1893) 69 L.T. 460; Phillips, E.A., *Practice of the Divorce Division*, London, 1951, p. 34; S.V. Gupte, *Hindu Law of Marriage*, Bombay, 1961, p. 203.

24. *Bosworthick* v. *B.* (1902) 86 L.T. 121.

25. D. Tolstoy, *The Law and Practice of Divorce*, London, 1963, p. 69; *Thompson* v. *T.* (1901) 85 L.T. 172; S.K. Aiyar, *Commentaries on the Special Marriage Act* 1954,, Agra, 1956, p. 219.

26. R. v. *Ryan* (1846) 2 Cox's C. C. 115; *R.* v. *Pressy* (1867) 10 Cox's C.C. 635 (C.C.A.). A similar case, where the girl was an apparent idiot.

27. *R.* v. *Flatcher* (1859) Bell 63 = 169 E.R. 1168. For the protection of mental defectives see Ss. 7-9 of the Sexual Offences Act, 1956 as amended by S. 127 of the Mental Health Act, 1959.

28. *Lalu Kamumal* v. *State*, A.I.R. 1953 Ajmer 12 (N.U.C.).

ing party. The non-resistance on the part of the woman does not necessarily render the act consensual.

(ii) *Sodomy*

There is some evidence that in the ecclesiastical courts in England matrimonial relief by a decree of divorce *a mensa et thoro* was available to a wife on the ground that her husband had committed an unnatural offence against third parties. In *Bromley* v. *B.*[29] the wife sued her husband for a separation *a mensa et thoro* on the ground of unnatural practices committed by the husband. The libel merely pleaded that the husband had actually been convicted of an assault upon one George Stiff with intent to commit the offence and sentenced to two years imprisonment. She failed in the Consistory Court of the Lord Archboshop of York, from where she appealed to the High Court of Delegates, which held that attempted sodomy was sufficient and pronounced the decree in her favour.

However, a contrary view was taken in *Geils* v. *G.*[30], where the husband sought a decree of restitution of conjugal rights, to which the wife raised the defence that the husband had committed sodomy on her and had often attempted to commit the offence on her. It was held that it must be proved that the offence of sodomy was committed and consummated and that a mere attempt was not sufficient. On evidence the commission of the offence was not proved, so the defence failed. In view of *Bromley* v. *B.*[31] it is difficult to explain why an attempt at sodomy with a third party is sufficient to ground a separation *a mensa et thoro*, but an attempt to commit the offence on the wife is not. Possibly an attempt to commit the offence against third parties was regarded as cruelty to the wife.

S. 27 of the Matrimonial Causes Act, 1857 made sodomy a ground for divorce on a petition by the wife but it was not stated whether this included sodomy committed on the wife herself. However, the courts have interpreted the section as including it. In *C.* v. *C.*[32] the wife petitioned for divorce on the ground of her husband's sodomy with her against her consent. It was contended on behalf of the husband that

29. *Bromley* v. *B.* (1793) 2 Add. 158, Note = 162 E.R. 252 Note.
30. *Geils* v. *G.* (1848) 6 N.C. 97.
31. *Bromley* v. *B.* (1793) 2 Add. 158, Note=162 E.R. 252 Note.
32. *C.* v. *C.* (1905) 22 T.L.R. 26.

sodomy with a wife was not a matrimonial offence under S. 27 of the (English) Matrimonial Causes Act, 1857. Mr. Justice Bargrave Deane stated that within his own knowledge many decrees had been pronounced in similar cases, although these cases had not been reported. The court found the charges proved and granted a decree of divorce. By section 7 of the Act the court was empowered to give a decree of judicial separation on the same grounds as would entitle a spouse to a separation *a mensa et thoro*. According to *Bromley* v. *B.* (*supra*) sodomy or attempted sodomy of the husband with a third party and according to *Geils* v. *G.*[33] sodomy with the wife were grounds for divorce *a mensa et thoro*, so after the enactment of the (English) Matrimonial Causes Act, 1857, it remained a ground for judicial separation as well as for divorce.[34] Both at English law and Hindu law under S. 13 (2) (ii) of the Hindu Marriage Act, 1955 when divorce is sought on this ground, it must be proved that the offence of sodomy has been committed by the husband; a mere attempt will not suffice.

When a wife petitions for divorce on the ground that her husband committed sodomy on her, her consent to the act is fatal. In *Statham* v. *S.*[35] a wife petitioned for divorce on the ground that her husband had committed sodomy on her and was guilty of cruelty by shameless uncleanness and invitations to repeat the offence. The Court of Appeal held that although sodomy was proved, she could not succeed as she was a consenting party. Greer, L. J., in the course of his judgement stated that she understood what the respondent was doing; she turned over to enable him to do what he wanted. She made no protest until she found that it hurt her so much that she could not stand it. The act was not done by force or against her will. She must have known that it was wrong, improper and unnatural; she did not venture to say that she did not. There was no indication of any sort of duress exercised by the husband. The wife, being a willing party, was not entitled to the relief sought.

33. *Geils* v. *G.* (1848) 6 N.C. 97.

34. S. 27 of the (English) Matrimonial Causes Act, 1857; J. M. Biggs, *The Concept of Matrimonial Cruelty*, London, 1962, pp. 182-183.

35. *Statham* v *S.* (1929) P. 131, 145 (C.A.).

This case was followed in *Bampton* v. *B.*[36] where a wife's petition for divorce on the ground of sodomy was dismissed, the court holding that the wife was a consenting party. The evidence showed that the wife submitted to abnormal practices of her husband, because she was in fear of losing her husband. Hodson, L. J., in the course of his judgement stated that there was no question of consent being compelled by fraud or duress; there was no threat, nothing of that kind. The decision[37] has been criticised on the ground that there the wife was actuated by the good motive of retaining the affection of her husband and preserving the marriage. The relationship of the husband and wife being very intimate and tender, motive, love and jealousy should be carefully considered while determining the question of consent. The wife had adopted the correct attitude in submitting to the unnatural practices of her husband in the hope that the happy state of the marriage would be restored. This criticism is not wholly justifiable, because once a wife is allowed to repudiate her consent if given with intent to keep the marriage intact, her consent will become irrelevant, because she can allege a variety of reasons for repudiating it. It has been contended that since the House of Lords' decisions in *Williams* v. *W.*[38] and *Gollins* v. *G.*[39] intention or motive is no longer an essential element in cruelty and the same should apply by analogy to the question of consent in case of sodomy. It is submitted that *Bampton* v. *B.* (supra) was rightly decided and that the special and intimate relations between husband and wife were taken freely into account in deciding whether there had been a real consent.

The courts have carefully drawn the distinction between submission of the wife induced by the fradulent persuasion of the husband and real consent. Thus following a dictum of Hodson, L. J., in *Bampton* v. *B.* (supra) to the effect that consent must be real, it was held in *T.* v. *T.*[40] that, where the wife has been persuaded by the husband to submit to the act

36. *Bampton* v. *B.* (1959) 2 All E.R. 766, 767 (C.A.).

37. J. M. Biggs, *The Concept of Matrimonial Cruelty*, pp. 184-189; Alan Milner, "*Sodomy as a ground for divorce*" (1960) 23 M.L.R. pp. 49-50.

38. *Williams* v. *W.* (1963) 2 All E.R. 994, H.L.

39. *Gollins* v. *G.* (1963) 2 All E.R. 966, H.L.

40. *T.* v. *T.* (1963) 2 All E.R. 746 (C.A.).

of sodomy on the representation that it was part of her marital obligations and normal between married couples, her consent was not 'real' consent. A real consent involves knowledge of the relevant factors bearing on the question, and one of the chief of these is whether the act to which the consent is sought is right or wrong. In this case the wife testified that she thought instinctively that the practice was unnatural but not wrong. Thus there was not such consent on her part as would bar her from obtaining a divorce. A similar opinion was expressed in *Davidson* v. *D.*[41] by Karminski, J., when he said, "It is of course true that the assent of a wife, especially a young one, cannot be true assent, if the acts are forced upon her, either literally by overwhelming force or by some fraudulent persuasion that it was all right and only one of the normal incidents of married life." Where a wife seeks divorce on the ground that her husband has committed sodomy on her and the husband admits that the unnatural act had taken place but states that the wife was a consenting party, the onus of proving consent is on the husband.[42]

In *Lawson* v. *L.*[43] the wife issued a summons under the Summary Jurisdiction (Separation and Maintenance Acts 1895-1949) against the husband on the ground of his persistent cruelty, alleging that, contrary to her wish, the husband on two occasions had committed sodomy and on many occasions had tried to force her to the unnatural act. He also insisted on her masturbating him. The justices found the allegations proved and that the wife was not a consenting party. From there he appealed unsuccessfully to the Divisional Court and thence to the Court of Appeal. Lord Goddard, C. J., pointed out that, although the wife may have sumbitted to the unnatural practice she was not a consenting party.

When a wife seeks divorce on the ground of her husband's unnatural offence against her person, her evidence generally requires to be corroborated in some material way implicating

41. *Davidson* v. *D.* (1953) 1 W.L.R. 387, 392.

42. *Keogh* v. *K.* (1962) 1 W.L.R. 191.

43. *Lawson* v. *L.* (1955) 1 All E. R. 341 (C. A.); *K.* v. *K.* (1962) 106 Sol. Jour. 97 (the onus of proving consent where sodomy was admitted or proved to have occurred was upon the husband).

the husband.[44] The crime in such a case is so heinous and contrary to experience, that it would be most unreasomable to find a verdict of guilty, where there is simply oath against oath.[45] It was held in *R.* v. *Jellyman*[46] that a married woman who consents to her husband's committing an unnatural offence with her is an accomplice in the felony and as such other evidence requires confirmation. The position is similar in India, e.g., in *Smith* v. *S.*[47] the wife alleged cruelty against her husband and, among other instances of cruelty, stated that the husband frequently attempted to have unnatural intercourse with her. It was held that, where a charge of that nature is alleged, the court ought, generally speaking, to require some corroboration of the petitioner's story, because, if she in any degree assents to the unnatural practice, she becomes an accomplice to her husband.

Where persistent cruelty is alleged on the ground of sodomy and other abnormal practices, the justices must, as a judge warns the jury, direct themselves on the desirability, though not necessity, of corroboration; and, if sodomy be found after such direction, then they must consider the possibility of acquiescence of the wife.[48]

In divorce proceedings on the ground of sodomy the burden of proof is as high as in a criminal case and the same duty rests on the judge to warn the jury that they ought not to convict the accused on the uncorroborated evidence of an accomplice.[49] Once that warning has been given, corroboration is not essential as an absolute rule of law. It was held in *D.B.* v. *W.B.*[50] that it is advisable that the justices should look for some corroboration on the part of the wife, where she

44. Phipson, S.L. *Evidence,* 10th. ed., London, 1963, p. 1568 (thi is a rule of practice and not of law).

45. *N.* v. *N.* (1862) 3 Sw. & Tr. 234=164 E.R. 1264.

46. *R.* v. *Jellyman* (1838) 8 C. & P. 604=173 E.R. 637.

47. *Smith* v. *S.* (1932) 59 Cal. 945, 946 (a case under the Indian Divorce Act, 1869).

48. *Davidson* v. *D.* (1953) 1 W.L.R. 387.

49. *Statham* v. *S.* (1929) P. 131 (C.A.); *Revanna* v. *Suseelamma*, A.I.R. 1967 Mys. 165 at P. 169. Wife's sole and uncorroborated evidence not to be relied on.

50. *D. B.* v. *W.B.* (1935) P. 80 at 83.

alleges abnormal sexual acts on the part of her husband. The court demands that, when a matrimonial offence is charged, if possible the evidence of the spouse making the charge should be corroborated and it is safer to do so but, once that warning has been given in the fullest form, there is no rule of law which prevents the tribunal from finding the offence proved in the absence of corroboration.

There are no reported cases as yet on unnatural offences under the Hindu Marriage Act, 1955. However, where the provisions of Hindu law are identical with that of English, in practice the English cases are normally followed as they have a strong persuasive authority on the Indian courts. Thus in *Dr. Dwaraka Bai* v. *Prof. Nainan*[51] a wife sought dissolution of her marriage alleging adultery, sexual perversity, cruelty and desertion. Her previous petition on the ground of cruelty by sodomy and desertion had been dismissed. Relying on the English decisions of *Statham* v. *S.*,[52] and *N.* v. *N.*,[53] where cruelty by sodomy or even an attempt to commit sodomy was disbelieved, the court held that it is quite clear from the authorities cited that cogent evidence is required to overcome the presumption of innocence, where such a charge is made.

In order to constitute a ground for divorce both at English and Hindu law the crime of sodomy must be proved in full. A mere attempt will not suffice for this purpose. As in case of rape so in sodomy the crime becomes complete on proof that penetration took place.[54]

(iii) *Bestiality*

This is defined as the crime of men having carnal intercourse with beasts.[55] Sodomy is committed by anyone who carnally knows any animal; or being a male, carnally knows any man or woman *per anum*.[56] Under S. 377 of the Indian

51. *Dr. Dwaraka Bai* v. *Prof. Nainan*, A.I.R. 1953 Mad. 792 (a case under the Indian Divorce Act, 1869).

52. *Statham* v. *S.* (1929) P. 131 (C.A.).

53. *N.* v. *N.* (1862) 3 Sw. & Tr. 234 = 164 E.R. 1264.

54. *R.* v. *Robert Reekspear* (1832) 1 Mood. C.C. 342.

55. W.A. Jowitt, edited by, *The Dictionary of English Law*, London, 1959, vol. I.

56. Stephen's *Digest of the Criminal Law*, 9th ed., London, 1950, p. 169; see also Russell on *Crime*, Vol. I, ch. 42, London, 1964, p. 735; R. v. *Bourne* (1952) 36 Cr. App. R. 125 (where a husband compelled his wife to submit to bestiality with a dog).

Penal Code, 1860, a man commits sodomy or bestiality who voluntarily has carnal intercourse against the order of nature with any man, women or animal.

S. V. Gupte[57] states that even though an attempt to commit rape or sodomy may not amount to committing rape or sodomy, it may amount to bestiality and would constitute a ground for divorce. This is not so at English law. As in case of rape and sodomy, so in case of bestiality, it must be proved that the offence of bestiality was committed.[58] If no more than an attempt to commit the offence be proved, it will not provide a ground for divorce to the wife, although she can prove cruelty on the ground of attempt only[59]. However, it is not essential to prove a criminal conviction of the offence. The offence has to be proved *de novo* when a decree of divorce is sued for, as it is done in case of rape, e.g., in *R.* v. *R.*[60] a wife sought a decree of divorce on the ground of her husband's bestiality with a mare. The husband had been convicted at the Central Criminal Court of the attempt to commit the offence and sentenced to imprisonment. At the matrimonial suit evidence was given by an eye-witness of the act of bestiality and it was held that the wife was entitled to divorce.

Thus it is not necessary that the accused must be convicted of the offence at criminal law. What is required is proof of the offence at matrimonial law and not a mere attempt. Shiva Gopal[61] gives a wide jurisprudential meaning to the word 'bestiality' so as to include brutish, irrational, and degrading conduct. This is not correct. The word 'bestiality' has the same meaning under the matrimonial law as it has acquired under S. 377 of the Indian Penal Code, 1860 and in English law.

57. S. V. Gupte, *Hindu Law of Marriage*, Bombay, 1961, p. 204.

58. *R.* v. *Cozins* (1834) 6 C. & p. 351.

59. D. H. Chaudhari, *The Hindu Marriage Act*, 1955, Calcutta, 1957, p. 238; P.V. Deolalkar, *The Hindu Marriage Act*, 1955, Nasik City, 1959, p. 120.

60. *R.* v. *R.* (1932) 173 L.T. Jour. 264.

61. Shiva Gopal, *The Hindu Code*, Allahabad, 1964, p. 363.

Chapter X

RESIDUARY GROUNDS FOR DIVORCE IN HINDU LAW

So far we have been discussing Hindu grounds for divorce which are similar to English law. In this chapter those grounds for divorce will be dealt which do not have any counterparts in English law. These include renunciation of the world, conversion to a religion other than Hinduism, leprosy and venereal disease not contracted from the petitioner.

1. *RENUNCIATION OF THE WORLD*

At Hindu law either spouse can petition for divorce on the ground that the other party to the marriage has renounced the world by entering any religious order.[1] Similar provisions exist at Hindu law in Kenya[2] and Uganda,[3] with the diffeence that there the respondent must be shown to have remained in such order apart from the world for a period of at least three years immediately preceding the presentation of the petition. A person's entry into a religious order operates as a "civil death", effecting a complete severence from his relations and property. According to the *sastra*, when a householder sees his skin wrinkled, his hair white and the sons of his sons, he may resort to the forest, taking a vow not to eat any food raised by cultivation, abandoning all his belongings, either entrusting his wife to his sons or taking her along with him.[4] Manu[5] says that he should reside in the forest, properly controlling his senses and living on water, roots and fruits. He should wear a skin or tattered garment, the hair of his head should be braided and the hair on his body, his beard and his nails unclipped. He

1. S. 13 (1) (vi) of the Hindu Marriage Act, 1955.
2. S. 10 (1) (f) of the (Kenya) Hindu Marriage and Divorce Ordinance, 1960.
3. S. 9 (2) (a) (ii) of the (Uganda) Hindu Marriage and Divorce Ordinance, 1961.
4. Baudhayana II, 6. 11, 16, S.B.E., Vol. 14; Manu VI, 2, S.B.E., vol. 25; Vishnu XCIV, 1-3, S.B.E., vol. 7.
5. Manu VI, 5-7, 21-25, S.B.E., vol. 25.

should lead a life of great austerity, reciting the Veda and practising solitary meditation.

At night he should roll about on the ground and stand on tip-toe or alternately stand and sit down during the day. In summer he should expose himself to the heat of the five fires;[6] during the rainy season he should live under the open sky and in winter he should wear wet clothes. He should dry up his bodily frame by practising increasingly harsher austerities, living without a fire, without a house, remaining wholly silent and avoiding all things that give sensual pleasure. He should harbour enmity against no one; he should bless him who curses him. The duties of an ascetic are laid down by Gautama[7] in terms similar to those of Manu. According to him an ascetic should be indifferent to all creatures, whether they do him injury or kindness. He should take no interest in the joys and sorrows of others.

He should worship gods, manes, goblins and Rishis. He should employ his time in the study of Vedas and in the meditation on the miseries of life and rebirth. He must acquire a complete mastery of the secrets of life. His salvation lies in acquiring knowledge of ultimate Reality. When 'release' is obtained the gods rejoice and the soul's timeless wandering is over; it has been reunited to the Supreme.[8] His purity of life and realisation of the Real are lights for those, who are still involved in the meshes of *Maya*, i. e., the material and social worlds. By entering a religious order, man becomes a free and resurrected soul, no longer subject to worldly considerations.[9] He must not recall his past life, but pursue meditation, so as to withdraw his mind from the world and concentrate on the Self.

According to West and Bühler[10] the religious order may be entered at any time after the completion of the ceremony of

6. Five fires are lit around the *sanyasi*. These are symbolic of the fact that he has control over his five senses and indicate that he has become detached from worldly affairs by overcoming sex, anger, greed, love and pride. The footnote to Manu VI, 23 in S.B.E., vol. 25, p. 202 explains that there are four fires and the heat of the sun is the fifth.

7. Gautama III, 11-36, S.B.E., vol. 2; see also Vasishtha X, 17, S.B.E., vol. 14.

8. Baudhayana II. 6. 11, 15, S.B.E., vol. 14; Gautama III, 26-35, S.B.E., vol. 2; K.V. Rangaswami Aiyangar, *Some Aspects of Hindu View of Life according to Dharmasastra*, Baroda, 1952, pp. 152-153.

9. Kewal Motwani, *Manu Dharma Sastra*, Madras, 1958, pp. 60-63.

10. West, R. and Bühler, G., *A Digest of the Hindu Law*, London, 1919, p. 518.

the investiture with the sacred girdle. This is not correct, because investiture with the sacred thread signifies that a boy has reached manhood. He still has to pass through the three stages of life in order to become competent to enter a religious order. The age for such retirement is seventy years according to Baudhayana. This is reasonable because by the time a man has fulfilled his sacred duty of paying off the three debts, he must have reached about the age of seventy years. As we have seen Manu says that, when a householder sees his skin wrinkled, his hair turning white and the sons of his sons, he may resort to the forest. A twice- born man who seeks final liberation without having offered sacrifices to the gods, sinks downwards (i. e., goes to hell). According to the *sastras* a Hindu passes through four successive stages of life.[11] He spends the first stage in studying the Vedas, the second in being a married man and begetting sons, as enjoined by the sacred law, and the third in offering sacrifices to the gods. Renunciation of the world is the last stage of a man's life, and this is not open to one who has not passed through the above mentioned three stages. The violation of this rule leads to hell.

(i) *Kinds of Ascetic*

An ascetic is of three kinds, i. e., Naishthika Brahmachari, (life-long student) Vanaprastha, (hermit in a forest) Bhikshu, *yati* or *sanyasi* (religious mendicant).[12] The adoption of the first two orders is included under practices to be avoided in this Kali age (present age) but persons of the last category are still found. Bhattacharya[13] on the authority of Vaikhanasa Grihya-Sutra VIII, 9, mentions four kinds of ascetic, namely, Kuticaka, Bahudaka, Hamsa, and Paramahansa. Ascetics of the first category dwell in the hermitages of Gautama, Bharadvaja, Yajnavalkya, Harita and the like, go round eight villages for begging and are proficient in *yoga*. Those of the second type, who carry the three *dandas*, (the trident), the water vessel and

11. Apastamba II. 9. 21, 1, 8, S.B.E., vol. 2; Baudhayana II. 6. 11, 12, S.B.E., vol. 14; Manu VI, 35-37, S.B.E., vol. 25; Golapchandra Sarkar Sastri, *A Treatise on Hindu Law*, Calcutta, 1936, pp. 851-852.

12. Gautama III, 2, S.B.E., vol. 2; Golapchandra Sarkar Sastri, *A Treatise on Hindu Law*, *p*. 672.

13. B. Bhattacharya, *The 'Kalivarjyas' or Prohibitions in the 'Kali' Age*, Calcutta, 1943, p. 68.

the yellow robe, dwell in the houses of *Brahmarsis* and other saints, eschew meat, salt and stale food and beg from seven houses. An ascetic of the Hamsa order stays for one night only in a village for every five nights in towns. Members of the Paramahamsa order dwell under trees or in deserted habitations or on a cremation-ground.

The above-mentioned four kinds of *sanyasi* are again divided into two classes according to the type of staff they carry. The Kuticaka and the Bahudaka carry a Tri-danda (trident) and the other two eka-danda (single stick).[14] The word 'danda' ordinarily means a staff. The trident figuratively used signifies threefold restraint exercised by control of tongue, body and mind or word, deed and thought.[15] The Kuticaka and Bahudaka have a more or less fixed habitation. A member of the former order is maintained by his sons, while one of the latter would dwell in a holy place appointed by the sages. According to the distinction made in the Digests, membership of these two orders is prohibited in this 'Kali' age.[16] It should be noted that irrespective of their order, all ascetics have the same object, i. e., attainment of spiritual salvation and final liberation by which man is saved from the hell of life and rebirth. According to the Mahabharata, Kuticaka, Bahudaka, Hamsa and Paramahamsa each later of the orders is superior to preceding one. But to which of these orders a *sanyasi* belongs depends on his *acharana* (act or conduct) or the path he treads after becoming a sanyasi.[17] The man who becomes an ascetic severe his connection with the members of his natural family and, being adopted by his preceptor, becomes his spiritual son. The other disciples of his *guru* are regarded as his brothers, while the co-disciples of his *guru* are looked upon as uncles and in this way a spiritual family is established on the analogy of a natural family.[18]

14. B. Bhattacharya, *The 'Kalivarjyas' or Prohibitions in the 'Kali' Age*, p. 70; see also P. V. Kane, *The History of Dharmasastra*, vol. II, part II, Poona, 1941, pp. 937, 939.

15. The Asiatic Researches, vol. XVI, Calcutta, 1828, pp. 132-133.

16. B. Bhattacharya, *The 'Kalivarjyas' or Prohibitions in the 'Kali' Age*, p. 72.

17. *Ramakrishan* v. *Srinivasarao*, A.I.R. 1960 Andh. Pr. 449.

18. *Sital* v. *Sant*, A.I.R. 1954 S.C. 606 at p. 613.

The principle of succession upon which one member of an order of ascetics succeeds to another is based entirely upon fellowship and personal association with that other and a stranger, though of the same order, is excluded.[19] If an ascetic or a hermit is a *Brahmin,* he is called a *yati* or *sanyasi*; if a *Sudra,* he is called a *Paradesi.*[20]

(ii) *Who can become a Sanyasi ?*

According to the *Dharmasastra* the adoption of the Holy Orders, i. e., the renunciation of the world by entering the fourth stage of life is open to the twice-born classes.[21] Thus the fourth caste, the *Sudras,* cannot become *sanyasis.* It was held in *Dharmapuram* v. *Virapandiyam*[22] that a *Sudra* cannot enter the order of *yati* or *sanyasi,* so the special rules applicable to the inheritance of a Hindu ascetic do not apply to the estate of a *Sudra* ascetic, unless there is proof of any general or special usage. This case was followed in *Harish* v. *Atir,*[23] and in *Narasinhdas* v. *Khanderao,*[24] where a similar conclusion was reached in holding that a *Sudra* could not become a *sanyasi* or a *yati.*

Hindu *sastric* rules could be modified by custom or usage. It has been seen above that since a *Sudra* cannot become a *sanyasi,* the special rules of Hindu law by which succession to the property of a Hindu ascetic is regulated are not applicable to a *Sudra* ascetic but this law was not followed in *The Secretary of State for India* v. *Sambasivam,*[25] where it was held that a disciple of a *Sudra* ascetic who dies without leaving any blood relations, is an heir of the latter under the Hindu law. In this case the rules of Hindu law applicable to twice-born classes

19. *Khuggender* v. *Sharupgir* (1879) 4 Cal. 54?.
20. *Giyana* v. *Kandasami* (1887) 10 Mad. 375.
21. K. V. Rangaswami Aiyangar, *Some Aspects of the Hindu View of Life according to Dharmasastra,* p. 152 (*sanyasa* is open only to persons of the first *varna*).
22. *Dharmapuram* v. *Virapandiyam* (1899) 22 Mad. 302; see also *Somasundaram* v. *Vaithilinga* (1917) 40 Mad. 846; *Sobhaddi* v. *Gobind* (1924) 46 All. 616.
23. *Harish* v. *Atir* (1913) 40 Cal. 545; P. V. Kane, *History of Dhramasastra,* Vol. III, Poona, 1946, p. 765.
24. *Narasinhdas* v. *Khanderao,* A.I.R. 1922 Bom. 295; see also T. P. Gopalakrishnan, *Hindu Marriage Law* Allahabad, 1957, p. 15; J. R. Gharpure, *Hindu Law,* Poona, 1921, p. 321.
25. *The Secretary of State for India* v. *Sambasivam* (1921) 44 Mad. 704.

were applied to a *Sudra*. In the minority judgement of Kapur, J., in *V. V. Giri* v. *Suri Dora*[26] it was stated that a person may be judged by his actions and not by his birth only. If a *Sudra* has the qualities of a *Brahmin*, he is is not to be treated merely as a *Sudra*. On the contrary if a *Brahmin* is devoid of good qualities and virtues, he is to be treated as a *Sudra*. The view that caste in Hinduism is not dependent on birth alone but on actions finds support in the Bhagwat Gita and the Mahabharata. The caste system, which was originally based on the occupation of a man and according to which the *Sudras* ranked lowest in Hindu society, is inconsistent with present democratic ideas, so the old view that a *Sudra* cannot be a *sanyasi* is unlikely to be maintained. Moreover, there are Hindu sects which admit *Sudras* as ascetics, if they are qualified otherwise,[27] e. g., the religious sect known as Bairagis is not confined to the twice-born classes,[28] but the order of inheritance applicable to the estate of a Hindu ascetic, is applied to a Bairagi on the ground of custom.[29] The Hindu Marriage Act, 1955 provides no indication of what it means by "renunciation of the world", which may be a matter of fact or of law. If the latter, presumably the old decisions apply. *Ramakrishan* v. *Srinivasarao*[30] seems to suggest that it is a question of fact.

(iii) *Renunciation must be complete*

In order to be a ground for divorce renunciation must be final and complete withdrawal from earthly affairs. The mere fact that a person declares himself to be a *sanyasi* or dresses like one, will not suffice for this purpose. In order to be civilly dead it is necessary that his entry into the religious order should be irrevocable so as to make it certain that he will not change

26. *V. V. Giri* v. *Suri Dora*, A.I.R. 1959 S. C. 1318, p. 1331; see also Manu X, 64-65, S.B.E., vol. 25; Yaj. I, 96, *Yajnavalkya Smriti*, Book I, The Achara Adhyaya, translated by Srisa Chandra Vidyarnava, Allahabad, 1918; Golapchandra Sarkar Sastri, *A Treatise on Hindu Law*, pp. 144-145.

27. Golapachandra Sarkar Sastri, *A Treatise on Hindu Law*, pp. 853-854; R. West and G. Bühler, *A Digest of Hindu Law*, p. 519; P. V. Kane, *History of Dharmasastra*, vol. II, part II, p. 946 (women and *Sudras* may adopt sanyasa).

28. *Sadhu* v. *Baldevdasji* (1915) 39 Bom. 168.

29. *The Collector of Dacca* v. *Jagat Chunder* (1901) 28 Cal. 608.

30. *Ramakrishan* v. *Srinivasarao*, A.I.R. 1960 Andh. Pr. 449.

his mind and return to his family.[31] A man cannot, merely by calling himself a *sanyasi*, change his status and bring about his civil death; there must be initiation by a *guru* into the order of *sanyasis* by the appropriate *mantra*.[32]

The essential characteristic of an orthodox *sanyasi* is the relinquishment of all property and worldly concerns and even the desire for them. Therefore, when a person makes a will before becoming a *sanyasi* and the will expressly states that it is to take effect from the date of his death, not from the date of his becoming a *sanyasi*, and that during his lifetime he will retain control over his property, the terms of the will show that there is no complete and final renunciation such as the law requires.[33] Similarly in *Gouri* v. *Niader*[34] it was held that a *Brahmin*, who had left his home in early life and settled in Calcutta, where he lived the life of a Hindu mendicant and practised religious austerities but dressed himself in ordinary clothes, deposited money on interest and acquired property in the Punjab, cannot be taken to have renounced the world and was not a *yati* or religious ascetic in Hindu law. The very fact that he dealt with and had control over secular property was inconsistent with the duties of an ascetic.

In *Ramakrishan* v. *Srinivasarao*[35] the man whose renunciation was in dispute used to dress like a *sanyasi* but had not ceased to take interest in the worldly affairs. The evidence showed that he was the head of the family and used to keep account of the expenses for the maintenance of the family. He wrote a book, "Nectar of Grace"; it is a translation of the Rubayat of Omar Qayam and he received royalities therefrom. He had money in the bank and lived in a house with his family. It was held that he had not renounced the world. The publication of "Nectar of Grace" shows that it could not have been undertaken by a *sanyasi*, because any translation of Omar Qayam would involve the application and engagement of his mind to the worldly affairs.

31. *Krishnaji* v. *Hanmaraddi* (1934) 58 Bom. 436.
32. *Satyanarayana* v. *Hindu Religious Endowments Board*, A.I.R. 1957 Andh. Pr. 824.
33. *Parshottam* v. *Desaibhai*, A.I.R. 1932 Bom. 459.
34. *Gouri* v. *Niader* (1913-1914) 18 C.W.N. 59.
35. *Ramakrishan* v. *Srinivasarao*, A.I.R. 1960 Andh. Pr. 449.

Entry into the fourth stage of life by renunciation of the world is done by formal rites. An important and symbolic act in the ceremony is initiation by a *guru*. The whole procedure takes fortyfour days. The prospective *sanyasi* is required to perform the eight *shraddhas* or twelve according to some authorities. These eight *shraddhas* are said to be to *Devas, Rishis, Divyas, Manushas, Bhutas, Pitrus, Matrus,* and oneself. The performance of the *Jeeva Shraddham* or *Atma Shraddham* is the last of the preliminaries before civil death takes place. The renouncer should also perform the *Prajapati* sacrifice, which involves relinquishing of all the wealth and abandonment of worldly affairs, i.e., he must give up *Putreshana, Vitteshana, Lokeshana,* and take up to *Bhikshacharyam.* He should then recite the *Trivrit Prasanna Mantram,* after which there is no turning back. After this the *Presha Mantram,* which involves complete renunciation of the world, his family, his children and his property, is performed.

In *Kondal* v. *Swamulavaru*[36] it was held that the essentials of *Sanyasam* are that the postulant for *Sanyasam* should perform the necessary rites and ceremonies prescribed by the *sastras,* in particular the *Prajapathiyeshti* or *Agneshti* and the *Viraja Homam* and finally relinquish all property and worldly concerns and even all desire for them. At the end of these ceremonies the postulant has no property at all for even the sacrificial vessels, if they are of wood, must be burnt in the fire and, if they are of metal, must be given to the priest.

A *sanyasi* becomes dead to the world from the time of his entry into the holy order, therefore, a will made by him takes effect from the date of his renunciation of the world and not from his death. The position of an ascetic at Hindu law is similar to the status of a monk at English law. According to Pollock and Maitland[37] a monk or nun cannot acquire or have

36. *Kondal* v. *Swamulavaru,* A.I.R. 19 18 Mad. 402; *Baldeo* v. *Arya,* A.I.R. 1930 All. 643 (the performance of *Prajapathiyeshti Homam* is essential and is the final ceremony); *Ramdhan* v. *Dalmer* (1910) 14 C.W.N. 191 (the *Viraja Homam* ceremony is essential for the attainment of the status of a *sanyasi*); see also K. V. Rangaswami Aiyangar, *Aspects of the Social and Political System of Manusmriti,* Lucknow University, 1949, p. 140; *Sital* v. *Sant,* A.I.R. 1954 S. C. 606 (rites and ceremonies are essential for entry into the religious order).

37. F. Pollock and F. W. Maitland, *The History of English Law,* Cambridge, 1911, vol. I, p. 434.

any property rights; when a man becomes 'professed in religion', his heir at once inherits from him any land that he has, and, if he has made a will, it takes effect at once, as though he were dead. If after this a kinsman dies leaving land, which, according to the ordinary rules of inheritance would descend to him, he is overlooked, as though he were no longer in the land of the living; the inheritance misses him and passes to some more distant relatives; nothing descends to him, for he is already dead.

2. *CONVERSION TO ANOTHER RELIGION*

It has been shown in the second chapter that according to the *sastras* a Hindu marriage once performed before the nuptial fire with the sacred formulae is irrevocable and subsists not only during the lifetime of both the spouses, but also in the next world. The wife being a gift from gods and marriage being a sacrament, it could not be dissolved by human act so that conversion to another religion by one or both spouses did not dissolve the marriage. In *Gulmohammad* v. *Emperor*,[38] a Hindu married woman was fraudulently taken away from her Hindu husband and converted to Islam, under circumstances which amounted to compulsion. After the conversion, the accused a Mohammadan, married her according to Muslim rites. She remained at his place against her wish for about one year, until she was rescued from his custody under a warrant of a magistrate. The accused maintained that, by conversion to Islam, her Hindu marriage was dissolved and she was legally married to him. It was held that the conversion of a Hindu wife does not *ipso facto* dissolve her marriage and she cannot during her husband's life-time contract a valid marriage with another person. A similar view was taken by the Calcutta High Court in the matter of *Ram Kumari*,[39] where it was laid down that there is no authority in Hindu law for the proposi-

38. *Gulmohammad* v. *Emperor*, A.I.R. 1947 Nag. 121.

39. In the matter of *Ram Kumari* (1891) Cal. 246, 271; this case was followed by the Madras High Court in *Budansa* v. *Fatima* (1914) 22 Ind. Cas. 697; *Mt. Nandi* v. *Emperor*, A.I.R. 1920 Lah. 379 (the mere conversion does not dissolve the marriage, which could be dissolved by a court of law); see also Golapchandra Sarkar Sastri, *A Treatise on Hindu Law*, pp. 172, 661; J.D.M. Derrett, "*The Convert's Polygamous Marriage*" (1965) 67 Bom.. L.R, Journal, 71 at p. 73.

tion that an apostate is absolved from his marital obligations, so conversion to Mahommedanism does not dissolve a Hindu marriage. A sacred and solemn relation like marriage cannot be regarded as terminated simply by the change of faith by either spouse.

A Hindu marriage is not dissolved if both the spouses adopt Christianity.[40] Conversion to another religion operates as degradation at Hindu law and the convert is regarded as an outcaste. The unconverted spouse is fully justified in abandoning the other and refusing to cohabit, but this never operates as divorce. That is why the Native Converts' Marriage Dissolution Act, 1866 was passed,[41] under which a convert to Christianity could sue the other spouse for restitution of conjugal rights and, in case the unconverted spouse refused to comply with the order, the marriage was dissolved. This Act provided no reciprocal right to the unconverted spouse to sue for divorce. The position of the unconverted spouse has been improved by S. 13 (1) (ii) of the Hindu Marriage Act, 1955 under which either spouse can sue the other for divorce on the ground that the respondent has ceased to be a Hindu by conversion to another religion. The word 'Hindu' in this sense does not mean Hindu by religion, but covers various sects of Hinduism, e. g., Jains, Buddhists, Sikhs, etc. In other words 'Hindu' is to be understood so as to include those people who are subject to Hindu Marriage Act, 1955. A person of non-Hindu origin can also become a Hindu. In *Morarji* v. *Administrator-General of Madras*,[42] a European lady who had lived in India for thirteen years became formally converted to Hinduism. She adopted a Hindu name, Sulochana, and married a Hindu according to Vedic rites. She resided in India till her death, and was cremated in a Hindu crematorium. It was held that she was a Hindu and, therefore, subject to Hindu law.

It was held in *Resham* v. *Khuda*[43] that conversion to an-

40. *Thapita Peter* v. *Thapita Lakshmi* (1894) 17 Mad. 235; *Gobardhan* v. *Jasadamoni* (1891) 18 Cal. 252.

41. *Administrator-General of Madras* v. *Anandachari* (1886) 9 Mad. 466, 470; *The Government of Bombay* v. *Ganga* (1880) 4 Bom. 330.

42. *Morarji* v. *Administrator-General of Madras* (1929) Mad. 160.

43. *Resham* v. *Khuda*, A.I.R. 1938 Lah. 482; followed in *Mt. Ayesha* v. *Subodh*, A.I.R. 1949 Cal. 436, where it was held that the motive of the convert is immaterial in deciding whether there has been a conversion from one religion to another.

other religion requires no other proof than a person's declaration, the only condition being that the declaration should be definite and voluntary. A genuine conversion is one which has actually taken place with the necessary formalities. Once it is proved as an accomplished fact, the court is not concerned with the motive of the convert. A mere declaration of conversion is not enough.[44] Some religions, e. g., Christianity and Islam have essential ceremonies of conversion. In order to be effective, there must be real and complete conversion, accompanied by the necessary formalities, unless there is custom or usage to the contrary, in which case the emphasis is on the prevailing sentiment and usages of the community and it is its approval or disapproval which should be the governing factor.[45] Motive may be relevant where a person undergoes conversion for the purpose of committing a fraud upon the personal law. However, if a Hindu becomes a Christian, there is nothing to prevent him from reverting to Hinduism.[46] But if the unconverted spouse has got a decree of divorce under S. 13 (1) (ii) of the Hindu Marriage Act, 1955, he cannot claim his Hindu wife back.

3. *LEPROSY*

Under S. 10 (1) (c) of the Hindu Marriage Act, 1955 either party to the marriage can petition for a decree of judicial separation on the ground that the other spouse has been suffering from virulent form of leprosy for a period of not less than one year. If, however, the disease has been virulent and incurable and has persisted for a period of three years immediately preceding the presentation of the petition, a decree of divorce can be sued for under S. 13 (1) (iv) of the same Act. The practical result is the same, because, if judicial separation has been obtained on the ground of leprosy and the parties have failed to resume cohabitation, either[47] party can petition for

44. *Ramayya* v. *J. Elizabeth*, A.I.R. 1937 Mad. 172; see also *Vermani* v. *V.*, A.I.R. 1943 Lah. 51 at 52 (Special Bench).

45. Per Krishnaswami Ayyangar, J., in *Durgaprasada* v. *Sundarsanaswami* I.L.R. 1940 Mad. 653, 660, 668.

46. *Marthama* v. *Munuswamy* (1951) 1 M.L.J. 694; see also Golapchandra Sarkar Sastri, *A Treatise on Hindu Law*, p. 67.

47. Hindu Marriage Amendment Act, 1964 (Amendment of S. 13 of the Hindu Marriage Act, 1955).

divorce under S. 13 (1) (viii) of the Hindu Marriage Act, 1955. Thus a period of three years has to elapse before the marriage can be dissolved. Under both the clauses the petitioner has to prove that the leprosy is of virulent type. The word 'virulent' has been defined as 'poisonous, venomous, deadly, noxious, extremely severe, malignant, bitter, spiteful.'[48] It is 'characterised by the presence of corrupt or poisonous matter or by extreme malignancy or violence.'[49] Cases relating to exclusion from inheritance on the ground of the claimant's suffering from virulent and aggravated[50] form of leprosy show that, in order to operate as a disqualification for inheritance, the leprosy has to be of agonising, sanious or ulcerous type. Deformity and unfitness for social intercourse, arising from the virulent and disgusting nature of the disease, are the most satisfactory tests.[51]

Under S. 13 (1) (iv) of the Hindu Marriage Act, 1955, in addition to being virulent the leprosy must be incurable. In *Annapurnamma* v. *Appa*,[52] a wife petitioned for divorce on the ground that her husband had been suffering from a virulent and incurable form of leprosy. The husband's defence was that the leprosy from which he suffered was of a mild and non-infective type, that he was treated in the leprosy hospital and was cured of the symptoms of the disease. Medical evidence showed that the word 'cure' could not be applied to leprosy, but further advance could be arrested; a person suffering from the disease could improve his skin and the leprosy from which the respondent was suffering could be arrested by treatment. It was held that every type of leprosy cannot be considered 'virulent' which only applies when the disease is malignant or venomous; the respondent was not suffering from 'virulent' leprosy.

48. Henry Cecil Wyld. *The Universal Dictionary of the English Language*, London, 1932.

49. A. H. Murray, *A New English Dictionary on Historical Principles*, vol. X, Oxford, 1928.

50. *Janardhan* v. *Gopal* (1868) 5 Bom. H. Court 145, 146.

51. *Kayarohana* v. *Subbaraya* (1913) 19 Ind. Cas. 690 (Mad. H. Ct.); followed in *Raju* v. *Ramaswamy* (1914) 25 Ind. Cas. 968 (Mad. H. Ct.).

52. *Annapurnamma* v. *Appa*, A.I.R. 1963 Andh. Pr. 312.

The word 'incurable' according to Murray's[53] and the Oxford Dictionaries means 'incapable of being healed by medicine or medical skill'. As mentioned in the above case of *Annapurnamma* v. *Appa* leprosy cannot be cured but its advance can be arrested. Incurability can be established by evidence that continuous treatment has proved ineffective or by medical evidence as to the nature of the respondent's affliction.

In the recent case of *Annapurna* v. *Nabakishore*,[54] the husband petitioned for divorce on the ground that his wife had suffered from virulent and incurable leprosy for not less than three years. The fact that the wife had leprosy was not disputed but it was held that the onus of proof was on the husband to establish that the leprosy was not only virulent but also incurable. There is no provision in the Hindu Marriage Act, 1955, empowering the court to keep the patient under observation or to give the respondent the opportunity to undergo treatment before granting a decree of divorce. The petitioner has to prove the "incurability" of the disease. Very stringent conditions have been imposed by the Lagislature to prevent dissolution of marriage on frivolous grounds or without an attempt to cure of what may be a curable disease.

In addition to the remedies provided by the Hindu Marriage Act, 1955, a wife is justified in living separate from her husband and claim separate residence and maintenance on the ground that he is suffering from a loathsome and virulent leprosy.[55] Leprosy is a problem in India, and its cure is lengthy and costly. One of the ways of prevention is to reduce the chance of infection, so it is reasonable that a spouse should not be forced to run the risk of contracting this painful and disabling malady from the other spouse. It is in the interest of prevention of the disease as well as the interest of the healthy spouse that the Hindu Code provides the remedies mentioned.

53. A. H. Murray, *A New English Dictionary on Historical Principles*, Oxford, 1901. vol. v, William Little, H. W. Fowler & J. Coulson, *The Shorter Oxford English Dictionary on Historical Principles*, Oxford, 1933.

54. *Annapurna* V. *Nabakishore*, A.I.R. 1965 Orissa 72.

55. *Sheenappayya* v. *Rajamma*, A.I.R. 1922 Mad. 399=45 Mad. 812; see also S. 18 (2) (c) of the Hindu Adoptions and Maintenance Act, 1956.

4. *VENEREAL DISEASE*

Under S. 10 (1) (d) of the Hindu Marriage Act, 1955, either party to a marriage can petition for a decree of judicial separation on the ground that the other spouse, for a period of not less than three years,[56] has been suffering from a venereal disease in a communicable form, the disease not having been contracted from the petitioner.[57] A decree for divorce can be had on the same ground under S. 13 (1) (v) of the Hindu Marriage Act, 1955, the difference between the two clauses being that the provision, that the disease should not have been contracted from the petitioner does not appear under the latter. However, this deficiency is made up by S. 23 (1) (a) of the Hindu Marriage Act, 1955, under which the court is required to be satisfied that the petitioner is not taking advantage of his own wrong, therefore, if the petitioner himself has communicated the disease to the respondent, he (the petitioner) will not be entitled to relief under this clause.

Syphilis, gonorrohea and soft chancre have been defined as venereal diseases under the (English) Venereal Diseases Act, 1917. In order to be a ground for divorce or judicial separation, the venereal disease must be of communicable form. The word 'communicable' means communicable to any person, e.g., to the other spouse or to the child of the marriage. In *Lawrence* v. *L.*,[58] where the wife's syphilis was communicable to the child of the marriage but not to the husband, the husband was held entitled to a decree on the ground of his wife's venereal disease.

The petitioner must prove that the respondent has been suffering from such disease for a period of at least three years.

56. S. 10 (1) (d) as amended by the Hindu Marriage Amendment Act, 1956 (73 of 1956).

57. Identical grounds for judicial separation and divorce exist under sections 23 and 27 of the Special Marriage Act, 1954, but unlike S. 10 (1) (d) and S. 13 (1) (v) of the Hindu Marriage Act, 1955, the same wording has been used under both the sections 23 and 27 of the Special Marriage Act, 1954. Provisions for divorce or judicial separation on the grounds of leprosy and venereal diseases do not appear in the Kenya or Uganda Ordinances.

58. *Lawrence* v. *L.*, June 2, 1954 (unreported) cited in Rayden on *Divorce*, edited by J. Jackson and others, 9th edition, London, 1964, pp. 121-122.

This time-limit has been criticised on the ground that a person should not be compelled to live and cohabit with another for such a long period, in continuous danger of being infected with the disease. The time-limit is absurdly unreasonable.[59] However, it should be noted that the policy of the Legislature is to discourage premature recourse to divorce, when there is a possibility of the disease being cured by medical treatment. Moreover, the communication of a venereal disease by one spouse to another can be pleaded as cruelty if the latter petitions for a decree of judicial separation under S. 10 (1) (b) of the Hindu Marriage Act, 1955. If the parties do not resume cohabitation for a period of two years or upwards after the passing of such a decree, a petition for divorce can be presented under S. 13 (1) (viii) of the Hindu Marriage Act, 1955.

The (English) Matrimonial Causes Act, 1950, does not expressly make venereal disease a ground for divorce but cruelty can be based on the communication of such diseases. A married woman or a married man may apply to a magistrates' court for an order under the (English) Matrimonial Proceedings (Magistrates' Courts) Act, 1960, against the other party to the marriage, if the defendant, while knowingly suffering from a venereal disease, has insisted on, or has, without the complainant being aware of the presence of that disease, permitted sexual intercourse between the complaintant and the defendant.

It was held in *Foster* v. *F.*[60] that a successful attempt by a husband, who knows that he is suffering from venereal disease, to have connection against her will with his wife, who also knows, that he is so suffering, may be legal cruelty, although, in fact, the disease is not communicated. In *Ciocci* v. *C.*[61] it had been held that there could be no cruelty, unless the disease was actually communicated but this case was overruled. The situation is similar in India; in *Birendra* v. *Hemlata*[62] it was held that to constitute cruelty it is usually required that the disease should have been actually communicated to the complainant,

59. Shiva Gopal, *The Hindu Code*, Allahabad, 1964, p. 358.
60. *Foster* v. *F.* (1921) P. 438 (C.A.).
61. *Ciocci* v. *C.* (1853) 1 Sp. Ecc. Ad. 121 = 164 E.R. 70.
62. *Birendra* v. *Hemlata*, A.I.R. 1921 Cal. 459, 463 (a case under the Indian Divorce Act, 1869).

that the complainant should have been ignorant of the existence and nature of the defendant's disease at the time of its communication and that the defendant should have infected the petitioner knowingly and wilfully. The principle laid down in that decision has been modified in later cases.

In *Browning* v. *B.*,[63] a wife petitioned for divorce on the ground of her husband's adultery and cruelty, alleging that he had contracted a venereal disease and communicated it to her. It was held that a wife establishes *prima facie* a charge of legal cruelty against her husband when she proves that she is a guiltless woman and he has communicated a venereal disease to her. If that has been done, it is for the husband, if he can, to prove that he was ignorant or innocent or otherwise not guilty of legal cruelty. The disease communicated in this case was gonorrhoea but there was no allegation that it was communicated knowingly, wilfully or recklessly. Though the wife could not prove knowledge on the part of the husband, it would have been unreasonable to require affirmative proof of such knowledge, because the strong probability is that she never would be able to find it. In view of the House of Lords' decision of *Gollins* v. *G.*,[64] which established that intent to injure is not an essential ingredient of cruelty, proof that the respondent was ignorant of the fact that he suffered from a venereal disease, although material, would not now necessarily be a defence.

The fact that a wife has been infected with a venereal disease is *prima facie* evidence that the husband has committed adultery. In *Stead* v. *S.*[65] a wife petitioned for divorce on the ground of her husband's adultery and cruelty, alleging that he was suffering from 'crab lice' and had communicated the infection to her. She stated that she had not had intercourse with any man other than her husband. It was held that cruelty and adultery was proved. Similarly in *Nagle* v. *N.*,[66] where a husband had contracted gonorrhoea and com-

63. *Browning* v. *B.* (1911) P. 161, 163, 172.

64. *Gollins* v. *G.* (1963) 2 All E.R. 966, H.L.; see also Rayden on *Divorce* at pp. 132-133.

65. *Stead* v. *S.* (1927) 71 Sol. Jour. 391.

66. *Nagle* v. *N.*, A.I.R. 1933 Lah. 507 (a case under the Indian Divorce Act. 1869); *Hardless* v. *H.*, A.I.R. 1933 All. 56 (the fact that a husband has communicated a venereal disease to his wife is in law sufficient evidence of adultery and it also amounts to legal cruelty).

municated it to his wife, she was entitled to a decree of divorce, on the ground of his adultery and cruelty.

It should be noted that infection with the venereal disease is only *prima facie* evidence of cruelty and capable of being rebutted. In *K.* v. *K.*,[67] the marriage took place in 1933. The wife never had cause to believe that the husband had committed adultery until, in 1953, he was found to be suffering from tabo-paresis, a disease caused by syphilis. The wife had never suffered from syphilis. In a suit for divorce the wife asked the court to infer that the husband had committed adultery. The husband now being a person of unsound mind, was represented by the official solicitor as guardian *ad litem*. In the circumstances the husband must have contracted syphilis from sexual intercourse with a woman infected with that disease but the question was whether that sexual intercourse had taken place during the marriage or whether it occurred before that. The medical evidence indicated that the husband's infection was probably contracted more than twenty years before 1953, so the court could not say that it had been established beyond reasonable doubt that the husband had become infected after the date of the marriage and held that adultery had not been proved.

Cruelty, like adultery based on venereal disease, can be condoned. In *N.* v. *N.*,[68] it was held that the wife knew that her husband had contracted a venereal disease but had condoned it by subsequent cohabitation. Similarly in *Birendra* v. *Hemlata*[69] it was held that, where communication of the venereal disease has been established no question can arise as to the propriety of granting the divorce, unless condonation of the offence is shown.

5. *SECOND MARRIAGE OF THE HUSBAND*

Under S. 13 (2) (i) of the Hindu Marriage Act, 1955

67. *K.* v. *K.* (1963) 107 Sol. Jour. 57; see also comments in Medicine, Science and the Law (1962-1964) vols. 3-4 at pp. 660-661.

68. *N.* v. *N.* (1862) 3 Sw. & Tr. 234, 240 = 164 E.R. 1264, 1266.

69. *Birendra* v. *Hemlata*, A.I.R. 1921 Cal. 459, 463 (a case under the Indian Divorce Act, 1869).

and the relevant provisions of the Kenya[70] and Uganda[71] Ordinances a wife may also present a petition for the dissolution of her marriage on the ground, in the case of any marriage solemnised before the commencement of this Act, that the husband had married again before such commencement or that any other wife of the husband married before such commencement was alive at the time of the solemnisation of the marriage of the petitioner, provided that in either case the other wife is alive at the time of the presentation of the petition. This ground of divorce is open to both the wives. In both the cases the other wife must be living at the time of the presentation of the petition.

In *Naganna* v. *Lachmi*[72] a wife petitioned for divorce on the ground that her husband had married again; the husband admitted the second marriage but resisted the petition on the ground that, subsequent to the filing of the petition, he had divorced the second wife. This defence failed and the court held that the crucial date is the time of the presentation of the petition, so the first wife was held entitled to a decree of divorce under S. 13 (2) of the Hindu Marriage Act, 1955.

The question of divorce on the ground of second marriage of the husband only arises where both the marriages were contracted before the commencement of the Hindu Marriage Act, 1955. The legislature has taken account of the state of Hindu society before 1955, where except possibly in certain parts of the country, it was not legally forbidden for a Hindu to take a second wife while the first was living. When the Act came into force, the legislature left it to the choice of the wife of a polygamous husband either to remain with him or to seek divorce on that ground.[73] After the commencement of the Hindu Marriage Act, 1955 a second marriage is null and void under Ss. 5 and 11 and the offence of bigamy is also committed under S. 17, which renders the bigamous marriage void and

70. S.10 (1) (g) (i) (ii)of the (Kenya) Hindu Marriage and Divorce Ordinance, 1960.

71. S. 9 (1) (b)(i) (ii)of the (Uganda) Hindu Marriage and Divorce Ordinance, 1961.

72. *Naganna* v. *Lachmi*, A.I.R. 1963 Andh. Pr. 82.

73. *Chanda* v. *Nandu*, A.I.R. 1965 Madh. Pr. 268.

punishable under Ss. 494 and 495 of the Indian Penal Code, 1860.[74] What is prohibited is the taking of the second spouse in the life-time of the first for the Hindu Marriage Act, 1955 aims at enforcing monogamy.[75] Bigamous marriages contracted before the commencement of the Act do not become *ipso facto* void, but continue to be valid. At the same time a right is given to the wife to seek divorce under S. 13 (2) (i) of the Act.

There is no provision in the Hindu Marriage Act, 1955 under which a wife apprehending her husband's taking a second wife, can apply for and obtain an injunction restraining the husband from doing so. But if the apprehended marriage actually takes place, she can bring proceedings for bigamy under Ss. 494 and 495 of the Indian Penal Code 1860 which are made applicable by S. 17 of the Act.[76] In order to establish the offence of bigamy, the prosecution must prove that the second marriage was solemnised in accordance with law or custom applicable to the parties and was celebrated with proper ceremonies and in due form. In the absence of such evidence mere admission by the husband that he married the second wife will not be sufficient to render him liable for bigamy.[77] In addition to the above remedies, a wife has just cause for leaving her husband and living apart from him on the ground of his second marriage.[78]

The defence of condonation, which operates as forgiveness either express or implied of a matrimonial offence with the implied condition that the offence will not be repeated, has no application to the above mentioned section, because in such a case the ground for divorce is based on the status of the

74. *Mohd. Ikram* v. *State of U.P.*, A.I.R. 1964 S. C. 1625 at p. 1631; followed in *Naurang* v. *Sapla*, A.I.R. 1968 All. 412; *Gitabai* v. *Fattoo*, A.I.R. 1966 Madh. Pr. 130; *Bhaurao* v. *State of Maharashtra*, A.I.R. 1965 S. C. 1564; *Dutta* v. *State*, A.I.R. 1969 Cal. 55 at p. 57.

75. *Bodemma* v. *Veeraiah*, A.I.R. 1962 Andh. Pr. 446; *Lalithamma* v. *Kannan*, A.I.R. 1966 Mys. 178 at p. 185; followed in *Nirmoo* v. *Nikka Ram*, A.I.R. 1968 Delhi 260.

76. *Umashankar* v. *Radha*, A.I.R. 1967 Pat. 220.

77. *Boloram* v. *Surjya*, A.I.R. 1969 Assam 90.

78. *Pulliah* v. *Rushingamma*, A.I.R. 1963 Andh. Pr. 323.

parties and not on any matrimonial offence.[79] The status of the husband as a twice married man cannot be restored by forgiveness. In a case where the husband married a second wife with the consent or at the instigation of the first wife, it is doubtful whether she would be successful in obtaining divorce, if she later decided to make use of the provision under S. 13 (2) of the Hindu Marriage, Act, 1955. Similar considerations apply where the second wife married the husband with full knowledge and approbation that his first wife was alive at the time of the second marriage. S. 23 (1) (e) of the Act, which provides that notwithstanding the existence of grounds for divorce, the court should be satisfied that there is no other legal ground why relief should not be granted, may be a bar to a decree, for a spouse should not be heard to complain of an act which he or she has fully approbated or acquiesced in.[80]

6. *FAILURE TO COMPLY WITH A DECREE FOR RESTITUTION OF CONJUGAL RIGHTS*

It has been shown in chapter two that separation between husband and wife was not countenanced by the *sastra*. The civil courts of British India continued to apply the *sastric* texts of Hindu law relating to conjugal cohabitation. It was held in *Binda* v. *Kaunsilia*[81] that these texts were not merely moral precepts, but rules of law, so a husband could bring a suit for the restitution of conjugal rights, when his wife had deserted him. This is now embodied in S. 9 of the Hindu Marriage Act, 1955. The essence of a decree for restitution of conjugal rights is that the aggrieved party desiring the company of his spouse makes an effort through the court to get the latter back so that they may be able to lead conjugal life. It does not impose a continuing obligation on the wife to stay with her husband till one of them dies. Thus where a wife returns to

79. *Chandrabhagabai* v. *Rajaram*, A.I.R. 1956 Bom. 91 (a case under the Bombay Prevention of Hindu Bigamous Marriages Act, 1946); followed in *Deepo* v. *Kher*, A.I.R. 1962 Punj. 183. 185.

80. J.D.M. Derret, *Introduction to Modern Hindu Law* pp. 236-237; Shiva Gopal, *The Hindu Code*, p. 362.

81. *Binda* v. *Kaunsilia* (1891) 13 All. 126.

the matrimonial home, lives there with a genuine intention to resume cohabitation with her husband and has to leave after some time because of the hostile attitude of the latter, it cannot be said that there is no compliance with such decree.[82] When a husband gets a decree for restitution of conjugal rights against his wife, but fails to execute it for more than 2 years, the wife is entitled to petition for divorce and the decree for restitution of conjugal rights becomes ineffective when she does so.[83]

By S. 13 (1) (ix) of the Hindu Marriage Act, 1955 a marriage may be dissolved on the ground that the other party has failed to comply with a decree for restitution of conjugal rights for a period of two years or upwards after the passing of the decree. From the language used in the section it is clear that the party against whom the decree has been passed cannot apply for a divorce. In *Kamlesh* v. *Kartar*[84] the husband was granted a decree for restitution of conjugal rights on the ground that his wife had deliberately brought the matrimonial cohabitation to an end. Later under clause (ix), subsection (1), section 13 of the Hindu Marriage Act, 1955, she petitioned for divorce on the ground of non-compliance by the husband with the decree for restitution of conjugal rights. It was contended that the absence of the words 'against that party' in clause (ix) indicates that it is open to either the husband or the wife to seek dissolution of marriage,wh en a decree for restitution of conjugal rights has been passed irrespective of the fact against whom it was decreed. It was held that the husband was under no obligation to execute the decree or make efforts to persuade the wife, who was the guilty party in this case, to comply with the decree. In accordance with the provisions of S. 23 (1) (a) of the Hindu Marriage Act, 1955, the court has to be satisfied that apart from the existence of the grounds for divorce the petitioner is not in any way taking advantage of his or her wrong. From this it is evident that only the successful petitioner for restitution can sue for divorce on this ground.

82. *Someswara* v. *Leelavathi*, A.I.R. 1968 Mys. 274.

83. *Shanti* v. *Ramesh*, A.I.R. 1969 Pat. 27.

84. *Kamlesh* v. *Kartar*, A.I.R. 1962 Punj. 156; see also J.D.M. Derrett, *Introduction to Modern Hindu Law*, pp. 235-236; S. V. Gupte, *Hindu Law of Marriage*, p. 200.

If, however, the party, against whom a decree for restitution of conjugal rights has been made, is rendered incapable by the act of the successful petitioner of complying with the decree, the latter cannot get a decree for divorce under S. 13 (1) (ix) of the Hindu Marriage Act, 1955. In *Ishwar* v. *Pomilla*,[85] after a decree for restitution of conjugal rights had been passed, the husband filed a petition for annulment of the marriage, which was dismissed. After the expiry of two years, he petitioned for divorce on the ground of non-compliance with the decree by the wife. It was held that, as it was impossible for the wife to make any attempt to comply with the decree for restitution of conjugal rights while the husband was proceeding with the petition for nullity of the marriage, the husband was not entitled to a decree for divorce.

S. 13 (1)(ix) of the Hindu Marriage Act, 1955 has been amended by the Hindu Marriage Amendment Act, 1964 (44 of 1964) under which either party can sue for divorce after a decree for restitution of conjugal rights has been passed. The amendment has extended the right to petition for divorce to the party against whom such decree was granted. This right is subject to the overriding provision that the petitioner is not taking advantage of his own wrong.[86] In *Syal* v. *S.*[87] where a husband resorted to proceedings under S. 9 of the Hindu Marriage Act, 1955 as a device for obtaining divorce from his wife who was free from blame and blemish. His petition for divorce was dismissed as he had throughout the proceedings been taking advantage of his own wrong. The recourse to law by petitioning under S. 9 was not for the purpose of getting his wife to stay with him, but with the object of treating this as a step towards final dissolution of the marriage. The remedy of restitution has been borrowed from English matrimonial law. Failure to comply with the decree for restitution of conjugal rights is a ground for judicial separation in Kenya,[88] where the position appears to be closer to that in England than in India.

85. *Ishwar* v. *Pomilla*, A.I.R. 1962 Punj. 432.

86. *Laxmibai* v. *Laxmichand*, A.I.R. 1968 Bom. 332.

87. *Syal* v. *S.*, A.I.R. 1968 Punj. 489

88. S. 12 (d) of the (Kenya) Hindu Marriage and Divorce Ordinance, 1960.

7. *FAILURE TO RESUME COHABITATION AFTER A DECREE FOR JUDICIAL SEPARATION*

Under S. 13 (1) (viii) of the Hindu Marriage Act, 1955 as amended by the Hindu Marriage Amendment Act, 1964 and under the analogous provision in S. 10 (1) (g) of the (Kenya) Hindu Marriage and Divorce Ordinance, 1960, either party can petition for divorce on the ground that there has been no resumption of Cohabitation as between the parties to the marriage for a period of two years or upwards after the passing of a decree for judicial separation in a proceeding to which they were parties. S. 13 (1)(viii) of the Hindu Marriage Act, 1955 was amended in its application in Uttar Pradesh by the Hindu Marriage Act (Uttar Pradesh Sanshodhan) Adhiniyam, 1962 which substituted "has not resumed cohabitation after the passing of a period of two years has elapsed since the passing of such decree" for the words set out above. It was held in *Waryam* v. *Pritpal*[89] that a decree for dissolution of marriage cannot be granted at the instance of the spouse against whom judicial separation was decreed. The remedy of divorce on the ground of non-resumption of cohabitation for a period of two years or upwards is not available to a spouse who had been found guilty of a matrimonial fault in the previous proceedings for judicial separation. But since the Hindu Marriage Amendment Act, 1964, either party can sue for the dissolution of the marriage.

In *Tej* v. *Hakim*,[90] a wife got a decree of judicial separation on the ground of her husband's cruelty; after the lapse of two years, she was granted a divorce, as there had been no resumption of cohabitation within that time. Under S. 23 (2) of the Hindu Marriage Act, 1955, where the relief of judicial separation or divorce is asked for the court is under a duty to endeavour to bring about reconciliation between the spouses.[91] The section states that such endeavour at reconciliation is to

89. *Waryam* v. *Pritpal*, A.I.R. 1961 Punj. 320.

90. *Tej* v. *Hakim*, A.I.R. 1965 J. & K. 111.

91. *Lakshmi* v. *Ravena*, A.I.R. 1966 And. Pr. 73 at p. 76.

be made 'in the first instance', but it cannot be said from this that the court cannot make use of its good offices at any later stage. If no endeavour is made by the trial court, it will be a serious omission, which has to be taken into account, but the appellate court also has jurisdiction to make such efforts at reconciliation. The intention is to ensure that all reasonable steps are taken to maintain the marriage and, if at any stage the circumstances are propitious for reconciliation, it will be the court's duty to take advantage of the opportunity, as was pointed out in *Jivubai* v. *Ningappa*,[92] where a husband was granted a decree of judicial separation on the ground of his wife's desertion. It was contended on behalf of the wife-appellant that only the trial court has jurisdiction to try to bring about a reconciliation but this plea was rejected.

But judicial separation would be a valuable remedy in India even if it did not pave the way for a petition for divorce, because it is a remedy appropriate to communities where divorce and remarriage are disliked or are economically impracticable.[93] The vast majority of the Indians still live in villages, where the joint family system prevails. In such cases the intrigues and jealousies of the relatives and misunderstandings between the spouses may result in premature appeals to the court to relieve them of the duty of cohabitation. A decree of judicial separation will provide a *locus poenetentiae*, an opportunity to reflect on the consequences. Even in modern England the matrimonial law provides opportunities for the parties seeking divorce to get reconciled. This is evident from S. 1 (2) of the (English) Matrimonial Causes Act, 1965, which says that, in calculating the period for which the respondent has deserted the petitioner without cause and in considering whether the desertion has been continuous, no account shall be taken of any one period, not exceeding three months, during which the parties resumed cohabitation with a view to reconciliation.

92. *Jivubai* v. *Ningappa*, A.I.R. 1963 Mys. 3 at p. 4.

93. J.D.M.Derrett, *Introduction to Modern Hindu Law*, p. 206; Amarendra Nath Mukherjee, "*Social Legislation with special reference to the Law of Marriage*"; 1 Law Quarterly (Journal of the Indian Law Institute, West Bengal) (1964), No. 4, 321 at p. 325.

A warning to guard against the danger of divorce is also found in the following remarks of Sir J. P. Wilde in *Sidney* v. *S.*[94] "It is the foremost duty of this court, in dispensing the remedy of divorce, to uphold the institution of marriage. The possibility of freedom begets the desire to be set free, and the great evil of a marriage dissolved, but it loosens the bonds of so many others. The powers of this court will be turned to good account if, while meting out justice to the parties, such order should be taken in the matter as to stay and quench this desire and repress this evil."

However, a contrary view is held by some authors,[95] who regard judicial separation as something strange and unnecessary. If a marriage is to be dissolved, they say, let it be dissolved altogether and set the parties free. It is a terrible thing that people should go about the world neither married nor unmarried, possibly liable to contract fresh and illegal unions[96] and certainly exposed to temptation to commit adultery. The grounds for judicial separation in S. 10 of the Hindu Marriage Act, 1955 are misplaced. They should be grounds for divorce under S. 13 of the same Act.[97]

A brief survey of the history of English divorce, as we have seen in chapter III, shows that in the nineteenth century and early twentieth century in England the grounds for divorce were very rigid. The restricted remedy of judicial separation was allowed so that the stability of marriage could be maintained. At present Hindus are making social, economic and educational progress by the same stages as the English did in the past. Until this progress and the independence of women have been fully achieved, a direct and ready remedy of divorce is likely to be misused by the people. The uneducated villagers in Hindu community need the paternal supervision of the courts. In this respect the provision for judicial separation

94. *Sidney* v. *S.* (1734) 34 L.J.P.M. 122.

95. N.D. Patnaik, "*Divorce in India, how it is and how it should be,*" A.I.R. 1959, Journal, p. 86, Vallabhdas P. Parekh, "*Desertion is no Ground for Dissolution of Marriage under the Hindu Code Bill—its effects*", A.I.R. 1951. Journal, p. 48.

96. Sir F. Jeune, P., in *Johnson* v. *J.* (1901) P. 193 at 195.

97. Surinder Singh, "*The Hindu Law of Marriage : Old and New*" (1965) XVII, The Law Review, Panjab University Law College, 24 at pp 153, 220.

is serving a useful purpose. Divorce is a concession to human weakness and should be granted only when a marriage has so completely broken down that it is a practical impossibility to keep the spouses together. As the same view is prevalent in Hindu society, the law has rightly made divorce more rigid than it is in England today.

Chapter XI

CONCLUSION

Hindu *sastric* law, as we have seen, attached great sanctity to the concept of marriage by considering it as a sacrament and holding it as an indissoluble bond between a husband and his wife, which was supposed to subsist not only during their lifetimes but also in the next existence in heaven. From the religious and spiritual point of view even the death of one of the marriage partners was not seen as dissolving the marriage. That is why a Hindu widow was not allowed to remarry, although there are some *sastric* texts, which are capable of being construed either as authorising a woman to take a second husband in some cases, e.g., when her husband is impotent, lost, dead or becomes a religious ascetic, or as countenancing customs permitting remarriage provided those conditions obtained. Such and other analogous texts may alternatively be interpreted, in part, as cases of presumption of death—actual death or civil death— and could conceivably be seen by the orthodox as venial breaches of the *sastric* pattern of the indissolubility of marriage.

Apastamba says, "He who has unjustly forsaken his wife shall put on an ass's skin with the hair turned outside and beg in seven houses saying, 'Give alms to him who forsook his wife'. That shall be his livelihood for six months."[1] Manu, Narada and Vasishtha also provide sanctions against the unjust abandonment of a wife.[2] This shows that even 'abandonment', which is comparable to judicial separation in English law, was not recognised at Hindu *sastric* law. In fact the prevailing sentiment of Hindu society has always been repugnant to the idea of divorce and remarriage of females, excepting the regions where divorce is practised by custom.[3]

1. Apastamba I. 10. 28, 19-20, S.B.E., Vol. 2.
2. Manu IX, 30, S.B.E., vol. 25; Narada XII, 95, S.B.E., vol. 33; Vasishtha XXVIII, 2-3, S.B.E., vol. 14; these texts are discussed earlier at Chapter II.
3. See also J.D.M. Derrett, *Religion, Law and the State in India*, London, 1968, pp. 356-358.

The existence of rigid orthodox *sastric* rules against permitting divorce inevitably created cases of real hardship which necessitated legislative measures, e.g., Baroda Hindu Nibandha, 1937; Bombay Hindu Divorce Act, 1947; Madras Hindu (Bigamy Prevention and Divorce) Act, 1949 and Saurashtra Hindu Divorce Act, 1952. Finally the Hindu Marriage Act, 1955 provided a uniform system for all Hindus in India. It is under this Act that the grounds for divorce have been discussed and compared with English law. Hindu law of divorce is by no means identical with English law, which is resorted to for the sake of clarification of legal terms. In interpreting the concept of desertion, cruelty and other matrimonial faults Indian courts frequently look at the English case-law in order to find out how English judges have construed the same words. Consequently English decisions seem to have a strong persuasive authority in this respect. Where there are no judicial precedents, not only English decisions but also Indian decisions under different statutes, e.g., the Indian Divorce Act, 1869 and Special Marriage Act, 1954, are referred to if they throw light on a similar point. This is obvious from a study of case-law.

"Living in adultery" is a ground for divorce under S. 13 (1) (i) of the Hindu Marriage Act, 1955. Here this term has a wider meaning than in S. 497 of the Indian Penal Code and S. 488 of the Criminal Procedure Code. It denotes an adulterous course of conduct pursued for a continuous period as distinguished from one or two lapses from virtue. It must be shown that the period during which the guilty spouse was living in adultery was so related in proximity of time, from the commencement of adulterous association to the filing of the petition, that it could reasonably be inferred that he or she was living in adultery at the time of the petition. It is not enough for a petitioner to prove that his spouse has led an adulterous life for a year or so at some time in the past. Keeping a concubine or a mistress (including a bigamously married 'wife') will suffice for this purpose. Where a Hindu contracts a second marriage, which is void at law, and lives with the bigamously married wife, this will amount to living in adultery.[4]

Since proof of 'adultery' or "living in adultery" is a question

4. *Chanda* v. *Nandu*, A.I.R. 1965 Madh. Pr. 268.

of evidence, the legislature has deliberately left these phrases undefined. The social status of the parties, their relationship to each other and the surrounding circumstances have to be taken into account, for social conduct among Indians of the professional classes differs from that which is normal among people living in a village, whose livelihood depends directly or indirectly upon agriculture. The matrimonial offence must be proved beyond reasonable doubt. The fact that there were opportunities for committing adultery is not sufficient in itself unless it can be shown by documents or antecedent conduct that the association of the parties was so intimate and their mutual passion so clear that adultery might reasonably be assumed as the result of an opportunity for its occurrence.[5]

Modern Hindu law gives a right of divorce on the ground of "living in adultery", while a single act of sexual intercourse with a person other than his or her spouse entitles the innocent party to a decree of judicial separation. It is interesting to compare this with the situation at Hindu *sastric* law and see what amounted to adultery in those days. *Sastric* law, being religious and divinely inspired, naturally considered adultery as a heinous offence, and provided heavy penalties for its offenders, which varied from cutting off limbs to death. Winking at a woman, smiling at her, sending her messages, touching her dress and ornaments were termed an adulterous act[6] of the first degree. Sending perfumes, garlands of flowers, spirituous liquor, clothes, fruit or food and conversing with a woman in secret were considered as an adulterous act of the second degree. Sitting on the same bed, kissing and embracing each other was regarded as adultery of the highest degree.[7] The classification into first, second and highest degree is relevant for the purpose of punishment.

5. *Sachindranath* v. *Nilima*, A.I.R. 1970 Cal. 38 pp. 55, 68 citing with approval *Ross* v. *R.* (1930) A.C. 1 pp. 7, 23.

6. The original is *stri-samgrahana*=guilty attempt upon a woman, or assault on a female.

7. Brihaspati XXIII, 3-8 = Manu VIII, 354-358 =Narada XII, 62-68, S.B.E., vol. 33, Oxford, 1889, p. 178;G. Jha, *Hindu Law in its Sources*, vol. I, Allahabad, 1930, pp. 472-475; this topic is skilfully discussed by Ludo Rocher, "*The Theory of Matrimonial Causes According to the Dharmasastra*" in J.N.D. Anderson, edited by, *Family Law in Asia and Africa*, London, 1968, pp. 105-108.

Unlike English law[8] desertion is not a ground for divorce but the petitioner can ask for a decree of judicial separation on the ground that the other party has deserted him for a continuous period of two years. Such desertion has to be without reasonable cause and without the consent or against the wish of the petitioner, and includes wilful neglect. When interpreting the legal concept of desertion Indian courts seek help from English cases. Having done so they must apply the law against the social background of Hindu society, which is so different from the English that similar facts in the two countries may not lead to the same conclusion, e.g., in *Dunn* v. *D.*[9] it was held that neither spouse has a casting vote to the choice of a matrimonial home. Such matters have to be settled by agreement and not by imposition of the will of one partner over that of the other. On the other hand Hindu law regards it as the bounden duty of a wife to live with her husband, wherever he may choose to reside.[10] Consequently, what is just cause for leaving in case of an English wife may not necessarily be so for her Hindu sister. However, this trend is not likely to continue in view of the education of women in India, resulting in their economic and social independence which is fast approaching.

Like desertion, cruelty is a ground for judicial separation under the Hindu Marriage Act, 1955. The nature of cruelty has to be such as to cause a reasonable apprehension in the mind of the petitioner that it will be harmful or injurious for him to live with the other party. This definition is virtually the same as laid down in the celebrated case, *Russell* v. *R.*[11] Here English decisions are useful for basic principles but should not be extended any further. This is for the compelling reason that social conditions and unwritten ethics of conduct in the two countries may be widely different. In fact Indian judges have warned against the danger of relying on the facts of foreign judicial precedents.[12]

8. As it stood before, the (English) Divorce Reform Act, 1969.
9. *Dunn*. v. *D.* (1949) P. 98, C.A.
10. See views of P. Diwan *Law Review* (University of Panjab Law College, Chandigarh) 22 (1968) 1-10 also at Annual Survey of Indian Law, 1966, 345.
11. *Russell* v. *R.* (1897) A. C. 395, H. L.
12. *Subbarama* v. *Saraswathi*, A.I.R. 1967 Mad. 85 p. 88; *Umari Bai* v. *Chittar*, A.I.R. 1966 Madh. Pr. 225.

At one time it was the rule that intent to injure is an essential ingredient of cruelty and to prove intent recourse was frequently had to the presumption that a person intends the natural and probable consequences of his acts. The test was hardly satisfactory, especially when the cruel conduct of the husband was not directly aimed at the wife but directed towards a third party, as for instance, brutally beating a child of the marriage or indecent assualts on females, which had an injurious effect on the mental health of the wife. The concept of cruelty was fully reviewed by the House of Lords in *Gollins* v. *G.*[13] which established that intention to injure is not essential, if it can be reasonably inferred, having regard to all the circumstances of the case, that the victim has been cruelly treated. The criterion is whether the conduct of the respondent has a cruel effect on the petitioner, and not whether he has the intent to be cruel.

The decision is a remarkable one, and has been relied on by courts in India. In creating the matrimonial offence of cruelty, the Hindu Marriage Act, 1955 has not only provided relief for hard cases, but also revived the spirit of Hindu *sastric* law, which condemned cruelty. A popular verse relates that gods rejoice where women are happy and honoured, but those families in which females live in grief perish as though destroyed by magic.[14] 'Therefore, men who seek their own welfare should always honour their womenfolk with gifts and ornaments'.

The next ground for divorce is incurable unsoundness of mind for a continuous period of not less than three years immediately preceding the presentation of the petition. Unlike English law the provision of care and treatment in an approved mental institution does not appear under the Hindu statute. This is probably due to the fact that facilities for medical aid are not adequate in India and society tolerates the presence of mental defectives more easily. The expression 'incurably unsound mind' cannot be so widely construed as to cover feebleminded persons or those of dull intellect who understand the nature and consequences of their acts. The test of unsoundness of mind is whether the person concerned is incapable of managing himself and his affairs, bearing in mind that 'affairs' in-

13. *Gollins* v. *G.* (1963) 2 All E.R. 966, H.L.; relied on in *Bhagwat* v. *B.*, A.I.R. 1967 Bom. 80.

14. Manu III, 55-60, S.B.E., vol. 25, pp. 85-86; Yaj. I, 82.

clude the problem of society, employment and married life and this has to be judged by the standard of the reasonable man, but without reference to the cause of such incapacity. If a mentally deranged person recovers from insanity but has to take a drug to maintain his cure and lead a normal life, this will not class him as of incurably unsound mind. 'Incurable' is tantamount to 'irrecoverable.'

The unsoundness of mind must be continuous and two separate periods cannot be added together to make the required period of three years under the statute. A petitioner is not entitled to a decree if his conduct has conduced to the insanity of the respondent. A decree of divorce or judicial separation presupposes that relief is granted to the petitioner on proof of guilt on the part of the respondent. If that is so, it is questionable whether the victim of insanity is to be blamed for his misfortune. The true reason in such a case is that marriage partners are unable to fulfil their marital obligations because of the insanity of one of them.

Either spouse can petition for divorce on the ground that the other has not been heard of as being alive for a period of 7 years or more by those who would naturally have heard of him, had that party been alive.[15] The provision is not novel. As we have seen before, some Hindu *sastric* texts allowed or appeared to allow a woman to remarry, as where her husband had gone abroad and was unheard of or was dead. These were cases of presumption of death—actual death or civil death – which were supposed to have dissolved the marriage. The presumption of death is also embodied in S.108 of the Indian Evidence Act, 1872. The objection against the ground for divorce on the presumption of death is that where a marriage is dissolved but after some years the spouse whose death was presumed is proved to be alive and actually returns, this will amount to divorcing him against his will without any element of guilt or blame on his part. Hence the doctrine of matrimonial offence has no application here.

Renunciation of the world by entry into an order and ceasing to be a Hindu by conversion to another religion are grounds for divorce, representative of Hindu religion, the paral-

15. S. 13 (1) (vii) of the Hindu Marriage Act, 1955.

lels of which are not to be found in English law. Renunciation which amounts to civil death, is the last *asrama* and final stage in a Hindu's life. It is true that entry into the *sanyasa asrama* is irrevocable and return to the worldly affairs is not permissible,[16] but whether it dissolved the marriage of the renouncer was doubtful. Consequently one could envisage a situation when a *sanyasi* after some years changes his mind and leaves the *asrama*. The question in such a case is whether, on his returning to family life, he should be able to claim his wife back. The answer would seem to be in the affirmative, if his marriage was not legally dissolved. It is against this contingency that the Hindu Marriage Act, 1955 has provided.

Conversion to another religion like Islam or Christianity does not *ipso facto* dissolve a Hindu marriage, which is a sacrament and as such incapable of being undone. However, the convert becomes degraded and an outcaste at Hindu *sastric* law, which act entitles the unconverted spouse to refuse to cohabit with the former. In such a case, under the Native Converts Marriage Dissolution Act, 1866, a convert to Christianity could sue the other spouse for restitution of conjugal rights and, in case the other spouse failed to comply with the decree, their marriage was dissolved. This Act provided, curiously, no reciprocal right to the unconverted spouse to sue for divorce.

The hardship of the unconverted spouse has been removed by S. 13 (1) (ii) of the Hindu Marriage Act, 1955 under which either spouse can petition for divorce on the ground that the other has ceased to be a Hindu by conversion to another religion. The mere fact that a person becomes an agnostic or an admirer of another religion, or goes to church or prays in a mosque will not be sufficient for this section. In order to be effective the act of conversion must be complete and attended by formal rites and ceremonies, if they are essential, according to the custom and usage of the religion concerned. Once it is proved to have taken place, the court is not concerned with the motive of the convert.[17] But motive may of course be relevant

16. This is discussed earlier at Chapter X; see also Y. Krishan, "Was *it permissible for sanyasi (monk) to revert to lay life* ?" Annals of the Bhandarkar Oriental Research Institute, 50 (1969) Poona, p. 75 ff.

17. A Christian, Hindu or any non-Muslim may, while married to a

when a person gets converted for the purpose of committing fraud on the personal laws. The reason for making conversion to another religion a ground for divorce is not difficult to see. One can envisage a situation in which the change of religion by one spouse without the consent of the other could create such a state of affairs in the family home that it would adversely affect the health of the other. Consequently divorce or lesser matrimonial relief, e.g., on the ground of cruelty is an appropriate remedy.

The grounds for divorce, as we have discussed, are based on the doctrine of matrimonial offence, namely, the commission by one spouse (the guilty) of a matrimonial offence on which the other (the innocent spouse) petitions for relief by way of dissolution of marriage. The relief may be refused if the petitioner is not so innocent, as for instance, where he has committed adultery or other matrimonial offence and the court's discretion is not exercised in his favour. Although about 93 per cent of all divorce suits brought in England and Wales are undefended, the legal procedure is based on the assumption that litigation is contentious.[18]

Of recent years this doctrine has been subject to severe criticisms, which have resulted in the passing of the (English) Divorce Reform Act 1969. Numerous exceptions had already been created to the basic principle of the matrimonial offence, e.g., divorce can be granted on the ground of incurable insanity, which obviously is no offence at all but rather a misfortune. The same criticisms can be directed against some of the Hindu grounds for divorce as where the respondent has renounced the world or becomes converted to another religion or is suffering from a venereal disease or incurable leprosy. Such acts do not involve the taint of guilt but are acts having only an indirect bearing on marriage or are unfortunate afflictions.

In cases where the petitioner discloses his own adultery and asks the court to exercise its discretion, which is exercised

wife of his former religion, be converted to Islam, and marry a second, Muslim wife, who may herself have been converted for the purpose. See J.D.M. Derrett, "*The Convert's Polygamous Marriage*", (1965) 67 Bom. L.R., Journal, 71-74.

18. Law Commission's Report, *The Field of Choice* (Cmnd. 3123), para 20.

against him only in rare circumstances, the judge takes into consideration the interests of all concerned—the parties to the suit, their partners in adultery, any children, whether of the marriage or of adulterous unions, and the interest of the society at large. Consequently judgement on an offence should lead to an inquiry into the total situation.[19]

Recent decisions[20] in the House of Lords have laid down that cruelty can be established without the intention to be cruel. Consequently a divorce can be granted on the ground of cruelty—simply because the respondent's conduct has produced an intolerable situation for the petitioner. The reason for the conduct—whether it be due to habitual and incurable laziness or insanity—is not essential. Thus a matrimonial offence can be established without proving any guilt or guilty intent of the offending spouse, and this is clearly inconsistent with the doctrine of matrimonial offence.

The notion that a marriage breaks up because one spouse has committed an offence against the other is false because in the majority of cases both parties are at fault, as for instance, a wife who nags her husband out of the matrimonial home is as much at fault as he is in leaving her for another woman. In such cases it is difficult to find out who the real culprit is. The commission of a matrimonial offence usually takes place after the breakdown and is seldom the cause of it. Happily married couples rarely commit adultery. Even if they do, a divorce suit is unlikely to be instituted as a result of this unless the marriage has already broken down. One spouse does not deert the other for a number of years unless the marriage has faised. Cruelty as a ground for divorce stands midway, for sometimes it is a cause of breakdown, while at other times it is a sympltom of it.[21]

Under the present system, the underlying causes, which may be emotional or psychological and which in reality lead to the failure of the marriage, are not investigated. Instead the parties have to fit their case within one of the matrimonial

19. *Putting Asunder: A Divorce Law for Contemporary Society*, S.P.C.K., 1966, p. 35.

20. *Gollins* v. *G.* (1963) 2 All E.R. 966; *Williams* v. *W.* (1963) 2 All E.R. 944; these cases are discussed earlier at Chapter VI.

21. Cmnd. 3123, para 25 (a), (b).

offences in order to get a divorce. Sometimes their legal advisers can conjure up a suitable offence from the history of the marriage or one is contrived. In fact an artificial, elaborate and dramatic legal performance is put up in the court to prove a matrimonial offence. The branding of one spouse as 'guilty' and the other as 'innocent' leads to unnecessary bitterness between the parties and has harmful effects on the children of the marriage, if there are any.

All this brings the law and the machinery of justice into disrepute. It encourages hypocrisy and perjury, e.g., evidence is brought before the court to suggest adultery which in reality did not take plce. In other cases offences are committed deliberately for the purpose of securing a ground for divorce. Cases of consensual separation are dressed up to look like real desertion. The fact is that when a married couple has decided to divorce each other, they use fair or foul means to obtain a decree. The truth is not brought before the court and the judge is asked to pronounce on the artificial state of affairs. Remarks of Denning, L. J., in *Trestain* v. *T.*[22] throw some light on the situation. "The fact that the husband has obtained this decree does not give a true picture of the conduct of the parties. I agree that the marriage has irretrievably broken down and that it is better dissolved. So let it be dissolved."

A law of divorce founded solely on the concept of matrimonial offence is unsatisfactory, and gives no remedy where it is needed most, namely, where a husband leaves his wife, who has committed no offence, for another attractive woman with whom he cohabits and has children, and wishes to legalise this second union and the children thereof, but is prevented from doing so because his wife would not divorce him. In such a situation it is unrealistic and unfair that law should keep a marriage alive, which is an empty shell and dead for all practical purposes except in name, and at the same time refuse legal validity to a *de facto* union and its children. Husbands in this type of difficulty, not knowing how to get out of their marriage tie decently, angry with themselves for letting their wives down often direct their aggression towards those wives.[23] They find

22. *Trestain* v. *T.* (1950) P. 198, p. 202 cited with approval by the C.A. in *Trumath* v. *T.* (1970) I All E.R. 111 at p. 114.

23. F.E. Mostyn, "*The Present Divorce System*", The New Law Journal, May 21, 1970, p. 485.

no way of ending their marriage except by behaving badly. The law, as it stands at present, is on the side of least scrupulous, the least honourable and the least sensitive.[24]

How law should operate is well defined by Lord Walker as, "The true significance of marriage as I see it is lifelong cohabitation in the home for the family. But when the prospect of continuing cohabitation has ceased the true view as to the significance of marriage seems to require that the legal tie should be dissolved. Each empty tie—as empty ties accumulate—adds increasing harm to the community and injury to the ideal of marriage."[25] This view is commendable and underlies the doctrine of 'breakdown', which has now been enacted in England in the Divorce Reform Act, 1969, under which the sole ground for divorce is that the marriage has broken down irretrievably. However, the court shall not hold the marriage to have broken down irretrievably unless the petitioner satisfies one or more of the following five facts.

(a) that the respondent has committed adultery and the petitioner finds it intolerable to live with the respondent. This provision takes account of the surrounding circumstances which precede the commission of adultery and gives effect to the Law Commission's observation that the commission of such a matrimonial offence follows the breakdown of the marriage and is not the cause of it. Here adultery operates as a symptom, pointing out that a marriage has broken down. In addition the petitioner is required to prove that he or she finds it intolerable to live with the respondent. The word 'petitioner' indicates that the test is subjective, i.e., the finding of 'intoleration' has to be measured by reference to the victim and not by the standard of hypothetical reasonable spouse.

(b) that the respondent has behaved in such a way that the petitioner cannot reasonably be expected to live with him. This provision extends to a very large field of acts and may cover most of the matrimonial offences, which are termed as grounds for divorce under the former law, e.g., cruelty will fall within the ambit of these words, but it will not be essential to estab-

24. *The Field of Choice* : Cmnd. 3123, para 25 (g).

25. Report (Cmd) 9678) p. 341; *Putting Asunder*, London, S.P.C.K., London, 1966, p. 37.

lish cruelty within the principle laid down in *Russell* v. *R.*[26] that the conduct complained of must be such as to cause injury, or a reasonable apprehension of injury, to life limb or health, bodily or mental. However, trivialities will not suffice for this purpose. The act or default on the part of the respondent will have to be grave and weighty. Under the former law, in cases of constructive desertion what amounts to just and reasonable cause for leaving may well come within S. 2 (1) (b) of the Act. Unnatural offences like sodomy, bestiality or insanity of the other spouse can provide strong evidence to establish that the respondent has behaved in such a way that the petitioner cannot reasonably be expected to live with him. Unlike the case of adultery, here the test is objective, namely, it is for the court to determine, having regard to all the circumstances of the case, whether the petitioner can reasonably be expected to live with the respondent.

(c) that the respondent has deserted the petitioner for a continuous period of at least two years immediately preceding the presentation of the petition. This differs from the former ground for divorce in that the requisite period is reduced from three years to two years, and desertion will be limited to actual desertion. Constructive desertion, that is to say where the respondent's conduct has caused the petitioner to withdraw from cohabitation, will be covered by (b) above.

(d) that since the celebration of the marriage the parties have lived apart for a continuous period of at least two years, being a period immediately preceding the presentation of the petition and the respondent consents to a decree being granted. For this purpose a husband and wife are to be treated as living apart unless they are living with each other in the same household.[27] This provision is entirely novel in English law and introduces consensual divorce, but is likely to be most beneficial to the parties and their children when used in making agreements between the spouses under S. 7 of the Act. Read in conjunction with S. 3 (5), it encourages attempts at reconciliation, for in calculating whether the period for which the parties have lived apart has been continuous, no account is to

26. *Russell* v. *R.* (1897) A.C. 395.

27. S. 2 (5) of the Divorce Reform Act, 1969.

be taken of any one period (not exceeding six months) or of any two or more periods (not exceeding six months in all) during which the parties resumed living with each other. A safeguard is provided under S. 5 in that the court has the power to rescind a decree before it is made absolute, if the respondent satisfies the court that the petitioner misled him (whether intentionally or unintentionally) about any matter which he took into account in deciding to consent to the grant of the decree.

(e) that since the celebration of the marriage the parties have lived apart for a continuous period of at least five years, being a period immediately preceding the presentation of the petition. This is the most controversial provision as it enables a blameworthy spouse to divorce the other, who may be completely innocent, against his wishes. However, the beneficial effect of it cannot be ignored. A husband, who has left his wife for another woman with whom he is cohabiting and has children, will be able to divorce his wife, regularise his illicit union by subsequent marriage and legitimise the children. Of course, it will be harsh for the innocent wife who does not want divorce because of her religious or conscientious convictions, but it is in the interest of all concerned in the situation and in the interest of the society at large that her marriage which for all practical purposes is dead and has become an empty shell should be dissolved and the other *de facto* union which promises stability should be regularised.[28] The continuing of such an empty legal tie will create more and more bitterness not only between the spouses but also third parties involved, e.g., the other woman and her children, whereas dissolution of the marriage in such circumstances will end the miserable relationship once for all.

From this discussion it must not be inferred that desertion and the formation of an illicit union would win a decree automatically, for the necessary safeguards are provided by S. 4 of the Act, under which the respondent may oppose the grant of a *decree nisi*. The court shall consider all the circumstances, including the conduct of the parties and their interests and those of any children or other persons concerned, and if of opinion

28. *Putting Asunder*, pp. 21, 28, 38.

that the dissolution of the marriage will result in grave financial or other hardship to the respondent and that it would in all the circumstances be wrong to dissolve the marriage, it shall dismiss the petition.

The Divorce Reform Act, 1969,[29] which abolishes the present grounds for divorce and substitutes for them irretrievable breakdown of marriage as the sole ground, is definitely an improvement both from the social and legal point of view. It is based on the concept that when a marriage has broken down beyond repair and there is no possibility that the spouses will ever again live together as husband and wife, they should be able to end it with the minimum of friction and maximum of justice to all concerned. When a marriage is dead in fact, it should be buried properly with decency and dignity. The ideal of law and justice should be upheld and respect for the legal profession maintained. Under the new law the courts will not be trying superficial issues in terms of guilt or innocence; a reward for marital virtue or a penalty for marital delinquency; a victory for one spouse or a reverse for the other, but will require the estabiishing of facts, which have led to the failure of the marriage—a defeat for both.[30]

The Act maintains the stability of marriage as an institution by ensuring the overriding necessity to satisfy the court that the marriage has broken down irretrievably, and by providing for reconciliation. The solicitor acting for the petitioner in a divorce suit shall certify whether he has discussed with the petitioner the possibility of a reconciliation and given him or her the names and addresses of persons qualified to help effect a reconciliation. At any stage of the proceedings, the court may adjourn for such period as it thinks, fit, if it considers that there is a reasonable possibility of a reconciliation attempt succeeding.[31] This shows that the new law aims at saving a marriage, if it is possible, and terminating it only in the last resort. It certainly does not encourage divorce or make it easier.

29. Each section of the Act is discussed in detail by B. Passingham, *The Divorce Reform Act*, 1969, London, 1970.

30. *Putting Asunder*, p. 18.

31. S. 3 (1) (2) of the Divorce Reform Act, 1969; in view of this section it is likely that extensive use will be made of the social services like Marriage Guidance Councils.

We have seen the inconsistencies and social difficulties occurring under the doctrine of matrimonial offence, on which rest the present grounds for divorce, which are abolished by the Divorce Reform Act, 1969. It is quite likely that India would be moving towards reforming her divorce law, for the Hindu Marriage Act, 1955 is not completely free from anomalies. As under the former English law, a petitioner at Hindu law has to prove one of the matrimonial offences enumerated under S. 13, which is rigid. Some of them like insanity, suffering from a venereal disease or a virulent and incurable form of leprosy do not contain the taint or the element of guilt on the part of the respondent, who under no circumstances is responsible for his affliction. Renunciation of the world by entering into a religious order is a meritorius actand in consonance with the commands of the *sastra* and should not be treated on the same footing as faults like adultery or cruelty by putting all of them in the same category. The fact in such cases is that the respondent is not at fault but the marriage has been frustrated.

"Living in adultery" as a ground for divorce is commonly used by the parties as it provides a large scope for fabricating evidence. Recent decisions[32] indicate that documents are forged and false witnesses are brought to court to commit perjury to support the case that the respondent is living in adultery.

As shown in Chapter X, failure to resume cohabitation for a period of two years or upwards after the passing of a decree of judicial separation entitles either party to petition for divorce. This section was meant to encourage reconciliation by providing ample time for the parties to think over the consequences of their action before petitioning for divorce. However, in practice it is not fulfilling its purpose as it is used by the litigants with the ultimate object of obtaining a divorce.

The remedy of restitution of conjugal rights is archaic and is of no practical use in modern England. Consequently it has been abolished under the Matrimonial Proceedings and Property Act, 1970. At Hindu law failure to comply with a decree for restitution gives either spouse the right to petition for divorce. Like judicial separation above, it is used as a means

32 *Sachindranath* v. *Nilima,* A.I.R. 1970 Cal. 38: *Rajalingam* v. *Lingayya,* A.I.R. 1964 Andh. Pr. 308.

of obtaining divorce after the lapse of two years, and in effect helps unscrupulous spouses to take advantage of their own wrong, which the law aims to prevent. In *Joginder* v. *Pushpa*[33] the husband petitioned for restitution of conjugal rights under S. 9 of the Hindu Marriage Act, 1955. At the time of framing the issues, the parties appeared before the court and made the following statements. The husband said, I want to keep the respondent (wife) with me. I will never maltreat her in future, but it should not be taken that I have maltreated her. I am ready to settle her happily after forgetting all the previous matters." The wife stated that she was maltreated and turned out of the house, but she was prepared to go along and stay with her husband. On the basis of this compromise the court made an order under S. 9 of the Hindu Marriage Act, 1955. But for the compromise the court had to determine the disputed question of fact as to whether the husband had maltreated his wife or whether the wife had withdrawn from his society without reasonable excuse. On the material before the court, it could not be satisfied one way or the other, and without determining this, a decree under S. 9 could not have been passed. The husband wanted his wife back and she had agreed to that. This being so, the petition under S. 9 had become infructuous and should have been dismissed.

It was contended that the compromise between the parties was the result of the efforts of reconciliation having been effected by the court under S. 23 (2) of the Hindu Marriage Act, 1955 and the order that followed was not a consent decree. This contention has no merits. If the court succeeded in reconciling the parties, it should have dismissed the petition for restitution of conjugal rights as having become infructuous. If on the other hand it failed to effect reconciliation, it should have tried the issues on the merits. No other conclusion is possible except that the decree was based on the consent of the parties, and was wrong in law.

If the decision is wrong in law it could be set aside on appeal under S. 28 or by a separate suit, but it is not a nullity. Accordingly the subsequent divorce based on the ground that the other party had failed to comply with a decree for restitution

33. *Joginder* v. *Pushpa*, A.I.R. 1969 P. & H. 397, F.B.

of conjugal rights was valid. There were, it seems, signs that the petition under S. 9 of the Act was being pursued with the collusion of the wife, as she refused to go with her husband soon after they left the court. It is superfluous to comment that experience still needs to be gained in the handling of these very difficult matters, unless the court is simply to be manipulated by the spouses and/or their families.

In *Syal* v. *S.*[34] a wife was completely innocent and no charges justifying a divorce could be brought against her. The husband, who wished to dissolve the marriage, drove her out of the matrimonial home without any cause, and later instituted restitution proceedings as a device for attaining his purpose. His resort to law under S. 9 was not with the intention of getting his wife to stay with him, but with the object of treating this as a step to a final divorce.

Cases of this type surely defeat or attempt to defeat the purpose of the law. The rigidity of the grounds for divorce and the inability of the law to provide remedy where it is desired tend to encourage married couples to manufacture grounds by forgery and perjury in order to bring their facts under S. 13 of the Hindu Marriage Act, 1955. If the individual grounds are abolished, and a new test based on the breakdown of marriage is introduced, a clear, consistent and reasonable reform of matrimonial litigation could be expected. This is particularly hoped, especially if the court is obliged to investigate the true cause of 'breakdown', which could be inter-familial,[35] and it would be impossible for the spouses or their advisers or patrons to manufacture prefered cases.

The law is already treading in the direction of substituting breakdown for matrimonial offence. This is evident from the statement of objects and reasons for the Amendment Act XLIV

34. *Syal* v. *S.*, A.I.R. 1968 Punj. 489; another illustration is *Laxmibai* v. *Laxmichand*, A.I.R. 1963 Bom. 332. The decision is correct but the facts show how litigants tend to use the law. See J.D.M. Derrett, "*May a spouse who is in desertion obtain a divorce on the basis of his own wrong*' ?" (1968) 70 Bom. L.R., Journal, pp. 117-122, 152. For contrary opinion see B.R. Dolia, "*Hindu Marriage Act*, 1955, *S.* 13 (1-*A*)," (1968) II M.L.J., Journal, pp. 83-86.

35. J.D.M. Derrett, *Religion, Law and the State in India*, London, 1968, pp. 352-399 and *A Critique of Modern Hindu Law*, Bombay, 1970, Appendix IV

of 1964. These read as follows : "The right to apply for divorce on the ground that cohabitation has not been resumed for a period of two years or more after the passing of the decree for judicial separation, or on the ground that conjugal life has not been restored after the expiry of two years or more from the date of decree, for restitution of conjugal rights should be available to both the husband and wife, as in such cases it is clear that the marriage has proved a complete failure. There is, therefore, no justification for making the right available only to the party who has obtained the decree in each case." Irrespective of the conflicting ways in which S. 13 (1A) has been construed by the courts it is evident that the Law Ministry in 1964 was already considerably influenced by the 'breakdown' theory.

BIBLIOGRAPHY

Abram, A., *English Life and Manners in the later Middle Ages*, London, 1913.

Agarwala, Rajkumari, "*Hindu Divorce Law—its History*" (1959) 2 M.L.J., p. 45.

Aiyangar, K. T. Bhashyam, *Women in Hindu Law*, Madras, 1928.

Aiyangar, K.V. Rangaswami, *Aspects of the Social and Political System of Manusmriti*, Lucknow University, 1949.

Aiyangar, K. V. Rangaswami, *Some Aspects of the Hindu View of Life according to Dharmasastra*, Baroda, 1952.

Aiyar, S. K., *Commentaries on Special Marriage Act*, 1954, Agra, 1956.

Allen, Sir C. K., "*Matrimonial Cruelty*" (1957) 73 L. Q. R. 316.

Altekar, A. S., *The Position of Women in Hindu Civilisation*, Banaras, 1956.

Anderson, J. N. D., edited by, *Family Law in Asia and Africa*, London, 1968.

Andrews, J. A., "*Evidence of Adultery*" (1961) 77 L.Q.R. 390.

Apte, V. M., *Social and Religious Life in the Grihya Sutras*, Bombay, 1954.

Ayyar, A. S. Nataraja, *Mimāmsa Jurisprudence*, Allahabad, 1952.

Bader, Clarisse, *Women in Ancient India*, London, 1925.

Banerjee, S. C., *Dharma-Sutras, A Study in their Origin and Development*, Calcutta, 1972.

Banerji, Sir Gooroodas, *The Hindu Law of Marriage and Stridhana*, Calcutta, 1923.

Bevan, H. K., "*Belief in the other Spouse's Adultery*" (1957) 73 L. Q. R. 225.

Bhattacharya, B., *The 'Kalivarjyas' or Prohibitions in the 'Kali' Age*, University of Calcutta, 1943.

Biggs, J. M., *The Concept of Matrimonial Cruelty*, London, 1962.

Bishop, J. P., *Marriage and Divorce*, 2nd. ed., vol. I., Chicago, 1891.

Blackstone, William, *Commentaries on the Laws of England*, 4th. ed., Bk. I, vol. I. Oxford,

Blair, Donald, "*Proof in Matrimonial Proceedings : the Medical Aspect*" (1965) 5 Medicine, Science and the Law. 65.

Blom-Cooper, L. J., "*Separation Agreements and Grounds for Divorce*" 19 M. L. R. 638.

Blom-Cooper, L. J., "*A Century of Divorce*" (1958) 25, The Solicitor, p. 19.

Bose, Shib Chunder, *The Hindoos As They Are*, Calcutta, 1883.

Bromley, P. M., *Family Law*, London, 1963.

Brown, L. Neville, "*Cruelty without Culpability or Divorce without Fault*" (1963) 26 M.L.R. 625.

Chagla, M. C., "*Indian Law: An Introduction*", Some Aspects of Indian Law Today, published by the British Institute of International and Comparative Law, London.

Chakladar, H. C., *Social Life in Ancient India*, Calcutta, 1954.

Chaudhari, D. H., *The Hindu Marriage Act*, 1955, Calcutta, 1957.

Chety, M. K. Lakshmipathi, "*A Survey of the Hindu Code Bill*" (1953) 105 M.L.J., Journal, p. 1 ff.

Colebrooke, H. T., *Digest of Hindu Law*, Madras, 1874.

Corbett, Jim, *My India*, O.U.P., 1954.

Coutts, J. A., "*The Standard of Proof of Adultery*" (1949) 65 L.Q.R. 220.

Cowell, H., *The Hindu Law*, Calcutta, 1870.

Dalton, E.J., *Descriptive Ethnology of Bengal*, Calcutta, 1872.

Das, R. M., *Women in Manu and his Seven Commentators*, Arrah, 1962.

Denning, A. T., "*Presumptions and Burdens*" (1945) 61 L.Q.R. 379, 381.

Deolalkar, P. V., *The Hindu Marriage Act*, 1955, Nasik City, 1959.

Derrett, J. D. M., *Hindu Law Past and Present*, Calcutta, 1957.

Derrett, J. D. M., "*Comments, Recent Legislation*" (1962) vol. II, Am. Jour. Comp. Law, p. 396.

Derrett, J. D. M., "*Divorce by Caste Custom*" (1963) 65 Bom. L. R., Journal, p. 161.

Derrett, J.D.M., *Introduction to Modern Hindu Law*, O. U. P., 1963.

Derrett, J.D.M., "*The Discussion of Marriage by Gadadhara*", The Adyar Library Bulletin, 1963, vol. XXVII, p. 171 ff.

Derrett, J.D.M., "*The Convert's Polygamous Marriage*" (1965) 67 Bom. L. R., Journal, 71 at p. 73.

Derrett, J. D. M., *Religion, Law and the State in India*, London, 1968.

Derrett, J. D. M., "*May a spouse who is in desertion obtain a divorce* on *the basis of his own 'wrong'* ? (1968) 70 Bom, L. R., Journal. pp. 117-122, 152.

Derrett, J. D. M., *A Critique of Modern Hindu, Law*. Bombay, 1970.

Dibdin, Sir Lewis, and E.H. Chadwyck Healey, *English Church Law and Divorce*, London, 1912.

Diwan, Paras, "*Divorce Law of Hindus, contemplated reform and a few Suggestions*" A.I.R. 1953, Journal, pp. 7, 9.

Dolia, B. R., "*Hindu Marriage Act*, 1955, S. 13 (1-A",) (1968) II M. L. J., Journal, pp. 83—86.

Dubey, Bhagwant Rao, "*Widow Re-marriage in Madhya Pradesh*" Man in India (1965), vol. 45, p. 50 (a quarterly anthropological journal).

Dutt, Nripendra Kumar, *Origin and Growth of Caste in India*, London, 1931.

Flood, Dom Peter, *The Dissolution of Marriage*, London, 1962.

Funk, I.K. Editor-in-Chief, *A Standard Dictionary of the English Language*, vol. II., New York, and London, 1920.

Gajendragadakar, P. B., "*Hindu Code Bill*" (1951) 53 Bom. L. R., Journal, pp. 77, 99.

Gharpure, J. R., *Hindu Code*, Poona, 1921.

Gharpure, J. R., *Hindu Law*, Bombay, 1931.

Gharpure, J. R., translated by, *Yajnavalkya Smriti*, Bombay, 1936.

Gharpure, J. R., translated by, *Yajnavalkya Smriti*, Bombay, 1939, vol. II.

Ghose, J. C., *The Principles of Hindu Law*, Calcutta, 1906.

Ghose, J. C., *The Principles of Hindu Law—The Commentaries*, vol. II, Calcutta, 1917.

Goodhart, A.L., "*Constructive Desertion*"(1955)71 L.Q.R.32.

Goodhart, A. L., "*Cruelty, Desertion and Insanity in Matrimonial Law*" (1963) 79 L.Q.R. 98, pp. 110-116.

Gopalakrishnan, T. P., *Hindu Marriage Law*, Allahabad, 1957.

Graveson, R. H. and Crane, F. R., *A Century of Family Law*, London, 1957.

Griffith, R. T. H., *The Hymns of the Atharva-Veda*, vol. II, Benaras, 1917.

Gulick, George S., and William S. Anderson, *American Jurisprudence*, vol. 17, New York, 1957.

Gupte, S. V., *Hindu Law of Marriage*, Bombay, 1961.

Gyan Prakash, *The Hindu Code*, Allahabad, 1958.

Hall, J. C., "*Matrimonial Cruelty and Mens Rea*" (1963) 104 Cambridge Law Journal 104, p. 106.

Halsbury, H. S. G., *Laws of England*, 3rd. ed., vol. 12, London.

Hammick, J. T., *The Marriage Law of England*, London, 1887.

Harris, S. F., *Criminal Law*, London, 1954.

Hartley, C. Gasquoine, *Divorce (Today and Tomorrow)*, London, 1921.

Hastings, James, *Encyclopedia of Religion and Ethics*, 1918.

Hirschfeld, Julius, "*The Law of Divorce in England and Germany*" (1897) 13 L.Q.R. 395, 397.

Holdsworth, W. S., *History of English Law*, vols. I, II. London, 1956.

Indra, Vidya-Vachaspati, *The Status of Women in Ancient India*, Banaras, 1955.

Iyengar, K. Ramaswami, translated by, *The Kama-Sutra of Sri Vatsyayana*, Lahore, 1921.

Iyengar, K. Srinivasa, "*Powers of the Managing Member of a Mitakshara Joint Hindu Family*" (1905) 15 M.L.J., Journal, 211 at p. 224.

Jackson, J., *The Formation and Annulment of Marriage*, London, 1951.

Jain, M. L., "*Validity of Hindu Marriage solemnised without performing any customary ritual or ceremony*" A.I.R. 1961, Journal, p. 84.

Jain, M. P., "*Matrimonial Law in India*" (1962) J. I. L. I., p. 71.

Jain, Chinuprasad V., "*Hindu Marriage Act and Divorce*" A.I.R. 1964, Journal, p. 116.

Jayaswal, K. P., *Manu and Yajnavalkya*, Calcutta, 1930.

Jha, Ganganath translated by, *Manu-Smriti* vol. II part I Calcutta 1921.

Jha, Ganganath, *Hindu Law in its Sources*, Allahabad, 1930.

Joshi, L.D., *Khasa Family Law*, Allahabad 1929.

Jowitt, W.A., *The Dictionary of English Law*, vol. I. London, 1959,

Joyce, G.H., *Christian Marriage*, London, 1948.

Kahn-Freund, O., "*Mental Cruelty*" (1953) 16 M.L.R. 68-70.

Kane, P. V., *History of Dharmasastra*, vol. I, part I, Poona, 1941.

Kane, P. V. *History of Dharmasastra*, vol. II, part II, Poona, 1941.

Kane, P. V., *History of Dharmasastra*, vol. III Poona, 1946.

Kangle, R. P., *The Kautilya Arthasastra*, part II, University of Bombay, 1954.

Kapadia, K. M., *Marriage and Family in India*, O.U.P., 1959.

Khetarpal, S. P., "*Cruelty and Insanity in Divorce Law*" (1964) Malayan Law Journal, p. LXXX.

Kirk, K. E., *Marriage and Divorce*, London, 1948.

Kitchin, S. B., *A History of Divorce*, London, 1912.

Krishan, Y., "*Was it permissible for a sanyasi monk to revert to lay life* ?" Annals of the Bhandarkar, Research Institute, 50 (1969) Poona, p. 75,ff.

Lacey, T. A., *Marriage in Church and State*, London, 1947.

Lakshman Svarup, *Sarupa-Bharati*, Hoshiarpur, 1954.

Lasok, Dominik, "*The Grounds of Divorce in Transition*" (1963) 2 Solicitor Quarterly 297, 311-318

Latey, W., *Divorce*, 14th. ed., 1952.

Little, William, H. W. Fowler and J. Coulson, *The Shorter Oxford English Dictionary on Historical Principles*, Oxford, 1933.

Lowe, R., "*A New Look at Cruelty*" (1963) 113 Law Journal, p. 683.

Maitland, F. W., *Roman Canon Law in the Church of England*, London, 1898.

Mathur, Kailash Sahai, "*Validity of Hindu Marriage solemnised without performing any customary ritual or ceremony*" A.I.R. 1962, Journal, p. 27.

Mayne, J. D., *Treatise on Hindu Law and Usage*, 11th. ed., Madras, 1950.

McCurdy, W.E., "*Insanity as a Ground for Divorce*" in *Selected Essays on Family Law*, by the Association of American Law Schools, 1950.

McGregor, O. R., *Divorce in England*, London, 1957.

Mehta, H., *The Woman under the Hindu Law of Marriage and Succession*, Bombay, 1943.

Mehta, Lehar Singh, "*Some Implications of the Hindu Code Bill*, 1948" A.I.R. 1950, Journal, pp. 26-27.

Milner, Alan, "*Sodomy as a Ground for Divorce*" (1960) 23 M.L.R. 43.

Mitra, T., *The Law Relating to the Hindu Widow*, Calcutta, 1881.

Mitter, Dwarka Nath, *The Position of Women in Hindu Law*, Calcutta, 1913.

Modi, J. P., *The Medical Jurisprudence and Toxicology*, 10th. ed., 1949, cited in D. H. Chaudhari, *The Hindu Marriage Act*, 1955, Calcutta, 1957.

Mostyn, F. E., "*The present Divorce System*", The New Law Journal, May 21, 1970. P. 485.

Motwani, K., *Manu Dharmasastra*, Madras, 1958.

Mukherjee, A. N. "*Social Legislation with special reference to the Law of Marriage*" 1 Law Quarterly (Journal of the Indian Law Institute, West Bengal) No. 4 (1964) 321, 325.

Mulla, D. F., *Principles of Hindu Law*, Bombay, 1960.

Müller, F. Max., edited by, *Sacred Books of the East*, vols. 2, 7, 14, 25, 29, 30, 33, Oxford.

Murray, James A. H., *A New English Dictionary on Historical Principles*, Oxford, 1888.

Murray, A.H., *A New English Dictionary on Historical Principles*, vol. V, Oxford, 1901.

Murray, A. H., *A New English Dictionary on Historical Principles*, vol. X,Oxford, 1928.

Nigam, S. S., "*Hindu Law*"(1964)6 J.I.L. I. 545 at 550.

Nigam, S. S., "*Annual Survey—Hindu Law*" (1964) 6 J. I. L. I. at p. 548 ff.

Ogle, A., *Canon Law in Medieval England*, London, 1912.

O'Malley, L.S.S., *Indian Caste Customs*, Cambridge U.P., 1932.

Pandey, R. B., *Hindu Samskaras*, Banaras, 1949.

Parekh, Vallabhdas P., "*Desertion is no Ground for Dissolution of Marriage under the Hindu Code Bill—its Effects*" A.I.R. 1951, Journal, p. 48.

Passinggham. B., *The Divorce Reform Act*, 1969. London, 1970.

Patnaik, N. D., "*Divorce in India how it is and how it should be*" A.I.R. 1959, Journal, p. 86.

Phillips, E.A., *Practice of the Divorce Division*, London, 1951.

Phipson, S. L., *Evidence*, 10th ed., London, 1963.

Pollock, F., and F. W. Maitland, *The History of English Law*, vol. I, Cambridge, 1911.

Powell, Raphael,"*The Concept of Marriage in Ancient and Modern Law*" (1950) vol. III, Current Legal Problems, p. 46.

Prabhu, P. H., *Hindu Social Organisation*, Bombay, 1949.

Pratapa Rudra Deva, *Sarasvati-Vilasa*, translated from the original Sanskrit by Thomas Foulkes, London, 1881.

Puxon, M., "*Cruel means Cruel*" (1964) 108 Sol. Jour. 786.

Puxon, M., "*The Changing Face of Cruelty*" (1962) 106 Sol. Jour. 579, 602.

Raghavachariar, N. V., *Hindu Law Principles and Precedents*, Madras, 1960.

Ranade, Ram Keshav, "*The Hindu Code*, 1948" A.I.R. 1949, Journal, pp. 12, 13.

Ranade, Ram Keshav, "*Widow Remarriage (whether an approved form or an unapproved form)*" A.I.R. 1950, Journal, p. 59.

Rao, M. V. Krishna, *Studies in Kautilya*, Delhi, 1958.

Rao, V. Suryanarayana, *Women under Hindu Law*, Mylapore, 1941.

Rattigan, Sir Henry, *Law of Divorce applicable to Christians in India*, London, 1897.

Rayden, W., *Practice and Law of Divorce*, 9th ed., edited by Joseph Jackson London, 1964.

Rege, P. W., "*The Development of Woman's Property in India*" in *Legal Essays—I* by T. K. Tope, Bombay, (1961-1962) 46 at pp. 49-50.

Ridley, J., "*The Refusal of Sexual Intercourse and the Law of Desertion*" (1948) 64 L.Q.R. 243.

Rose, H.A., *A Compendium of the Punjab Customary Law*, Lahore, 1911.

Rosen, Lionel, "*Cruelty in Matrimonial Causes*" (1949) 12 M.L.R. 324.

Rosen, Lionel, "*Cruelty and Constructive Desertion*" (1954) 17 M.L.R. 432.

Rosen, Lionel, *Matrimonial Offences, London*, 1962.

Rosen, Lionel, "*Legal Cruelty and Cruelty*" (1964) 108 Sol. Jour. 887.

Roy, A. G., *Commentary on Hindu Law*, Patna, 1960.

Russell, on *Crime*, vol. I, edited by J. W. Cecil Turner London, 1964.

Saldanha, Jerome A., *Civil-Ecclesiastical Law*, Trichinopoly, 1935.

Samson, K. T., "*Motive as an Element of Cruelty in Divorce*" (1948) 11 M.L.R. 88.

Samuels, A., "*Cruelty and Mental Illness*" (1963) a Solicitor Quarterly 97.

Sarkar, U. C., *Epochs in Hindu Legal History*, Hoshiarpur, 1958.

Sarkar, U. C., "*Hindu Law: Its Character and Evolution*", The Law Review, Panjab University Law College, 1965, vol. XVII, 1 at pp. 3, 16-17.

Sastri, Golapchandra Sarkar, *A Treatise on Hindu Law*, Calcutta, 1927.

Sastri, S. R., *Woman in Sacred Laws*, 1950.

Sen, P. N., *The General Principles of Hindu Jurisprudence*,Calcutta, 1918.

Sen-Gupta, N. C., *Evolution of Ancient Indian Law*, London, 1953.

Seth, H. L., *Matrimonial Muddle in India*, Lahore.

Sethna, M. J., edited by, *Synthetic Jurisprudence*, Bombay, 1962.

Shelford, L., *The Law of Marriage and Divorce*, London, 1841.

Shiva Gopal, *The Hindu Code*, Allahabad, 1964.

Siromani, J.S., *Commentary on the Hindu Law*, Calcutta, 1885.

Steele, A., *The Law and Custom of Hindoo Castes*, London, 1868.

Stephen, Sir James Fitzjames, A *Digest of the Criminal Law*, 9th. ed., edited by Lewis Frederick Sturge, London, 1950.

Sternbach, Ludwick, *Juridical Studies in Ancient Indian Law*, Delhi, 1965.

Strange, Sir Thomas, *Hindu Law*, vol. I, London, 1830.

Surinder Singh, "*The Hindu Law of Marriage : Old and New*", The Law Review, Panjab University Law College, 1965, vol. XVII, 24 at pp. 111-112.

Tarlo, H., "*Intention and Insanity in Divorce Law*" (1963) 37 Aust. L. J. 3.

Tewari, S. K., *Nullity of Marriage in Modern Hindu Law.* (unpublished) Thesis, Ph. D. London, 1965.

Tolstoy, D., *The Law and Practice of Divorce*, 1963.

Tomlins, Sir Thomas, *The Law-Dictionary*, London, 1820.

Tope, T. K. and H. S. Ursekar *Why Hindu Code* ?, Poona, 1950.

Venkataraman, S., "*The Hindu Marriage Act*, 1955" (1955) 2 M.L.J., Journal, pp. 33-34.

Venkataraman, S., "*Matrimonial Causes among Hindus*" (1962) 1 M.L.J., Journal, p. 1.

Vidyarnava, Srisa Chandra, translated by, *Yajnavalkya Smriti*, Allahabad, 1918.

Vora, D. P., *Evolution of Morals in the Epics*, Bombay, 1959.

Warmington, L. C., *Divorce Law*, London, 1951.

Webb, P.R.H., "*Insanity as a Defence in Proceedings for Divorce and Judicial Separation*" (1966) 6 Medicine, Science and the Law, p. 102 ff.

West, R. and Bühler, G., *A Digest of the Hindu Law*, London, 1919.

Whitlock, F. W., "*Insanity, Drunkenness and Divorce*" (1964) 4 Medicine, Science and the Law 81, 87.

Wyld, H. C., *The Universal Dictionary of the English Language*, London, 1932.

Young, P. V., "*Separately and Apart*" (1964) 5 Australian Lawyer 145.

COMMENTS IN NOTES

(1890) 34 Sol. Jour. 247.
(1922) 66 Sol. Jour. 735.
(1946) 62 L.Q.R. 7.
(1948) 64 L.Q.R. pp. 8, 16.
(1947) 10 M.L.R. 98, 198.
(1948) 92 Sol. Jour. 318.
(1952) 62 Yale Law Journal P. 55.
(1953) 69 L.Q.R. 439.
(1953) 216 Law Times 587 (Journal Record).
(1954) 17 M.L.R. 76.
(1955) 71 L.Q.R. 11.
(1956) 58 Bom. L.R., Journal, 105.
(1962) 106 Sol. Jour. 293-294.
(1962) 106 Sol. Jour. 377-378.
(1962) 106 Sol. Jour. 886.
(1964) 108 Sol. Jour. 925.
(1965) 67 Bom. L. R., Journal, p. 11.

The Report of the Royal Commission on Marriage and Divorce, 1951-1955 (Cmd. 9678).

The Report (*Putting Asunder*) of a Group appointed by the Archbishop, of Canterbury in January 1964, S. P. C. K, London, 1966.

The Report of the Law Commission, *The Field of Choice*, London, 1966 Cmnd 3123..

Medicine, Science and the Law (1962-1964) vols. 3-4 at pp. 660-661.

The Asiatic Researches, vol. XVI, Calcutta, 1828, pp. 132-133.

TABLE OF STATUTES

TABLE OF CASES

ABBREVIATIONS

A.C.	..	Appeal Cases.
A.I.R.	..	All India Reporter.
Ad. & El.	..	Adolphus & Ellis.
Add.	..	Addam's Ecclesiastical Reports.
All E.R.	..	All England Law Reports.
All.	..	Allahabad.
All. L.J.	..	Allahabad Law Journal.
Am. Jour. Comp. Law		American Journal of Comparative Law.
An. W. R.	..	Andhra Weekly Reporter.
And. or Andh. Pr.		Andhra Pradesh.
Aust. L.J.	..	Australian Law Journal.
Beav.	..	Beavan Reports.
Bom.	..	Bombay.
Bom. H. Ct.	..	Bombay High Court.
Bom. L.R.	..	Bombay Law Reporter.
C.A.	..	Court of Appeal.
C.C.A.	..	Court of Criminal Appeal.
C.C.R.	..	Crown Cases Reserved.
C. & P.	..	Carrington & Payne.
C.W.N.	..	Calcutta Weekly Notes.
Cal.	..	Calcutta.
Cal. L.J.	..	Calcutta Law Journal.
Ch. Ap.	..	Chancery Appeals.
Ch. D.	..	Chancery Division.
Cl. & Fin.	..	Clark & Finnelly.
Cox's C.C.	..	Cox's Criminal Cases.
Cr. App. R.	..	Criminal Appeal Reports.
Cr. L.J.	..	Criminal Law Journal.
D.L.R.	..	Dominion Law Reports.
Dea. & Sw.	..	Deane & Swabey.
Den.	..	Denison.
E. Punj.	...	East Punjab.
E.R.	..	English Reports (Reprint).
F.B.	..	Full Bench.

H.L.	..	House of Lords.
H.L.C.	..	House of Lords Cases (Clark's).
H.L. Cas.	..	House of Lords Cases.
Hag. Cons.	..	Haggard Consistory Reports.
Hag. Ecc.	..	Haggard Ecclesiastical Reports.
Him. Pr.	..	Himachal Pradesh.
Hyd.	..	Hyderabad.
I.A.	..	Indian Appeals.
I.L.R.	..	Indian Law Reports.
Ind. Cas. or I.C.		Indian Cases.
J.I.L.I.	..	Journal of the Indian Law Institute.
J. & K.	..	Jammu & Kashmir.
J.P.	..	Justice of the Peace (and Local Government Review Reports).
K.B.	..	King's Bench Division.
K.L.R.	..	Kenya Law Reports.
Ker.	..	Kerala.
L.J.P. & M.	..	Probate and Matrimonial (Law Journal Reports).
L.J.P.M. & A.	..	Probate, Matrimonial and Admiralty (Law Journal Reports).
L.Q.R.	..	Law Quarterly Review.
L.R.	..	Law Reports.
L.T.	..	Law Times.
L.T. Jour.	..	Law Times Journal.
L.T.R.	..	Law Times Reports.
Lah.	..	Lahore.
Lah. H. Ct.	..	Lahore High Court.
Lee	..	Sir G. Lee's Ecclesiastical Judgements.
Low. Bur.	..	Lower Burma.
M.I.A.	..	Moore's Indian Appeals.
M.L.J.	..	Madras Law Journal.
M.L.R.	..	Modern Law Review.
M.P.L.J.	..	Madhya Pradesh Law Journal.
M. & W.	..	Meeson & Welsby.
Mad.	..	Madras.
Mad. H. Ct.	..	Madras High Court.
Mad. L.J.	..	Madras Law Journal.
Madh. Pr.	..	Madhya Pradesh.
Mitak.	..	Mitaksara.

Mood. C.C.	..	Moody's Crown Cases.
Mys.	..	Mysore.
N.C.	..	Notes of Cases.
N.U.C.	..	Notes of Unreported Cases.
N.Y.S.	..	New York Supplement.
Nag.	..	Nagpur.
Ont. L.R.	..	Ontario Law Reports.
Or.	..	Orissa.
Oudh.	..	Oudhyapur.
P.; P.D.; P. & D.		Probate and Divorce Division.
P.C.	..	Privy Council.
P. & H.	..	Punjab & Haryana.
P.R	..	Punjab Records.
Pat.	..	Patna.
Phill. Ecc.	..	Phillimore's Ecclesiastical Reports.
Punj.	..	Punjab.
Q.B.	..	Queen's Bench Division.
Raj.	..	Rajasthan.
Rang.	..	Rangoon.
Rob. Ecc.	..	Robertson's Ecclesiastical Reports.
S.B.E.	..	Sacred Books of the East.
S.C.	..	Supreme Court.
Saur.	..	Saurashtra.
Sol. Jour.	..	Solicitor's Journal.
Sp. Ecc. Ad.	..	Spinks' Ecclesiastical and Admiralty Reports.
Sw. & Tr.	..	Swabey & Tristram Reports.
T.L.R.	..	Times Law Reports.
Tra. C.	..	Travancore Cochin.
V.L.R.	..	Victorian Law Reports.
V.P.	..	Vindhya Pradesh.
Ves.	..	Vesey (Chancery Series).
W.L.R.	..	Weekly Law Reports.
W.R.	..	Weekly Reporter (Sutherland).
Wk. Rep.	..	Weekly Reporter.
Yaj.	..	Yajnavalkya.

INDEX